# MADE IN
## MANITOBA

BY JOHN      EINARSON

# A MUSICAL LEGACY

Lee Aaron, Randy Bachman, Tal Bachman, Bachman Turner Overdrive, Steve Bell, Bif Naked,
Heather Bishop, Lenny Breau, Tom Cochrane, Crash Test Dummies, Terry Crawford, Crescendos,
Crowcuss, Burton Cummings, C-Weed / Errol Ranville, Doc Walker, The Duhks, Eagle & Hawk,
Foster Martin Band, Fresh IE, Joey Gregorash, The Guess Who, Harlequin, Hart-Rouge,
Tara Lyn Hart, Dianne Heatherington, Tom Jackson, Terry Jacks, Angela Kelman, Kilowatt,
Chantal Kreviazuk, Joel Kroeker, Daniel Lavoie, Alana Levandoski, MacLean & MacLean,
Robbie McDougall, Loreena McKennitt, Big Dave McLean, McMaster & James,
Holly McNarland, Mood Jga Jga, Mae Moore, Rick Neufeld, Orphan / The Pumps,
Fred Penner, Scrubbaloe Caine, Remy Shand, Graham Shaw, Al Simmons,
Ray St. Germain, Lucille Starr, Amanda Stott, Streetheart,
Sugar & Spice, Swing Soniq, Wailin' Jennys, The Watchmen,
The Weakerthans, Jane Vasey, Neil Young

Great Plains Publications
420 – 70 Arthur Street
Winnipeg, MB  R3B 1G7
www.greatplains.mb.ca

Great Plains Publications gratefully acknowledges the financial support provided for its
publishing program by the Government of Canada through the Book Publishing Industry
Development Program (BPIDP); the Canada Council for the Arts; as well as the Manitoba
Department of Culture, Heritage and Tourism; and the Manitoba Arts Council.

Design & Typography by Relish Design Studio Inc.

Printed in Canada by Friesens


CANADIAN CATALOGUING IN PUBLICATION DATA

Main entry under title:

Einarson, John, 1952-
  Made in Manitoba : a musical legacy / John Einarson.

  ISBN  1-894283-56-2

Musicians—Manitoba—Biography. 2. Popular music—Canada.
I.   Title

ML394.E355   2005   781.64'092'2     C2005-900125-9

Respectfully dedicated to all those local musicians and bands who inspired me when I was growing up in Winnipeg and all the current musicians and bands who continue to inspire me today. And to my Mom and Dad who bought me my first guitar and encouraged my passion for music.

# TABLE OF CONTENTS

• Neil Young, 1968

# ACKNOWLEDGEMENTS

## ACKNOWLEDGEMENTS

**A** SINCERE THANK YOU TO ALL THOSE who willingly agreed to be interviewed for this book and whose names appear throughout. Special thanks to the following for assisting with information, contacts, photographs, or arranging interviews: my good friends Larry Leblanc (*Billboard*), Larry Delaney (*Country Music News*) and Holger Peterson (Stony Plain Records, Edmonton) for their invaluable support and encouragement; Todd Jordan (no longer simply 'Fab's nephew'– Paquin Entertainment, Winnipeg); Roland Stringer (Folle Avoine Productions, Montreal); Shelley Stertz and Jake Gold (The Management Trust, Toronto); Gord Osland; Bart Kives (*Winnipeg Free Press*); my best friend Glenn MacRae (Long & McQuade Ltd., Winnipeg); Steve Warden (Panic Media + Communications Inc.); Shelley Wilde (Tomali Productions, Calgary); Winnipeg-based writer Bonnie Baltessen; Martin Melhuish (for his Juno Awards history book); Kathleene Cochrane; Jessica Johnston and Jannah Stone (Quinlan Road Ltd., Stratford, ON); Sandy Rogers (Swell Management, Toronto); Josh Glover (Sony Music, Canada); Paula Danylevich (Hype Music, Vancouver); 'Captain' Jim Drysdale (James Portley) for the feedback and suggestions; Christine Corthey and Amrit Singh (Paquin Entertainment, Winnipeg); Mort Goss (The Duhks), Leonard 'Lewsh' Shaw and Sandy Chochinov; Carolyn Berthelet and Suzanne Erdelyi at SJR for the insights and translations and Jeff Hiebert for computer expertise.

• The Crescendos

Thank you to the following for assisting with photographs: Cara Luft; Rick Johnson; Blair MacLean; Danny Casavant; photographers David Lee and Angela Browne, Cyril Stott; Perry Hart; Stéphanie Parkin (GSI Musique); my friends John Cody and Mark Doble; Gary Taylor; Henry Small; Joey Gregorash; Ray St. Germain; Bill Dergousoff; Phil O'Connell; Hermann Frühm; Lucille Starr; Kathleene Cochrane; Suzanne Little (Bachman Headquarters); Jessica Johnston; Robbie McDougall; Roland Stringer; Christine Corthey; Amrit Singh; Al Simmons; Paul G. Kohler at Art of Life Records (www.artofliferecords.com); Kelly Fairchild; Terry Neplyk; Mrs. Dorothy Vasey; Larry Leblanc; Joel Kroeker; and Pete Watson.

Special thanks to Catherine Gerbasi (Portage & Main Press) for passing the concept along to Gregg Shilliday at Great Plains Publications. Also my sincere appreciation to Ron Robinson and Jan Harding at CBC Radio 990 in Winnipeg for doggedly pursuing me to do the "From the 45s Cupboard" series Saturday mornings which, besides being a heap o' fun, served as inspiration and early research for this book.

As always, thank you to my wife Harriett and children Matt and Lynsey for their patience and support. ■

• CJAY TV's Teen Dance Party hosted by Bob Burns

### *Born and raised in a prairie town, just a kid full of dreams.*

### ("Prairie Town", Randy Bachman, 1992)

**W**HY MANITOBA? WHY WINNIPEG? How is it that a province of barely a million, with most of those people living in the capital city of Winnipeg, could consistently produce some of this country's greatest musical talent? The artists profiled in the following pages all have direct connections to Manitoba, have also achieved national or international acclaim, and account for a staggering 100 million records sold worldwide. But why here? It's a question pondered by music journalists, in the same way that London scribes contemplated an out-of-the-way city like Liverpool dominating the British Invasion in the 1960s.

• **'The Galaxies' Bill Jaques**

Winnipeg has much in common with Liverpool. The key factor is geography. Both cities are isolated from mainstream pop culture and entertainment industry meccas (London or Toronto), and often overlooked or bypassed by touring artists and productions. Winnipeg is dead centre in the North American continent, our nearest large urban centres being Toronto and Minneapolis, and the closest of these is a good seven hour drive away, if the highways are clear.

"You're isolated in Winnipeg," notes ex-Winnipegger Terry Jacks. "It's like the British Isles. That's why the best rock 'n' roll came out of England. They're holed up on this little island. And the best Canadian rock 'n' roll came out of Winnipeg. I think it's the containment thing. It's somewhere that you have to get out of. You're not in Vancouver, you're not in Toronto; you're in Winnipeg and you've got to explode."

As well, for a good portion of the year Winnipeg is socked in by winter. If you don't play hockey what else are you going to do except make music? And the chances are, in a city where it's too cold for garage bands, it will be in your basement. "You don't realize how much you are indoors compared to other people," notes singer/songwriter Chantal Kreviazuk on the influence of winter on the music scene, "and how much music is a focal point in your life." Adds singer/songwriter Holly McNarland, "If you look at how many great musicians come out of Winnipeg, and how many people play instruments, I think it's because of the cold. You can go nuts or become creative."

These factors contribute to an insular environment; instead of following trends, Winnipeggers tend to create their own. There has always been an 'us against the world' air about Winnipeg and its inhabitants, a spirit of staunch independence. We chart our own course. And that spirit permeates the province and affects the music created here. "In Manitoba, we kind of know what's going on but we're not directly influenced as fast as other cities, so we have time to think about what we want to do," suggests Doc Walker singer/songwriter Chris Thorsteinson.

"When I listen to the Guess Who," says the Weakerthans' John K. Samson, "musically there is so much force of will, a fierceness to it somehow, and I see that as a line that runs through Winnipeg music. Maybe everyone sees that in the places they come from. Geography does mysterious things that we don't entirely understand. It certainly has a profound effect on the art people make."

"To this day my Winnipeg work ethic benefits me," asserts punk rocker Bif Naked, raised as Beth Torbert. "I believe a lot of Manitobans who toured in a band in

• Al Simmons

**FOR BUDDING MUSICIANS, THE COMMUNITY CLUB OFFERED NOT ONLY SPORTS AND BINGO, BUT ALSO THE FIRST CHANCE TO PERFORM AT A CANTEEN DANCE AND GAIN LOCAL CELEBRITY.**

winter, rehearsed in cramped spaces with no heat, peed in a cup and threw it outside in the snow, acquired a work ethic and perseverance that stayed with them. I think it's important for young bands to cut their teeth on the prairies."

The absence of a major music industry presence in Manitoba is a further factor in shaping the artists who have emerged from here. Chantal Kreviazuk says, "If I can describe one of the differences I see between myself, being from Winnipeg, and other artists I meet, is that there wasn't this entertainment business quality that is pretty competitive and contrived in LA or New York or generally in the entertainment world. In Winnipeg, making music was just so real. There was no industry. That's really rare and beautiful. I never thought I was aspiring to become somebody or be something in Winnipeg, it was just very genuine."

In addition, the multicultural character of both the city and province encourage a diversity reflected in the arts community. "Another factor, I think, is the multicultural nature of the population, the diverse ethnic mix," suggests Randy Bachman. "To this day each ethnic group retains a distinct identity within the city. There are Polish clubs, Ukrainian clubs, Italian clubs, and Belgian clubs where they hold weddings and socials. So in my day when teenagers got together to form bands in their basement they had all these venues available right in their own neighbourhoods. On any given weekend there were literally hundreds of dances organized throughout Winnipeg."

And then there are the bands playing, to this day, at community clubs. Ask any middle-aged Winnipegger which community club was theirs and see the wistfulness in the voice, the longing look on the face. Every neighbourhood had its own community club and loyalties were fierce. For budding musicians, the community club offered not only sports and bingo, but also the first chance to perform at a canteen dance and gain local celebrity. Imagine a teenage Neil Young spinning 45s at Earl Grey Community Club in Fort Rouge on a Friday evening, then taking the stage the following evening with the Jades, his first band. Neil has always said his passion for playing live was ignited that night on the tiny community club stage. Or imagine Randy Bachman playing his

• The Balladeers (Pat Riordan, top left), (Photo Right) Joey Gregorash with The Mongrels

big orange Gretsch guitar with Mickey Brown & the Velvetones at Weston Memorial Community Club; Burton Cummings fronting the Deverons perched on top of a piano at Luxton Community Club; Fred Turner with Roy Miki and the Downbeats playing for a chocolate bar and a Coke at Orioles Community Club. And at each club a throng of teens crowding the stage or dancing up a storm. It was music at a grassroots level, and that's always what Winnipeg has been about. Winnipeg's rock 'n' roll pioneers like Ray St. Germain, Wayne Walker, Club 63 Galaxies, the Balladeers, Triads, Swingtones and Del Royals inaugurated the community club canteen dances in the '50s, playing for bobby soxers throughout the city. Other venues included car shows, sporting events, high schools, even car dealerships and movie theatres ("Sunday Shindigs" at the Rialto) between features. The Champs Kentucky Fried Chicken drive-in on Henderson Highway featured bands on its roof.

In the 1950s and '60s it was the community clubs, high schools, teen clubs like the Cellar, Twilight Zone, Pink Panther, Elks Hall, and church basement

soirees. In the 1970s, '80s and '90s it was pubs like the Zoo (the Plaza Hotel, later known as the Osborne Village Inn), the St. Vital, Norlander, Royal Albert, Wellingtons, and the Downs, and clubs like the Spectrum (later the Pyramid), Blue Note, Tom Tom Club, Marble Club, Times Change, Corner Boys, and the Bella Vista. Then there were socials — another unique Manitoba institution, with plenty of beer, kolbasa, Old Dutch potato chips and loud music — at spots like Le Rendez-Vous in St. Boniface, the Native Club in Fort Rouge and UMSU at the University of Manitoba. Lowering the drinking age to eighteen in September 1970 transformed pubs like the Marion, Village Inn and Voyageur from staid beverage rooms to wild parties with live bands such as Katerpillar, Dianne Heatherington & the Merry-Go-Round, Fabulous George & the Zodiacs, and Next appearing nightly.

Radio in Winnipeg has always supported local talent. Early on, CKY, CKRC and later CFRW recognized the potential in connecting with bands and dances. Disk jockeys like Doc Steen, Darryl Burlingham, Jim Paulson, PJ the DJ (Peter Jackson), Boyd Kozak, Ron Legge, Jim Christie and Bobby 'Boom Boom' Branigan spent every weekend hosting a dance somewhere, often venturing outside Winnipeg. Local records were given airplay and became hits, frequently at the expense of better-known artists. I recall attending a concert by Toronto's Ugly Ducklings, who enjoyed several hits across Canada, and being among a handful of patrons at the St. James Civic Centre. Down the road, local favourites the Fifth were turning people away with standing room only at Silver Heights Community Club. Those trends continued through the next decades as 92 CITI FM, POWER 97, and the university radio stations supported homegrown music and artists by playing their recordings — sometimes even their demo tapes — and promoting live shows.

Television weighed in as well with CBC's *Music Hop*, featuring Ray St. Germain and Lenny Breau, and later *Let's Go* (hosted by Chad Allan and his former

band the Guess Who) in the '60s and shows like *10:30 Live* in the '70s offering opportunities for local artists to appear on your TV screens throughout the province and across Canada. CJAY (now CKY) TV's *Teen Dance Party* became a popular and influential local music showcase for bands, with host Bob Burns playing a star maker role for a number of local groups, including the Guess Who and Sugar & Spice, as manager and record producer. Bob & the Hits and Young As You Are also featured local talent.

The 1960s was the golden age of Winnipeg rock 'n' roll, beginning in early 1965 when Chad Allan & the Expressions, re-christened the Guess Who, scored a surprise North American hit with their raucous rendition of Johnny Kidd & the Pirates' "Shakin' All Over". Suddenly all eyes and ears were on this prairie city in the middle of nowhere. Boasting over 250 working bands, record labels weighed in and groups like The Lovin' Kind, Quid, Jury, Shondels, Eternals, Mongrels, Fifth, Sugar & Spice and Gettysbyrg Address (all using locally made Garnet 'BTO' amplifiers) enjoyed hits beyond Winnipeg's perimeter highway. For a few years Winnipeg was the undisputed rock 'n' roll capital of Canada. In 1970, when the Guess Who single-handedly outsold everyone in the Canadian music industry combined to that point, once again Winnipeg was home to Canada's reigning rock monarchy. Bachman-Turner Overdrive, Harlequin, Streetheart, Scrubbaloe Caine and Crash Test Dummies all continued the dynasty.

Artists such as the Fuse, Popular Mechanix, Woodwork, Holy Hannah, Streetheart, Harlequin, the Pumps, Queen City Kids, the Freeze, Les Pucks, the Cheer, Frank Soda, Combo Combo, Stagmummer, Liquid Bone Dance, the Watchmen, and the New Meanies carried the torch into the next decades, keeping the clubs jumping. While Winnipeg was always a hard 'n' heavy rock city, punk rock and New Wave found favour with bands like Chocolate Bunnies From Hell (with perennial punker PJ Burton), Personality Crisis, the Red Fisher Show, Gorilla Gorilla, and Dash & the Dots.

"There has always been a very strong punk rock scene in Winnipeg beginning around the Personality Crisis years of the early '80s," says John K. Samson, "which led to musician-run venues that had originally flourished in the '60s Winnipeg scene. There was always the Albert and Wellington's downtown. Then there were basement shows, and house parties. That's the parallel to those community club shows in the '60s, this grassroots thing."

But while rock 'n' roll lit the lights, other forms of popular music found fertile ground throughout the city and province. Country music always held a firm foothold outside the city and became popular in Winnipeg as groups like the Henry Brothers, Double Eagle Band, Rhonda Hart, Cindi Cain & the Cheaters, and Byron O'Donnell started combining country with rock at boot-scootin' clubs

like the Palomino. From these influences would emerge Doc Walker, Foster Martin Band, Amanda Stott, C-Weed, and Tara Lyn Hart. Singer/songwriter Stu Clayton from Manitou and fiddler Andy Desjarlis helped keep traditional country music alive and well. Folk music enjoyed a strong following in the many coffeehouses throughout the city such as the 4-D (where Neil Young met Joni Mitchell), Wise I, Wing'd Ox, Ting, and Cro Magnon, where you could find eclectic fare, everything from brothers Jim and Dan Donahue's folk songs to Billy Graham's jazz trio, electric blues from Pig Iron to bluegrass from the Chicken Flats String Band.

The significance of the annual Winnipeg Folk Festival held every July out at Birds Hill Park cannot be underestimated in the evolution of Manitoba music. From its inception in 1974, founder Mitch Podolak sought not only to present the widest possible range of folk and ethnic

sounds, allowing attendees to experience the best in international folk fare, but also to showcase local talent, both established and up-and-comers. The event has become the premier folk festival in North America. For many Manitoba artists including Loreena McKennitt, Crash Test Dummies, The Wailin' Jennys, Fubuki Daiko, and Alana Levandoski, a Folk Festival appearance is a seminal moment in their careers.

"There are a lot of songwriters in Winnipeg and a lot of really interesting musicians, too, and a lot of it has to do with the Folk Festival," says The Duhks' Leonard Podolak, son of Folk Festival founder Mitch Podolak. "People go to the festival and their world gets transformed."

Across the Red River in St. Boniface, a unique Francophone music scene quite separate from the rest of the city thrived, nurturing the likes of Daniel Lavoie, Gerry & Ziz, Hart-Rouge and Marcel Soloudre at St. Boniface College, Louis Riel Collegiate and clubs like Les Cent Nons and Le Canot. Francophone musicians from throughout the province were drawn to this scene. "Being in a French college, I had much more contact with the French culture and what was happening," recalls singer/song-writer Daniel Lavoie on enrolling at St. Boniface College in the 1960s, "so we just started playing French music. I didn't really get into the English music scene at all. It was a very strong movement that involved all young Francophones in southern Manitoba because we branched out to all the Francophone communities."

Similarly, a parallel Aboriginal music community, originating from the Purple Pit at the Indian & Métis Friendship Centre on Donald Street, offered opportunities for Native musicians to get their start. "The Aboriginal music scene is a real community," says Errol 'C-Weed' Ranville. "It's just a mesh that has interwoven between everyone. We support each other and rally together."

By the 1980s the various individual music strands were becoming more integrated as artists began to merge genres, creating a melting pot of unique styles. For example, Eagle & Hawk

• **Bob Burns, Doc Steen and the Guess Who with silver disks for "Shakin' All Over" (1965)**

brought together traditional Aboriginal music and hard rock, while Fresh I.E. and Mood Ruff took the sound of urban hip-hop and placed it in a Winnipeg context. Doc Walker's infectious mix of country and rock has won them dozens of awards. Propagandhi espouse an unwavering socially and politically–conscious message in their proto-punk rock. Loreena McKennitt draws on a wide musical palette of international influences, past and present. "There were so many different kinds of bands and it was a very fertile, creative time, a real breeding ground for talent," recalls Scrubbaloe Caine's Henry Small. "Bands like Mood Jga Jga and Graham Shaw were great. I can remember thinking that there seemed to be so many original-sounding bands in Winnipeg."

Added to this has been the emergence of children's and family entertainers, making the province the leader in this field, with artists like Fred Penner, Al Simmons, Heather Bishop, Jake Chenier, Bob King, Aaron Burnett and Just Kiddin'. The annual Winnipeg International Children's Festival, organized by veteran rock drummer Gord Osland, is nationally recognized and helped launch the careers of many entertainers in this field.

While this book focuses on rock, folk, pop and children's entertainers, I would be remiss in not mentioning the world-class Manitoba artists in other musical genres including opera singer extraordinaire Tracy Dahl, classical violinist and Juno Award winner James Ehnes, Broadway musical stars Jeremy Kushner and Ma Anne Dionisio, as well as jazz arranger and band leader Ron Paley and local jazz stalwarts such as Ron Halldorson, Reg Kelln, Walle Larson, Leonard 'Lewsh' Shaw and Larry Roy to name but a few. In addition, Klezmer ensemble Finjan have won awards for their blending of traditional European klezmer music in a contemporary context.

There is a proud musical legacy associated with Manitoba and Winnipeg that every artist is aware of. "Everywhere I go in Canada, whenever I mention I'm from Winnipeg, people say 'Oh, there's so many

• CBC *Music Hop* chorus: Carol West, Lucille Emond, Pat Harvey, Yvette, and Micki Allen

great artists there!'" says singer/songwriter Joel Kroeker. "Everyone across the country knows that Winnipeg has soul." Even if you leave Manitoba to pursue your career elsewhere, you carry that legacy with you. It's both inspiring and daunting.

When asked what motivated her decision to pursue a music career instead of her studies at the University of Manitoba, Loreena McKennitt cites the Guess Who as a shining example for her, demonstrating that if they could do it from a prairie city, so could she. "How can you not feel inspired when you see people like the Guess Who and others who at the time were already successful and you think 'I see them, they're at close proximity and the trajectory of their career was not given to them on a silver spoon.' So it does imply that if you work hard and you have some measure of talent you, too, could be successful."

Not every artist in this book made it from Manitoba; what they all have in common though is a connection, a spiritual bond, with this province and its capital city. In one way or another they were all made in Manitoba.

"It's pretty much all I write about," reflects John K. Samson. "Even on this last record I wrote about Paris, America and the Antarctic but all these places are filtered through my Winnipeg consciousness. When I think of Paris I'm probably really thinking of the Old Market Square. I think this place has had a profound effect on how I see the world. Growing up here and staying here, it's become a huge part of my identity. It's certainly something I think about a lot, this place and what it means, and how frustrating and wonderful it can be."

"I came of age in Manitoba. I fell in love, lost my virginity, and learned how to ice skate here," says Bif Naked. "I'm always really proud to be from Winnipeg and to consider it my home town. I always say, 'Home of the Winnipeg Jets' and wipe a tear from my eye."

John Einarson
January, 2005

• 70s rockers Barrelhouse

*ACRONYMS*

**BMI:** Broadcast Music, Incorporated, a performing rights organization

**BCCMA:** British Columbia Country Music Association

**CCMA:** Canadian Country Music Association

**MARIA:** Manitoba Audio Recording Industry Association

**CIDO:** Cultural Industries Development Office (now known as Manitoba Film and Sound)

**CMT:** Country Music Television, a Canadian cable channel that broadcasts country music videos

**SOCAN:** Society of Authors, Composers, and Music Publishers of Canada; the Canadian copyright collective administering performing rights for members who are composers, authors and publishers

**MTYP:** Manitoba Theatre for Young People, a theatre based in Winnipeg

**MCMA:** Manitoba Country Music Association

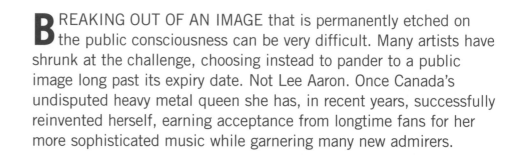

# LEE AARON

**B**REAKING OUT OF AN IMAGE that is permanently etched on the public consciousness can be very difficult. Many artists have shrunk at the challenge, choosing instead to pander to a public image long past its expiry date. Not Lee Aaron. Once Canada's undisputed heavy metal queen she has, in recent years, successfully reinvented herself, earning acceptance from longtime fans for her more sophisticated music while garnering many new admirers.

In the early 1990s you couldn't turn on *MuchMusic* without seeing Lee — all big hair, leather, body-hugging tights and pointy guitars — prancing across your television screen. Hits like "Whatcha Do To My Body", "Hands On" and "Some Girls Do" reinforced the sex kitten image. "I was the 'it' girl on *MuchMusic*," she says from her home in White Rock, BC. "I just happened to make a couple of strong videos the first couple of years *MuchMusic* was out of the gate and those had a major impact on people."

Born Karen Greening in Belleville, Ontario, she moved to Winnipeg with her family at age two. "We lived in Transcona on Dowling Avenue," she recalls, "and Blair MacLean [later of 'toilet rock' duo MacLean & MacLean] and his wife Ann lived two doors down. My parents knew them quite well. They would baby sit occasionally. We would all be out in the yard and Blair would pull out his guitar and sing. Blair and his brother Gary had a band, the Vicious Circle, and Burton Cummings would perform with them and crash at Blair and Ann's house.

"I got my love of singing from my mother," notes Lee. "She used to sing to me all the time and she's still very involved in church choirs." In a grade three production of *Heidi* at Radisson Elementary, Lee provided the off-stage singing voice for the lead. "I'd been singing since I was just a few years old, but another girl who looked like Shirley Temple but couldn't sing got the lead. The teacher had me stand behind a set and sing all the songs while this girl lip-synched. When the night of the production came, the teacher introduced everyone but neglected to introduce me. I was devastated. I was determined, from that point forward, that I was going to be noticed."

Moving to Brampton, Lee was spotted at age fifteen singing musical theatre by a local high school rock band, who invited her to join them. The band's name was

Lee Aaron. By seventeen Karen took the same name, and came to the attention of a manager who crafted the image that brought her to the top of the charts. "He was quite the Svengali," Lee admits. "Under his influence I did some pretty harsh growing up in the public eye, some of which was really embarrassing for me and not choices I would have made on my own." Posing nude for *Oui* magazine was one decision she regrets. "That took me years to live down, but I was a kid."

*The Lee Aaron Project*, released in 1982, launched the singer as a hard rock pin-up queen. "That whole image was created for me," she says. "I was naïve and didn't know anything about the music business. I figured I was supposed to do what they told me." More albums followed, including *Metal Queen* and *Call Of The Wild* (produced by Bob Ezrin of Alice Cooper and KISS fame) but by the latter 1980s Lee managed to extricate herself from her manager.

Signed to Attic Records, she found the label still expected the familiar image. Despite enjoying her greatest commercial success during this period, earning several Juno nominations and touring North America and Europe, Lee was dissatisfied with her sex kitten image. "I just didn't want to do that anymore."

She has ambivalent feelings about that period in her career. "It's really hard sometimes when your perception of yourself is so different from the way other people look at you. The *Metal Queen* video is a really strong image, but for me it's like watching a cartoon of myself."

The release of *Emotional Rain* marked a turning point, with a more sophisticated and mature sound. "That was the first album I put out on my own label and I was able to select the tunes I

wanted." An attempt to submerge her identity on *2precious* failed. "I started using my real name but it was like being a brand new artist right out of the gate. It was too hard to do that." Taking a year off to evaluate her career, Lee decided to be true to herself. "The only reason to stay in this business is because you love the music, never for the money. A friend of mine once said to me: 'Make every decision as if you've got a million dollars in the bank,' and that's the best advice I've ever been given."

A turn on the classic rock circuit in 1998 only stiffened her resolve. "I didn't think of myself as an oldies act. I really didn't want to get trapped as a caricature of myself doing my old hits at fifty. I still felt that I was a relatively young artist who had more to do."

An early passion for jazz motivated Lee's next move. "I was in a nightclub in my early twenties when I first heard Nina Simone and I couldn't believe how amazing she was." Remembering that feeling

for Simone's music she recorded *Slick Chick*, a jazz-inflected album of torch songs that garnered positive reviews across the country. Lee toured Canada and Europe to enthusiastic response at every stop.

Her recent album, *Beautiful Things*, continues her personal journey. "I wrote a bunch of songs that incorporate my jazz, blues and roots influences, more of a jazz-pop hybrid." On several tracks she collaborated with songwriter Joel Kroeker. Reviews have once again been ecstatic. "This is the direction that I much prefer."

How have her dedicated rock fans taken to the new Lee Aaron? "They've matured and are delighted to discover the Lee Aaron whom they were fans of a few years ago doing something that's palatable for them now."

Her stubborn determination to redefine herself comes as no surprise to those who know Lee Aaron. "If you can survive a Winnipeg winter you're going to grow up to be one tough chick," she laughs. ∎

Born Karen Greening in Belleville ON; moved to Winnipeg at age two

First public performance at Radisson Elementary School, Transcona

ALBUMS: The Lee Aaron Project (1982); Metal Queen (1984); Call Of The Wild (1985); Bodyrock (1989); Some Girls Do (1991); Emotional Rain (1994)

HIT SINGLES: "Whatcha Do To My Body", "Hands On", "Some Girls Do"

Toured with Bon Jovi, Uriah Heep and KISS

Launched jazz career with Slick Chick (2000) and Beautiful Things (2004)

Collaborating with ex-Winnipeg singer/songwriter Joel Kroeker

Appeared nude in *Oui* magazine early in career

Neighbour Blair MacLean of comedy duo MacLean & MacLean used to babysit her

# RANDY BACHMAN

**W**HEN GUITARIST/SONGWRITER RANDY BACHMAN stepped away from his namesake band Bachman-Turner Overdrive in 1977, he had few financial worries and could afford to dabble in projects near and dear to his heart. He had scaled the dizzying heights of rock success not once but twice, and if anyone deserved to rest on his laurels it was he. However Randy was not about to do that. Instead he set out on a strange and wonderful journey that would ultimately bring him right back to where he started in 1958.

Born and raised in West Kildonan, Randy's musical career began at the age of three when he won *King Of The Saddle*, an amateur show for pre-teens. Violin lessons followed until, at the age of thirteen, he saw Elvis Presley on television, and suddenly the guitar had more allure. His ability to adapt his dexterity on violin to the guitar allowed Randy to progress at light speed. A chance encounter at a car dealership a year later changed the course of his life.

"Saturday mornings I would listen to the CKY Caravan hosted by Hal Lone Pine," he recalls. "After a few numbers Lone Pine would say 'Now we're going to let Junior play.' The next thing you would hear was the most marvelous guitar music coming over the airways. It sounded like two or three guys playing, so I thought Junior was the name of a band. The following Saturday I rode my bike down to Gelhorn Motors on North Main and waited around to watch the group. There was this little guy about my age, very slight, playing the most beautiful guitar I had ever seen, an orange Gretsch Chet Atkins model. He played *Caravan*, playing all the parts simultaneously by himself. My eyeballs were fixed on his fret board. 'This sounds marvelous!' I thought."

Junior was Lenny Breau, and a profound musical bond formed between the two guitarists. Randy began cutting school to sit in Lenny's bedroom and watch him play. As Lenny became a sophisticated

Born in Winnipeg

BANDS: Mickey Brown & the Velvetones, Chad Allan & the Reflections (Expressions), Guess Who, Bachman-Turner Overdrive (BTO), Ironhorse, Union

ALBUMS: Axe (1970); Survivor (1978); Any Road (1993); Merge (1996); Every Song Tells A Story (2002); JazzThing (2004)

HIT SINGLES: "Prairie Town", "Made In Canada"

Numerous Junos, SOCAN and BMI awards

Won King Of The Saddle competition at age three

Holds Guinness Book of World Records for most performers playing one song, "Takin' Care of Business"

Possesses the largest collection of Gretsch guitars in the world

Created Guitarchives Records to release recordings by his mentor Lenny Breau

Digitally-simulated duet with Lenny Breau on JazzThing

Written songs for both Canadian Idol winners

jazz player, he took Randy along with him as he explored the intricacies of the genre. It was an education that would leave an indelible imprint. Recalling his informal lessons with Lenny some ten years later, Randy composed "Undun" for the Guess Who, drawing on chord patterns copped from the jazz great. He would return to Lenny's catalogue of progressions for BTO's "Looking Out For #1". Still, there was unfinished business.

**RECALLING HIS INFORMAL LESSONS WITH LENNY SOME TEN YEARS LATER, RANDY COMPOSED "UNDUN" FOR THE GUESS WHO, DRAWING ON CHORD PATTERNS COPPED FROM THE JAZZ GREAT.**

While still in the Guess Who, Randy cut what was intended merely as a side project in March 1970, a guitar instrumental album titled *Axe*. Never intended as a solo album from a solo artist, *Axe* was released in the wake of his sudden departure from the Guess Who and tagged as such. The album never had a chance, but it did allow the versatile guitarist to noodle about in a variety of genres from country to jazz rock. Instead of pursuing that avenue, Randy set his sights on the top of the rock pile and succeeded in spades with Bachman-Turner Overdrive.

Randy's first real solo venture was 1979's *Survivor*, based loosely on his own career. "I conceived it as a concept. The theme was someone climbing the ladder of success. Maybe it was my story subconsciously. It had a sense of wholeness

to it as opposed to random songs geared for the pop charts." *Survivor* was a labour of love if a commercial disappointment.

Wanting to play in a band again, Randy formed the groups Ironhorse and Union, the latter featuring ex-BTO cohort Fred Turner. Both groups enjoyed chart success and critical praise. Still unsatisfied, Randy convened reunions with the Guess Who and BTO before striking out on his own again in the 1990s. The fruits of that decision came on *Any Road*, a solo album with confident songwriting and a boost from Neil Young, who appeared on Randy's tribute to Winnipeg, "Prairie Town". "I faxed the lyrics to Neil and he called

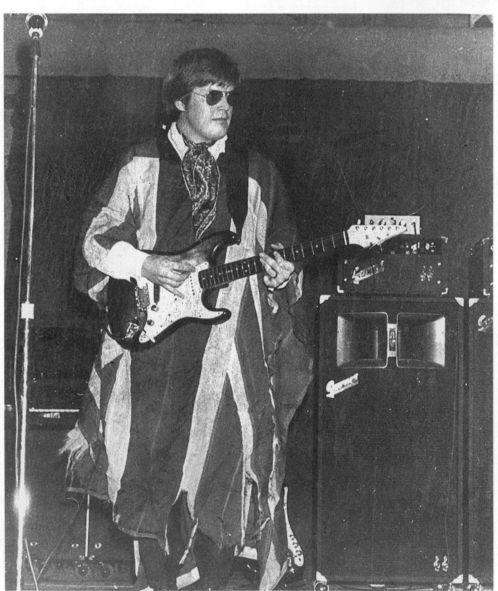

**THROUGHOUT HIS ENTIRE RECORDING CAREER RANDY HAD DABBLED IN JAZZ WITHOUT EVER RECORDING AN ALBUM EXCLUSIVELY IN THE GENRE.**

me up saying, 'That song is so honest. I want to play and sing on it.' Neil played like a man possessed singing 'Portage and Main fifty below' alongside me. That was such a thrill." The duo was a winning combination as *Any Road* and the "Prairie Town" video catapulted Randy back into the public consciousness. The two guitar warriors followed their first duet with a number together on the Shadows tribute album and "Made In Canada", a track from Randy's next solo venture, *Merge* (1996). *Merge* offered Randy's eldest son Tal the chance to play alongside his father.

Despite more work recording, writing, touring, and guesting on other artists' albums, Randy had more unfinished business to take care of. In 1996 he launched Guitarchives, dedicated exclusively to finding, restoring and releasing the recorded works of Lenny Breau. Lenny had gone on to be regarded as among the greatest of all guitar players, an innovator and inspiration in jazz music. His tragic death in 1984 left his recorded legacy in tatters until Randy lovingly resurrected it, paying royalties to Lenny's children. "I have always acknowledged Lenny Breau as my mentor. Everything I needed to know about guitar came in those eighteen months or so I spent hanging out with him. I felt I owed him something."

The acclaimed Guess Who reunion saw Randy reliving his glory days with Burton Cummings. Randy also continued writing with some of the top songwriters in the business, shuttling between Nashville, Los Angeles and London, England, and posting songs on a number of albums including *Canadian Idol* winner Ryan Malcolm's debut release. He also produced and/or guested on albums by Prairie Oyster, Farmer's Daughter, Lava Hay, Colin Arthur, Michael Carey, and Joel Kroeker.

His autobiography *Takin' Care of Business* inspired another project, *Every*

*Song Tells A Story*, a multimedia concept uniting his unique storytelling gifts in concert, television special, CD and DVD formats. The concerts were a sellout with Randy detailing the stories behind his best-known songs before performing each one, backed by his longstanding trio (Colin Arthur Wiebe, Rogé Belanger, and Mick Della Vee).

Still, unfinished business remained. Throughout his entire recording career Randy had dabbled in jazz without ever recording an album exclusively in the genre. Immersing himself in jazz music, and collaborating with respected jazz writers, the end result was *JazzThing*, released to critical acclaim in 2004 and complete with a digitally-created duet with Lenny Breau.

"I know my strength is as a songwriter, but Lenny always wanted me to do jazz. And now I'm doing it. It's just thirty years late." The guitar icon had finally come full circle. ∎

CARVING OUT YOUR OWN NICHE when you carry the name of one of the country's greatest musical heroes can be an overwhelming task. But Tal Bachman has succeeded in establishing his own identity and launching a successful career on his own terms, despite the weight of his father Randy's legend. He has earned respect and hit records as a singer/songwriter and recording artist in his own right. But a career in music wasn't his chosen path initially, despite public expectations.

**IRONICALLY, DESPITE ENJOYING AN ENORMOUS HIT RECORD RIGHT OUT OF THE CHUTE, TAL REMAINS LARGELY ANONYMOUS AND IS WORKING TO OVERCOME THAT WITH MORE PERSONAL APPEARANCES.**

TAL
BACHMAN
———
STARING
DOWN
THE SUN

"Dad was never overt about me following him into music until I went to college years later," recalls the soft-spoken father of eight, who resisted pressure to take up the family franchise. "Then he would call me and say, 'What are you doing wasting your time? Why don't you quit and form a rock 'n' roll band?' But that's kind of typical for Dad. When he gets an idea in his mind for what he thinks you should do he can't seem to get off it." Tal abandoned his pursuit of a master's degree in philosophy to join his father's band when the drummer was laid up. Music was Tal's destiny.

Born in Winnipeg in 1968 just as the Guess Who began their rise to the top, Tal's father was out on the road the day he was born. It would be a recurring theme throughout his young life. "For about three or four years he was gone an awful lot, but I think he felt he had to feed his growing family. It was just one of those things that was a given, his being away a lot. I don't really remember feeling neglected." At home, Randy worked in his basement studio on Scotia Street in Winnipeg's West Kildonan, writing songs. Tal would often wander down.

"He had a set of drums and I would try to play along to Led Zeppelin's 'Immigrant Song'. I used to hit the high hat in sync with the syllables of the vocal line. Then Dad showed me how to play an eighth note and to play that through the whole song. And it just seemed to click in my head."

In 1972 Randy moved his family, now including daughter Kezia, to Vancouver in the hope of getting his band Brave Belt steady work. A year later Bachman-Turner Overdrive was on the road constantly, with Randy leaving his family behind — first in New Westminster and later in a mansion in Lyndon, Washington — for months at a stretch. Eventually the pace, coupled with the enormity of BTO's success, resulted

in Tal's parents divorcing. In the ensuing custody battle Tal remained with Randy and a bond was formed through music. "Even though we have different personalities, I think there is some understanding there between us, because we spent more time together. And the musical connections are a part of it." Tal played drums and guitar, but never seriously enough to dream of a career. A devout Mormon, he set his sights on the world of academia, until a phone call from Randy in 1993. "I had a moment of clarity at college where I felt ready to rock. Dad called and said 'There's a job here. Do you want it?' That's why I quit school and moved back to BC to play with his band." For the next few years Tal toured as his father's drummer, all the while nurturing his own songwriting ambitions.

In 1999 he released his self-titled debut album on Sony/Columbia to rave reviews. The twelve original songs had catchy hooks and insightful lyrics. "I usually try to touch people in some way. I don't try to be cloying or write gushy

romantic things but I like to hone in on personal experiences and maybe shift it around a bit like when you write a short story or screenplay. Dad can be reluctant to share his innermost feelings in his writing. Perhaps it's because I have slightly different musical influences. I like U2 and was a big Smiths fan. I tend to like bands that pack an emotional punch." "She's So High", a song inspired by his brother's attempts to impress a girl, rocketed up the charts worldwide reaching #14 on *Billboard*.

"It was written because I thought that if I put my mind to it, I could write a #1 smash hit." The following year Tal picked up Juno awards for top song and top producer. He toured the US, opening for Barenaked Ladies and appeared on *Melrose Place* as well as the American Music Awards.

However, he was not able to follow up the success of that single and ultimately parted with his label. "I thought I had other songs with big hooks that people would like to hear on the radio." Toronto-

based manager Steve Warden agreed and signed Tal, negotiating a contract for a second album with independent Sextant Records, who released *Staring Down The Sun*, recorded at Tal's home studio, in 2004. "Aeroplane", the first single off the album, garnered considerable airplay across Canada, becoming a Top 20 hit in many markets. His follow up, "Broken", also earned attention.

Ironically, despite enjoying an enormous hit record right out of the chute, Tal remains largely anonymous and is working to overcome that with more personal appearances. "He's an artist who had a huge song but there's an anonymity about him," says Steve Warden. "We need to let people see who he is." A recent split with his longstanding Mormon faith received considerable publicity at the time the second album was released. "You go from thinking you're a member of an elite group that knows everything important, to wondering if you know anything that's important." His wife Tracy (Tal calls her "PW" for Perfect Woman), a devout follower of the Mormon faith, found his lapse difficult. "This was a bombshell for her."

Nonetheless, despite the setbacks in his career and his faith, Tal remains optimistic about the future. *Staring Down The Sun* once again reveals his gift for penning catchy, introspective pop songs and he is set for a major tour in the new year.

"I feel if you've got something catchy and compelling out there, it's going to find an audience," Tal says. "I just want a shot. My hope for this one is just to give my songs a chance. I feel like if they get a chance at radio, people will react. That's all I can really ask for." ∎

Born in Winnipeg, moved to British Columbia as a child

Drummed for his father Randy Bachman's backing band

ALBUMS: Tal Bachman (1999); Staring Down The Sun (2004)

HIT SINGLES: "She's So High", "Aeroplane", "Broken"

Juno Award for Single of the Year and Producer of the Year in 2000

Performed on *Melrose Place*

Played drums for Neil Young and Randy Bachman's recording "Made In Canada"

Norwegian Idol winner Kurt Nilsen enjoyed a #1 hit in Norway with "She's So High"

# BACHMAN-TURNER OVERDRIVE

BACHMAN-
TURNER
OVERDRIVE

**F**EW RECORDING ARTISTS have had their songs transcend the pop charts to become anthems in the lexicon of popular culture. Bachman-Turner Overdrive — BTO — accomplished that rare feat. Their 1974 recording "Takin' Care Of Business" is one of the most recognized tunes on the planet, used in movies, television, and to sell everything from office supplies to hamburgers. And it never fails to bring an audience to its feet, chanting, fists pounding the air.

When founding member Randy Bachman exited the Guess Who at the height of their success in 1970, he vowed to himself that he would prove all the naysayers, who questioned his decision, wrong. It took him a couple of years but, in the end, he triumphed, topping the Guess Who's success with the rock-solid BTO. "How many artists can say they went from a big band to an even bigger band?" notes former BTO manager Bruce Allen. Bachman-Turner Overdrive racked up sales in excess of 20 million records, earning over 100 platinum, gold and silver disks.

*...BTO's tours were marked by a spartan regimen that emphasized Gatorade over Southern Comfort, buses and semi's over Lear Jets, and Holiday Inns over Hilton Hotels.*

But while BTO's music was hard driving, the members of the band were far from hard living. At a time when excess characterized the music industry and status was measured by the size of your entourage and the weight of drugs you could ingest, BTO's tours were marked by a spartan regimen that emphasized Gatorade over Southern Comfort, buses and semi's over Lear Jets, and Holiday Inns over Hilton Hotels. It was a calculated move to maximize their bottom line. "We were the only band that was in the black on the road," says Fred Turner. "Everybody else was in the red. None of us was into the raucous rock 'n' roll atmosphere." BTO knew how to take care of business.

Following his contentious split from the Guess Who, Randy Bachman determined to forge a whole new musical identity for himself. But he wasn't yet ready for muscular BTO sound. "I knew that if I did a pop band it could never be as good as the Guess Who," states Randy. "I didn't want to be a second rate Guess Who. Instead, I went totally anti-pop. What else could I do?" Country rock was still in its infancy. Three years later the Eagles would make the genre commercially viable, but in 1970 it was a fringe movement and a risky venture. Nonetheless, Randy jumped in headfirst. What would emerge would be Brave Belt: an album, an image, and a band.

"Country music was always a big influence for me," he acknowledges, "and I always admired Neil Young and Buffalo Springfield because they were rockin' but they kept those country influences." Reunited with former Guess Who front man Chad Allan, the two friends set about recording a country rock album. Enlisting younger brother Robin to play drums, Randy and Chad augmented their sessions at Winnipeg's Century 21 Studios with fiddle, pedal steel guitar and accordion. But the trio lacked a name.

"I was looking for a name that was sort of like Buffalo Springfield, a name that would convey a western motif. Somebody said to me 'When an Indian becomes a brave he carries a brave belt to carry his scalps on, to show that he is a brave.' And I thought 'Brave Belt, that's the name!' I mentioned it to Neil Young and he said 'Cool name!' I played him the acetate of the album when he was back in Winnipeg in January 1971 and he liked it. Next thing I knew I had a contract on Reprise Records, Neil's label."

But there was one final piece to be added to the puzzle. "When I was in LA, the label executives told me I had to have four members in the band," recalls Randy. "I couldn't tour as a trio. I immediately thought of Fred Turner as the fourth guy." A veteran of a succession of local cover bands, Fred was the anchor Brave Belt needed. "I wanted a guy who could play both guitar and bass and who had a strong, distinctive voice, a gigantic Harley Davidson voice, and Fred Turner had it." Randy's brother Gary was enlisted to manage the band.

*Brave Belt* marked a dramatic departure from Randy's signature rock sound. Fans expecting the power-chording of "American Woman" were in for a shock. Brave Belt's mellow, acoustic, country-tinged songs found little favour. Chad Allan's "Rock And Roll Band" was released as a single, becoming a mild hit.

With his former group still riding high, Randy and Brave Belt found it an uphill battle winning converts to their new sound. "Radio stations wouldn't play us, magazines wouldn't do stories on us,"

Formed in Winnipeg in 1971 as Brave Belt; became BTO in 1973

Logged 27 rejections (and $97,000) before being signed to Mercury Records

ALBUMS: BTO I (1973); BTO II (1973); Not Fragile (1974, sold over 3 million copies); Four Wheel Drive (1975); Head On (1975)

HIT SINGLES: "Let It Ride", Takin' Care of Business", "Roll On Down The Highway", "You Ain't Seen

Nothin' Yet", "Hey You","Looking Out for #1"

AWARDS: over 100 gold, silver and platinum awards; Junos for Most Promising Group and Best Contemporary Album (1973); Group, Album and Producer (Randy Bachman) of the Year (1974); Group, Album and Single of the Year (1975)

Split up in 1977; reunited in 1984

The stuttering vocals on "You Ain't Seen Nothin' Yet" were a poke at brother Gary Bachman

Early on, all four Bachman brothers were involved with the band: Randy, Robbie and Timmy as musicians, and Gary as manager

"Takin' Care of Business" was based on a rejected Guess Who song called "White Collar Worker"

First Canadian group to be immortalized on The Simpsons (1999)

**THE GROUP LOGGED THE HIGHWAY MILES PLAYING OVER 300 DATES, FROM TRACTOR PULLS TO DRIVE-INS, WORKING THEIR WAY FROM OPENING ACT TO TOP BILLING.**

laments Randy. Chad Allan bowed out during sessions for a second album, allowing Randy to redefine the band's sound. "No matter how much you like something, if it isn't working you have to change it." At a gig in Thunder Bay, Brave Belt's laid back sound cleared the hall. Chastened, they returned to the drawing board and found the missing ingredient: good old rock 'n' roll. "That weekend we became Bachman-Turner Overdrive even though we didn't yet have the name," Randy says.

*Brave Belt II* offered a harder-edged rock sound dominated by Fred's throaty vocals and leaving little doubt that this was a new band with a rockin' attitude. Reprise released Chad's acoustic country "Dunrobin's Gone" as the leadoff single, contrasting sharply with the new rockier approach, and then Reprise dropped the band. The group found it needed another guitar to flesh out the live sound, and Randy turned to another brother, Tim, before relocating to Vancouver and hooking up with manager Bruce Allen.

By 1973 Randy had staked his Guess Who nest egg, some $97,000, keeping Brave Belt afloat. He had logged twenty-seven rejections from record labels for *Brave Belt III* and was ready to fold. But fate is strange. "My phone rang the next morning," continues Randy, "and it was Charlie Fach from Mercury Records calling from Chicago. I could hear 'Gimme Your Money Please' in the background. 'Everyone here loves it. I'll make you a two album deal and give you $50,000 per album.' That was it! I got my investment back." *Brave Belt III* became *BTO I* as the group adopted a heavier sounding name, inspired by a truckers' magazine, in keeping with their sound. "Bachman-Turner Overdrive was the closest thing to a metal band in Canada back then," notes Canadian journalist Larry LeBlanc. "There was nothing like them."

BTO was no frills, meat 'n' potatoes hard rock. "We were a blue-collar band," confirms Randy. "Our songs were about average guys. 'Takin' Care of Business' was about the average Joe going to work each day. The Guess Who sang love songs like 'These Eyes' whereas BTO was like a 'Tim Allen Tool Time' guys band."

The group logged the highway miles playing over 300 dates, from tractor pulls to drive-ins, working their way from opening act to top billing. "The master plan for breaking BTO was get out there, you get seen, you get records on the radio, and wherever the record is getting played you get in there and work. Simple," insists Bruce Allen. "And it paid off."

While *BTO I* set the template for their sound, *BTO II* gave them their first taste of success with the singles "Let It Ride" and "Takin' Care of Business". Their follow-up, *Not Fragile* launched the group into the rock stratosphere after "You Ain't Seen Nothin' Yet" topped the charts in over twenty-five countries worldwide, the song's stuttering vocal becoming its hook. Tim Bachman was replaced by Vancouverite Blair Thornton as the band carried on, releasing *Four Wheel Drive* and notching

another hit with "Hey You". "We had credibility in both markets because we had both AM pop radio on the one hand and FM rock on the other," maintains Bruce Allen. Wise investments ensured that the four band members would enjoy the fruits of their labour for years to come.

Conceived on-stage, "Takin' Care of Business" remains the group's best-known song. "In a club in Vancouver Fred lost his voice. Out of desperation I thought of 'White Collar Worker', a rejected Guess Who song, so I told the guys to play C, B♭, and F over and over. On my way to the club gig with my radio on I heard a deejay say, 'This is Daryl B takin' care of business' so when we got to the chorus I just sang "Takin' care of business" four times. When we finished people kept clapping, stomping, and shouting 'Takin' care of business' over and over."

European fans embraced the Canadian band with equal gusto. "We were perceived as the lumberjack rockers from Canada who'll blow the windshield out of your car," laughs Randy. "Loggers from the wilds of northern Canada whose music was used for knocking down trees. Our image matched our sound."

*Head On* was another fan favourite and included the jazzy "Looking Out For #1", but by 1976 the bloom was starting to wilt. The group found themselves type-cast. An attempt at a more contemporary sound on *Freeways* bombed and Randy soon departed, leaving BTO to Fred, Robbie and Blair, who recruited ex-April Wine bassist Jim Clench and recorded two more albums before folding.

Bachman-Turner Overdrive reunited in 1984 and carried on with various personnel changes through to 1990 when

Randy left once again. Today, BTO — Fred, Robbie, Blair, and guitarist Randy Murray — continue touring, giving fans that same brand of hard rock they have come to expect. While there have been feuds between the two camps, no one can deny the musical legacy the band forged in their heyday. Their songs remain staples of classic rock radio.

Randy Bachman is judicious about BTO's legacy. "The Guess Who and BTO are both very special to me," he muses. "I feel very fortunate to have been in these two incredible schools because they were an education. The Guess Who was an education in everything to do wrong business-wise. But with BTO, I got a second chance to do everything right. Not too many musicians get that second chance." ■

# STEVE BELL

**N**OT MANY CANADIAN RECORDING ARTISTS can credit our prison system for starting their careers. For Steve Bell, spending time with inmates at Drumheller Alberta's prison provided him with music lessons and a performing venue. "I honestly don't know if I would have been a musician if some of Canada's most unwanted men hadn't listened to me when I was little," he says, smiling.

As one of Canada's leading Christian contemporary singer/songwriters, Steve has carved out a niche on his own terms. He's sold over 200,000 recordings through his own label. Despite the success, he maintains a unique sense of authenticity.

"I'm a songwriter first, not a Christian songwriter," he points out. "I'm obligated to tell my life's truth, and since a large part of that is my faith, that needs to come out. I feel no obligation to write a Christian song, only an obligation to write an authentic song. I really hope that an atheist, a Muslim, or a Buddhist could come out and have a great time at my concerts."

Steve's father, a Baptist minister, moved his young family to Drumheller from Calgary when Steve was eight, to work as chaplain at the new prison. "That became my spiritual place, where I went to church." Steve's mother, a classically-trained pianist, would play late at night, everything from classics and hymns to Gershwin. "I would fall asleep hearing melodies. That's been important to my songwriting. It has to have melodic content."

The prison chapel hosted Saturday afternoon jam sessions where Steve became fascinated with the guitar. "The inmates heard I wanted to play guitar so they asked my dad if they could teach me. At eight years old I would sit with these guys in a circle with their guitars."

When Reverend Bell was transferred to Stony Mountain Penitentiary in Manitoba, the family moved onto the compound north of Winnipeg. Soon they became the Alf Bell Family Singers, traveling to churches to perform on weekends. "We had these matching outfits so it was like we were the Christian Partridge

Born in Calgary; moved to Stony Mountain, Manitoba at age twelve

BANDS: Elias, Schritt & Bell, Rocki Rolletti, Rhonda Hart Band, solo artist

Owns and operates Signpost Music with partner Dave Zeglinski

Learned guitar from inmates at Drumheller Penitentiary

ALBUMS: Burning Ember (1994); The Feast of Seasons (1995); Romantics & Mystics (1997); Simple Songs (2000); Waiting For Aidan (2001); Sons & Daughters (2003)

Borrowed $1,000 from thirty friends to finance his first major album

Sons & Daughters album recorded with children Sarah, Micah and Jesse

Juno Award for Best Contemporary Christian album (1997 and 2000); Prairie Music Award (2000 and 2001); Vibe Award — Male Vocalist of the Year (2003), Artist of the Year (2004), and Male Soloist of the Year (2003)

Family and I was Keith," laughs Steve. "Dad preached and we sang." They even recorded an album. Steve enrolled in music at Brandon University, only to withdraw a week before classes began, taking a job at a Winnipeg music store and joining jazz-fusion band Dega.

Steve had met Winkler natives Tim Elias and John Schritt at a folk fest in Treherne years earlier, but ran into the duo again coming out of Roade Studios on Grosvenor. Together they formed acoustic trio Elias, Schritt and Bell, one of the city's most popular early 1980s ensembles. "They had long hair and sang all this hippie music," he remembers of their duo the Mountain City Ramblers. The two singers introduced Steve to artists like Bruce Cockburn, Joni Mitchell and Neil Young. "I grew up listening to the Carpenters. What was fascinating about Bruce Cockburn was that he was a Christian but he was talking about social justice issues, which was not part of my framework." The trio began performing in Winnipeg clubs and came to the attention of CBC, who funded an album, *Awakenings,* in 1980.

"It was just the right time locally, but the wrong time internationally, because music had gotten very angry. When we sent the record out to the major labels they all said, 'Great record guys, but ten years too late.'" Elias, Schritt and Bell remained together three years before disbanding. Tim and Steve formed short-lived pop band Motet before Steve hit the bar circuit working with entertainers like Rocki Rolletti, Rhonda Hart, and Byron O'Donnell. Ready for something new, Steve began running a Youth For Christ worship service for street kids on

Sunday evenings, playing rock 'n' roll and reading the Bible.

Then Steve was approached to provide music for a Toronto-based religious TV program run by an old friend from Stony Mountain Penitentiary, Father Bob McDougall. "I wrote very little back then. In my teens I either wrote Christian songs or syrupy love songs. Then one day I decided I wasn't going to write a song again until I wrote one that wasn't about me. I didn't write for about ten years. But I started reading the Psalms around this time, and I heard melodies simultaneously.

**AS ONE OF CANADA'S LEADING CHRISTIAN CONTEMPORARY SINGER/SONGWRITERS, STEVE HAS CARVED OUT A NICHE ON HIS OWN TERMS. HE'S SOLD OVER 200,000 RECORDINGS THROUGH HIS OWN LABEL.**

Suddenly I was writing daily. In a six-month period I wrote ninety percent of my first four solo albums. But I didn't know what to do with the material."

The popularity of Steve's cassettes for Father McDougall encouraged him to finance a second album, borrowing $1,000 from thirty friends and distributing the album independently. But he had not considered performing. "Pastors invited me to sing at their churches and I'd say, 'No, I'm just a failed bar musician.' This one pastor would not give up. 'Why don't you come and sing just three songs at my church on Sunday night? You don't have to say anything.' I agreed. As I was

walking onstage this story came to me that was connected to the first song. So I told the story and it came out funny. I was up there forty minutes. As I walked off the stage I apologized to the pastor. He smiled and said, 'I knew that was going to happen.' I cried all the way home. That was the beginning. I'm a storyteller and songwriter. I think people are starving for stories and meaning."

Together with Mid-Ocean Studio owner Dave Zeglinski, Steve formed Signpost Music in 1989 to record his albums exclusively, later creating their own distribution arm. "I was tired of waiting for the big record deal." To date Steve has written and recorded ten albums of contemporary Christian pop/folk material. In 1997 he won a Best Gospel Album Juno for *Romantics & Mystics* and another in 2000 for *Simple Songs*, as well as two Prairie Music Awards and three Vibe Awards. Signpost's 20,000-strong direct mailing list offers a solid base but Steve relies on personal contact through performances. "It's a direct relation. You sing, you sell."

"I don't want people to buy or not buy my music because I'm a Christian," he stresses. "I want them to buy it because it's good." He recently recorded an album with his daughter Sarah, backed by his two sons, Micah and Jesse. "My goal is not to sell a million records or establish the biggest independent music company in Canada," he insists. "My goal is to be of musical value. I've been at this for 25 years. I hope when I die Canadians will say I contributed to the landscape. To me that's enough." ∎

# BIF NAKED

BIF NAKED

**I**N THE WORLD OF HARD ROCK MUSIC, image and substance rarely go hand in hand. Bif Naked is the exception. Her multi-tattooed, hard rockin', take no prisoners stage persona belies an insightful, soft-spoken woman as capable of quoting French poetry or Camille Paglia as churning out venomous rock lyrics. Her image is her own. She created it, she controls it, much as she does her own career.

Bif's personal history reads like a Hollywood script. Born in 1971 to an upscale Canadian teenager on a sojourn in India, Bif was adopted by two American missionaries working in New Delhi. Christened Beth, the Torberts returned to Minnesota with their infant. At age four, they moved to The Pas in northern Manitoba, where her father trained dental therapists. Following a two-year spell at the University of Kentucky in Lexington, the Torberts returned to Manitoba, settling in Dauphin as Beth entered junior high. "My first boyfriend was in Dauphin and he had a band. He gave me my first record, Judas Priest. I was a bit of a tomboy."

Despite the predilection for heavy metal, Beth's interests leaned towards theatre and an acting career. The family moved to Winnipeg where Beth studied drama at John Taylor Collegiate in St. James. "I was in a high school production of *Lil' Abner* and I was cast as Daisy Mae. That was my singing debut. I learned all about the 'confuse and distract

theory' of entertainment. My skirt was too short and my boobs too big so I think that may have distracted from my lack of pitch."

Upon graduation, Beth enrolled in drama at the University of Winnipeg, but dropped out after the first semester to join neo-punk avant garde ensemble Jungle Milk. "I thought it would be a good exercise in musical theatre, which I was studying at the Prairie Theatre Exchange. But I fell in love with all of it." She then joined punk band Gorilla Gorilla. "Again, it wasn't my goal in life but I enjoyed the catharsis of the live performance."

With Gorilla Gorilla, Beth Torbert transformed into Bif Naked. "PJ Burton from the Chocolate Bunnies From Hell was always calling me Bif. Gorilla Gorilla's first show was at the Royal Albert on Valentine's Day 1989, and they needed a gimmick to get people to come see the

band. So the gimmick was 'Come see Bif naked,' and it stuck. Gorilla Gorilla ended up doing an entire national tour called the 'See Bif Naked Tour'. So I've always gone with that name."

Gorilla Gorilla ultimately moved to Vancouver where, after two years of slogging it out, Bif split, hooking up with Chrome Dog and Dying To Be Violent before going out under her own name. John Dexter of Plum Records (an A&M Records affiliate) signed her to a recording contract, co-writing and produced her debut album. "He took a big chance on me because the guys at A&M didn't think I would ever be on the radio and told him so." When Plum folded, Bif and manager Peter Karrol formed Her Royal Majesty's Records to distribute her recordings, an astute business move that gave her control over her career.

The grueling pace of promoting her album had a life-altering affect on Bif. "I quit drinking," she admits. "The work schedule was so taxing that I realized on my first European tour that I couldn't party every night and be camera-ready every morning. I would have died if I had kept on like that."

*I Bificus* became her breakthrough release in the US on the Lava/Atlantic label. "I got my sorry ass in *Vogue* magazine and *Glamour* and *Teen People*. I did the Lilith Fair tour, toured with the Cult and Kid Rock, went on *Jay Leno* and my parents got to watch. Really, I could have died happy." Two singles, "Spaceman" and "Lucky" widened Bif's fan base.

Her third album, *Purge*, marked a turning point with a more radio-friendly dance-influenced sound that still retained her hard edge. From it came the single "I Love Myself Today", a signature song for Bif. "That came from a collaboration between Desmond Child and myself," she notes. "That feel was definitely Desmond and his rock sensibilities. It's an homage to Joan Jett and the 'I Love Rock 'n' Roll' stuff." The album was nominated for a Juno Award in 2000 for Best Rock Album, losing out to Nickelback. "I was the only female in the category and that

> ## "THE WORK SCHEDULE WAS SO TAXING THAT I REALIZED ON MY FIRST EUROPEAN TOUR THAT I COULDN'T PARTY EVERY NIGHT AND BE CAMERA-READY EVERY MORNING."

was important to me. I didn't want to be in a gender-specific category."

In her twenties, Bif railed at being categorized as a female performer. "Oh yeah, I was a real spitfire when it came to stuff like that. I definitely did not want to be objectified. But once I hit thirty I thought, 'Wait a minute. I'm kind of tired of being anorexic. I'm a woman now.' I'm a lot more comfortable in my own skin now. For the video for 'I Love Myself Today' I wore a skirt. It was a real shock to my fans and a delight to my mother."

With age, too, has come a greater appreciation for her craft. "I always hope to be a better singer. God knows I didn't have a lesson and I'm sure I could have used many. I remember I was on a really long, hard tour and I had no voice and I was on the phone to my friend Jann Arden saying, 'I just can't keep doing this.' And she said, 'Biffy, just go out there and sing like you don't need the money'. I take that advice to heart."

Currently recording her next album, Bif maintains her ties to Manitoba where her family continues to reside. "I was a northern Manitoban, middle and southern Manitoban at all different stages of my childhood. I'll always be a prairie girl. My music career began there. When people say 'Oh, you're from Winnipeg,' I just cock my head to one side, get this wild look in my eyes and reply, 'You know what they say about prairie girls!' and I give them a wink." ∎

Born in India; moved to Manitoba at age four

NAME: Beth Torbert; graduate of John Taylor Collegiate in Winnipeg

BANDS: Jungle Milk, Gorilla Gorilla, Chrome Dog, Dying To Be Violent, solo artist

ALBUMS: Bif Naked (1995), I Bificus (1999), Purge (2003); all on her own Her Royal Majesty's Records

HIT SINGLES: "Spaceman", "Lucky", "Daddy's Getting Married", "I Love Myself Today"

Toured with Lilith Fair in 1999; appeared in *Vogue, Glamour* and *Teen People* magazines

Hosted Western Canada Music Awards in 2004

# HEATHER BISHOP

**V**ERY FEW RECORDING ARTISTS have had the impact, not just on the music world but on society as a whole, that singer/songwriter Heather Bishop has. As her official biography notes, "Heather has dedicated her life to making a difference in the world. From fighting to save the environment, to struggling against racism, to fighting for women's rights and against homophobia, she has never been afraid to stand up for what she believes."

She has been honoured with awards and accolades, including the YM/YWCA Woman of Distinction and the Order of Manitoba, yet much of what Heather has contributed falls under the radar. Indeed, every young recording artist in Manitoba owes a debt to Heather's groundbreaking efforts to support and champion Manitoba music through the creation of the Manitoba Audio Recording Industry Association (MARIA) and her membership on the board of Manitoba Film and Sound.

"I had spent a lot of time in the States and overseas so I decided to devote my attention to the local music scene," explains Heather. "It has grown so enormously in the last few years. Manitoba is really making a mark not just nationally but internationally. We're a force to be reckoned with. There are so many great songwriters coming from Manitoba. We're producing some of the top Canadian children's performers. I take this very maternal pride in how great the young musicians coming out of Manitoba are and how well they're doing. And I don't think Manitobans are aware of the rich culture that comes out of this province. You have to get out of the province to see that we've made a huge mark on the world."

And Heather is part of that mark. As one of the first independent recording artists in the province she has released thirteen albums since 1979 on her own record label, with sales of over 200,000 units, pioneering the now-thriving indie music scene. She has been nominated for Junos, Prairie Music Awards and received the coveted US National Association of Parents Award twice, toured the world performing at children's festivals and folk festivals, appeared regularly on *Fred Penner's Place*, and played with symphony orchestras. Heck, she even built her own solar-powered home. "I've been blessed, that's for sure. Usually the music industry is a place where you do this for years without getting much recognition. So I feel very fortunate."

Heather began her musical career in her hometown of Regina in the early 1970s singing with a travelling dance band. "We played all the small towns in Saskatchewan so we had to play some old time music, but as the rye flowed more, I could get into some blues." Discovering folk music in the '60s led to an affinity for the blues. "When the Beatles hit, I was so immersed in the blues, Nina Simone and the records of black artists, that whole era kind of got by me."

Moving to Winnipeg in 1975, Heather launched her folk career with a performance at the Winnipeg Folk Festival the following year before heading out on the road. "The Winnipeg Folk Festival opened doors to the rest of Canada if not into the US as well. It's the premiere folk festival in North America and continues to influence young artists. It's still very relevant." Singing the songs of friend and fellow artist Connie Kaldor, Heather developed a following, and in 1979 launched Mother of Pearl Records to market her recordings, with Dan Donahue as producer. "Connie had this arsenal of great songs and no

**AS ONE OF THE FIRST INDEPENDENT RECORDING ARTISTS IN THE PROVINCE SHE HAS RELEASED THIRTEEN ALBUMS SINCE 1979 ON HER OWN RECORD LABEL, WITH SALES OF OVER 200,000 UNITS, PIONEERING THE NOW-THRIVING INDIE MUSIC SCENE.**

one having heard them before, I had this wonderful material to work with. I didn't really start writing myself until later on."

Over the next two decades Heather toured consistently, releasing both folk-oriented albums and children's recordings, carving out a separate career in that market with *Belly Button* (remaining her best selling album, going gold), *A Duck In New York* and *Chickee's On The Run*, nominated for a Juno. She credits her success not only to her talent and enthusiasm but also her business acumen. "I have a pretty good business sense. Whenever I'm mentoring young musicians I always tell them to pay attention to business. Your chances of survival are much greater then."

Despite her international stature, Heather continues to reside in Manitoba, living in tiny Woodmore, south of Winnipeg. "I made a conscious decision to stay in Manitoba. That decision has had a big impact on my career because it meant certain things about whom you worked with, what studios you'd work in, and what your influences would be. Had I moved to Toronto or Vancouver, I would have been influenced more by those cultures, which are very different. So I managed to stay rooted in a prairie culture and what is, for me, a deep and rich musical history here.

"If you look at the Jennys or the Duhks, there is a prairie thread, as diverse as the music is, that runs through it. And because they haven't left here it's alive and well. For young artists coming up, they can look at me and think, 'Heather did it. She survived all these years from here. We don't have to go to Toronto if we don't want to.'"

Recently Heather debuted another side of her multi-faceted career with *A*

*Tribute to Peggy Lee.* "Because I was influenced by Nina Simone and Billie Holiday, I've always loved that era of jazz. It's a show that I can take my band with me. Often I work alone but creating a show where I'm onstage, making music with some of the best musicians in Canada is such a privilege. And they're all Manitoba players. I don't have to go elsewhere to find good players."

Heather continues to marvel at her own success. "Every step of my career has been this little miracle. When I first started I didn't think I would get anywhere, but every year I would be surprised at

continuing to make a living at it. Then when I made an album and sold thousands of copies it was, 'Whoa, *that's* a surprise.' Then my career with children opened up.

"One of the ways I have survived is with diversity. After thirty years in the music business I have three completely different shows I can take on the road. What that has done is kept the music fresh for me so I don't get bored.

"I hit that stage each night and just smile to myself, thinking 'I love what I do.' It's quite a blessing to do what you love." ∎

Born in Regina; moved to Winnipeg in 1975

Appeared as a regular guest on CBC TV's *Fred Penner's Place*

ALBUMS: Grandmother's Song (1979); Belly Button (1982); Taste Of The Blues (1987); Old New Borrowed Blue (1992); Chickee's On The Run (1997); Daydream Me Home (1997); A Tribute to Peggy Lee (2004)

AWARDS: YM/YWCA Woman of Distinction (1997); The Order of Manitoba (2001), two U.S. Parent's Choice Gold Awards

Created her own label, Mother Of Pearl Records to distribute her recordings in 1979

Helped to found the Manitoba Audio Recording Industry Association (MARIA)

An activist for gender/pay equity, Aboriginal women's issues, founder of the first lesbian organization in Manitoba, taught the first Pre-Trades Training for Women courses in the country at Red River Community College, and founded the Women in Trades organization

Heather built her own solar home in 1979

# LENNY BREAU

**T**HE WORDS 'GENIUS' AND 'LEGENDARY' are applied far too often these days to musicians. However, in the case of guitarist extraordinaire Lenny Breau, the descriptors hardly do him justice. Lenny was, without doubt, a genius of the guitar, perhaps the greatest guitar player who ever lived. His tragic death at age 43 left a huge void in the music world.

Lenny Breau
*Boy Wonder*

Before Breau's death, Chet Atkins said: "He is one of the true geniuses of the guitar. I suppose he is a musician's musician. His knowledge of the instrument and the music is so vast, and I think that's what knocks people out about him. But he's such a tasty player too. I think if Chopin had played guitar, he would have sounded like Lenny Breau."

"It was such a loss," laments four-time Grammy winner Pat Metheny, about Lenny's premature death in 1984, "because he came up with a way of addressing the instrument technically that no one had done before, and nobody has actually done since." That's quite an endorsement, coming from Metheny, the outstanding jazz and fusion guitarist of his generation.

Born in Auburn, Maine in 1941, Lenny moved to Winnipeg with his parents in 1956, joining their travelling country music jamboree at the age of 14. Backing Hal Lone Pine and Betty Cody, Lenny, known as Lone Pine Junior, dazzled audiences with his self-taught mastery of the Chet Atkins/Merle Travis finger-picking guitar style. "All he wanted to do was play guitar," noted his mother Betty Cody, who recalls her son carrying his guitar to elementary school to practise during recess. As the CKY Caravan, Lone Pine and Betty Cody travelled throughout the Prairie provinces from their home base in St. Vital. Joining their road show on vocals was a young Ray St. Germain. Lenny backed Ray on what is regarded as Winnipeg's first rock 'n' roll single, "She's A Square."

"Lenny was always experimenting with different licks," says Ray, "but Pine always wanted the licks to be exactly the same. One time Pine slapped him after he improvised on the lick in 'Oh Lonesome Me'. But Lenny was just sick of playing the same thing over and over. He knew that he had to move on and he left his Dad's show. I always say that was the slap that changed the jazz world forever."

> "TO ME, LENNY BREAU WAS THE JOHNNY APPLESEED OF THE GUITAR. EVERY PLACE I GO IN THE WORLD TODAY I CAN FIND A GUITAR PLAYER WHO EITHER SAW LENNY PLAY, HUNG OUT WITH HIM, OR HAD A LESSON FROM HIM."

Ray witnessed firsthand Lenny's voracious appetite for music, progressing from country pickin' to jazz explorations. "It was Lenny's sixteenth or seventeenth birthday and I went down to Lowe's Music and asked 'Who's the big jazz guitar player?' and they said, 'Barney Kessel.' I gave Lenny a Barney Kessel album for his birthday. A couple of days later I was over to visit him and he said, 'Come in and listen' and he played me note-for-note the entire Barney Kessel album, both sides, all by ear. That was pretty amazing."

After the family moved to West Kildonan, novice guitarist Randy

Bachman became a frequent visitor, observing Lenny's technique and incorporating it into his own developing style. "Everything I needed to know about guitar came in those eighteen months or so I spent hanging out with him," acknowledges the Guess Who and BTO founder. "It was probably the greatest couple of years of my life in terms of my learning curve and it gave me the foundation for my playing style today because I started integrating those ideas and styles into my stage playing. Lenny was extremely disciplined. He would practise twelve hours a day." Randy would later adapt Lenny's lessons into hit songs like "Undun" and "Looking Out for #1".

By the early '60s Lenny abandoned country and rockabilly for jazz. "Lenny and I would go to the jazz clubs in town like the Stage Door on Fort Street and Jazz-a-Go Go on Edmonton," remembers Ray, "He started to play more jazz then." Married at age seventeen to Ray's sister Valerie, Lenny was also shuttling back and forth between Winnipeg and Toronto, the latter to play jazz in Yorkville clubs with singer/actor Don Francks, who Lenny backed on a 1962 album. In Toronto, Lenny recorded tracks backed by drummer Levon Helm and bass player Rick Danko both from Ronnie Hawkins' Hawks (later The Band) which were finally released over 40 years later.

In Yorkville, Lenny was beginning to experiment beyond the boundaries of contemporary music. "He had the chance to romp and play in the flowered fields of music," suggests Francks of their freeform jazz improvisations integrating classical music elements with blues and jazz. "Working the jazz clubs for me was like going to school," Lenny once remarked. Indeed, he had already synthesized his own unique guitar style, a blending of Chet Atkins, flamenco, East Indian ragas, and jazz that allowed him to play melody, accompaniment and bass all at the same time. His technique of employing crystal-clear octave harmonic arpeggios was unique to his style.

"One of the cornerstones of the Breau style," wrote Jim Ferguson in a Guitar Player retrospective entitled "Lenny Breau Remembered" in November 1984, "was his uncanny ability to play chords with his right-hand thumb and first two fingers, while superimposing single-note lines with the third finger and pinky. He occasionally added a bass line to this concept, resulting in a mind-boggling three-voice tapestry that made an indelible impression on all who heard it."

In Toronto, Lenny was also introduced to the world of drugs. At first, they were a means of musical inspiration for the quiet, introspective young man; later they took over his life.

CBC TV in Winnipeg kept Lenny busy through the early sixties performing on virtually every local music production from *Music Hop Hootenanny* with Ray St. Germain to *The George LaFleche Show.* In the off times he and his trio — Reg Keln on drums and bassist Ron Halldorson — played the jazz clubs. But Winnipeg's jazz scene was far too small for someone with such a prodigious talent so Lenny moved

on, leaving his wife and children behind. He returned to Toronto before heading south to Nashville to meet his mentor, Chet Atkins. Lenny's gypsy life was about to begin.

Under Atkins' tutelage Lenny recorded the albums *Guitar Sounds From Lenny Breau* and *The Velvet Touch of Lenny Breau — Live* in the latter '60s, both revolutionizing jazz guitar playing by breaking all the rules. His attempts to merge jazz pianist Bill Evans' chord structure into a guitar context expanded the range of the instrument. Although he released more than a dozen albums on a variety of independent labels in his short lifetime, few sold beyond the faithful. His increasing dependence on drugs made him a risk for record labels. Live performance sustained Lenny over the next decade. A brief stint backing pop singer Anne Murray offered a steady paycheque until the drugs intervened.

"Anne was going across Canada and they came through Winnipeg," recalls Ray St. Germain, who was looking after Lenny's children Chet and Melody (another daughter, Emily, was born in Edmonton), "and her manager called me and said, 'You have to come get Lenny.' I picked him up and took him to St. Boniface Hospital. He wasn't in very good condition." Ray was dismayed at his friend's deterioration. A late '70s concert at Winnipeg's Playhouse Theatre ended midway through after an incoherent Lenny was escorted offstage by Ray. "I didn't like

what he was doing and he knew it, but he got to the point where he didn't care anymore. That was the last time I saw him."

In 1981, now living in Nashville, Lenny teamed up with Chet Atkins for the duet album *Standard Brands*. However Lenny could not escape the specter of drugs, much to Chet's dismay. He would make frequent visits home to Maine to dry out only to hit the needle soon after. "It robs you of your soul," he once declared about heroin.

By the early eighties, Lenny had set himself up in Los Angeles. Married to wife Jewel, his appearance on the local jazz scene caused an immediate stir drawing lineups round the block at clubs like Donté's in Hollywood. Every guitar player of note would be there to take in Lenny's sets. By now, six strings were no longer enough for the guitar genius, who commissioned the design of a unique seven-string model to allow him to further explore his muse.

As his drug use spiralled, his performances deteriorated. Finally, on the morning of August 12, 1984, his body was found at the bottom of the swimming pool on the roof of his LA apartment block. He had just turned 43. Investigators immediately assumed foul play; friends all knew Lenny hated the water and was unlikely to be taking a swim. The case, considered a homicide, remains open to this day.

In recent years, Lenny Breau's legacy has been resurrected through the determined efforts of acolyte Randy Bachman, who created the Guitarchives label dedicated exclusively to issuing Breau recordings (Art of Life Records in Toronto has also re-released Lenny's early recordings). Randy has unearthed hundreds of hours of tape in the hands of family, friends and devotees. Royalties are distributed among Lenny's children. It is a way of returning to Lenny the valuable lessons he imparted on the young guitarist.

"To me, Lenny Breau was the Johnny Appleseed of the guitar," muses Randy. "Every place I go in the world today I can find a guitar player who either saw Lenny play, hung out with him, or had a lesson from him. He gave us more than just notes; he imparted a style that is recognizable no matter in what genre." ∎

# C-WEED/ERROL RANVILLE

**I**T'S A WONDER THAT SINGER/SONGWRITER Errol 'C-Weed' Ranville ever got the opportunity to start his music career at all. With eight brothers all playing guitar, getting his hands on the instrument wasn't easy. "There was just one guitar that we shared and it only had five strings," he laughs, recalling his younger years in rural Eddystone, Manitoba among a family of twelve siblings. Fortunately for Canadian country music, Errol managed to snag that coveted instrument. He's never looked back.

Errol acquired his lifelong nickname as a youngster. "It's just something the boys laid on me when I was a kid and it stuck," he concedes. "Even my professors at university called me C-Weed." Growing up on a diet of country music at home, Errol was turned on to the Beatles in the early sixties, and formed a band at age twelve with brothers Wally on bass, Donn on drums and Randy on guitar. C-Weed and the Weeds played around the vicinity, journeying as far as Winnipeg to play Club 376 at the Indian & Métis Friendship Centre.

Errol pursued his music career in tandem with his educational goals after the family relocated to Winnipeg in 1969, ultimately studying social work at the University of Manitoba. He began writing his songs early on, draw-ing inspiration from another Canadian singer/songwriter, Buffy Sainte-Marie. "I remember listening to her song 'Take My Hand For Awhile' and it made me cry. I thought to myself, 'If I can stir emotions like that in people, then that's what I want to do.'"

By 1975 the first C-Weed lineup (with Jim Flett replacing brother Randy on guitar) was playing regularly, but facing particular obstacles as an Aboriginal band in Winnipeg. "Club owners didn't like the Native crowd we drew at that point so we went on the road through to 1978, barely playing in the city. When we came back we were welcomed everywhere. It was

good music and cash is cash. We were *the* big country-rock band."

Signed to Winnipeg-based Sunshine Records, C-Weed's debut album, *The Finest You Can Buy*, included a cover of Canadian rock legend Robbie Robertson's "Evangeline". "I was a few credits away from graduating," he recalls, "when 'Evangeline' went to #1 and I got pulled out of school to go on the road because the demand for the band was just so huge. We were all over the country — Whitehorse one week and Toronto the next."

The group scored again with their next album *High And Dry* on their own Hawk Records label, the title track a cover of a Rolling Stones song that also rocketed up the charts to #1 in Manitoba and into the Top 10 on the national *RPM* magazine charts. "We got pretty big in the early '80s," says Errol. "In '83 it really blew out of the water with *Going The Distance*. Those were all songs I had written." The album yielded four Top 10 singles: "Play Me My Favorite Song", "Bringing Home The Good Times", "Pickup Truck Cowboy", and "Magic in The Music." That year C-Weed walked off with seven Manitoba Country Music Association awards. "We won everything except Female Vocalist," laughs Errol.

Amid the whirlwind surrounding the group, a couple of engagements stand out. One was the time they played Toronto's legendary Horseshoe Tavern. "We offered to play for nothing just to play there. We

had a free night in between touring. So the owner said sure. He had no expectations. We sold 465 seats that night. They had never seen so many Native people in their club before. And that was on short notice."

At a 1982 Center Of The Arts concert in Regina, Errol was thrilled to meet his early inspiration. "Buffy Sainte-Marie was playing at the Regina Folk Festival. We were doing our last set so she came over. I didn't know she was there. I was up front singing 'Can't You See'. Suddenly I heard this angelic voice coming out of my monitor. I looked around and there was Buffy on our stage." C-Weed played again with Buffy at the T'Saille Campus for the American Indian Music Festival.

Another engagement remains memorable for a different reason. In 1984 the group performed a free show at Edmonton's maximum security prison. "After our first song no one clapped; then another song and no one clapped. I was sweating, wondering what was going on. Then we played Johnny Paycheck's 'Eleven Months and Twenty-Nine Days' and finally one big guy in the middle started clapping and the whole place followed. That was probably one of the most awkward shows we ever did."

The group was nominated for Juno Awards in 1985 and 1986. But by the following year, Errol found the pace exhausting. He and brothers Wally and Donn parted company (Donn has since returned) while Errol assembled a new line-up including local hotshot players Craig Fotheringham and Randy Hiebert. Errol then cut a solo album of covers called *Tribute To Southern Rock*. The album included only one original song, "Old Rodeo Cowboys", which received airplay across Canada.

In 1990, Errol signed with Thunder Records, a Winnipeg-based venture founded by Fred Turner of BTO fame and lawyer David Wolinsky. The new partnership produced *I Wanna Fly*, whose

**...C-WEED WALKED OFF WITH SEVEN MANITOBA COUNTRY MUSIC ASSOCIATION AWARDS. "WE WON EVERYTHING EXCEPT FEMALE VOCALIST."**

title song returned C-Weed to the charts. Unfortunately the fledgling label could not extricate Errol from the mess that engulfed his business affairs. "We discovered I had a lien against my songwriting. It was too much of a legal battle to unravel then, so they ended up canning my project. I was left in limbo until 1995. But I've got all my songs back now."

C-Weed continued to tour further afield, appearing in Germany, Austria,

France, and the prestigious American Music Festival in Locarno, Switzerland. In 1992 Errol set aside his guitar to open C-Weed's Cabaret in north Winnipeg, later opening clubs in Edmonton and Saskatoon. It wasn't until his nephew, Mike Bruyere, joined Errol in Edmonton in 1997 that he returned to recording, releasing *Run As One* the following year. The title song remains a popular anthem among Aboriginal groups. "So many causes are using it for their theme song, so it's still growing and reaching people."

Recently, Errol joined the staff of MARIA (Manitoba Audio Recording Industry Association), sharing his expertise with up and coming artists. He was honoured with the Lifetime Achievement Award at the 2004 Canadian Aboriginal Music Awards. The recent commercial acceptance of Aboriginal music in North America is a source of pride for Errol. "It's an evolution," he suggests. "It's an amazing time in our history and songs like 'Run As One' play their part." ∎

Formed in Eddystone, Manitoba by the Ranville brothers

Moved to Winnipeg in 1969

ALBUMS: The Finest You Can Buy (1980); High And Dry (1982); Going The Distance (1983); Tribute To Southern Rock (1988); I Wanna Fly (1990); Run As One (2000)

HIT SINGLES: "Evangeline", "High And Dry", "Play Me My Favorite Song", "Bringing Home The Good Times", "Pickup Truck Cowboy", "Magic in The Music", "Old Rodeo Cowboys", "Run As One"

AWARDS: Seven MCMA awards in 1983, including Entertainer of the Year; Lifetime Achievement Award for Errol Ranville at the 2004 Canadian Aboriginal Music Awards

Performed at the Edmonton Maximum Security Prison in 1984

Appeared at the American Music Festival in Locarno, Switzerland in 1996

Errol 'C-Weed' Ranville owned a string of clubs in Western Canada called C-Weed's Cabaret

**C**OMMUNITY IS IMPORTANT to Canadian rock Hall-of-Famer Tom Cochrane. It resonates through songs like "Big League" or "Life Is A Highway". Growing up in an isolated northern Manitoba town, community remains central to how Tom defines himself as a Canadian.

"Why I've been successful has a lot to do with who I am, and who I am is because of where I'm from," he says. "If you don't have that sense of who you are, I don't think you'll have any longevity in this business. That sense of community has given me strength.

Born in the northern mining town of Lynn Lake, Tom's father, a Winnipegger, worked as a bush pilot. His mother hails from Gimli. The Cochranes remained in Lynn Lake until Tom was four, when they moved to Etobicoke in southern Ontario. Though the family would return to Manitoba often in the intervening years, the Lynn Lake experience left a profound impression. "You had to have a pretty independent, adventurous spirit to live in remote places like that. And if you're from one of those communities like I was, that stays with you."

Selling his father's train set for a guitar at age eleven, Tom began his music journey, like most 1960s era teens, emulating the Beatles and Stones, before being drawn more toward the folk music lyricism of Bob Dylan and Neil Young. "When I heard Dylan I realized there could be more than just singing simple pop songs. That's when I really started to go after it."

Driving a cab for a living, Tom cut a couple of long forgotten singles for a tiny Toronto label before joining rock group Red Rider, his arrival transforming the generic cover band into an innovative group that performed original tunes. Between 1979 and 1984 Red Rider released four acclaimed albums, all marked by Tom's thought-provoking lyrics, best illustrated on 1981's "Lunatic Fringe", recorded the night John Lennon died at the hands of a crazed fan. "That song tapped into the American psyche more than anything. It just keeps going."

*Neruda* in 1983 is regarded as the group's creative high water mark. A hasty follow-up, *Breaking Curfew*, failed to measure up to its predecessor and Red Rider folded, re-emerging three years later as Tom Cochrane & Red Rider with a revised lineup, and notching up hits "The Boy Inside The Man", "Victory Day", "Good Times" and in 1989 "Big League". Inspired by a true story told to Tom in a rural Canadian hockey arena, the song tapped into the hockey dreams at the heart of the Canadian psyche.

"What I'm most proud of is being able to tell a story like 'Big League'. And if that story is about where you're from or about something that's strongly identifiable with Canada or ties into something Canadians can understand, then it really works. Every community in Canada's got a hockey team."

Tom Cochrane & Red Rider picked up Junos in 1987 for Group of the Year, with Tom getting the nod for Composer of the Year in 1989 for "Big League".

The following year Tom went solo, releasing his breakthrough album *Mad Mad World*. The album's lead-off single, "Life Is A Highway", was the result of a recent fact-finding trip to Mozambique on behalf of World Vision, an experience that left an enduring impression on the song-writer. "I was able to tap into something joyous that came out of something very depressing. I saw people die in front of me and out of that comes the biggest success of my career."

"Life Is A Highway" became the anthem of 1991, generating sales in excess of two million copies for *Mad Mad World* and thrusting Tom into the rock stratosphere. "Things kind of start spinning out of control when you're in the maelstrom of that kind of success. Kathy [Tom's Winnipeg-born wife] and I separated for the better part of a year, but we got back together."

The strength of that song can be measured by the fact that it was used in a North American car commercial as well as on both *American Idol* and *Canadian Idol*, a point that brings a smile to the songwriter's face. "It's ironic. *American Idol* is the antithesis of where I started out and what I'm about. I wasn't American idol material."

In 1992, he walked away with four Juno Awards for Album of the Year, Song of the Year, Songwriter of the Year, and Male Vocalist of the Year.

Throughout his career Tom has championed his Canadian roots. "When I started out the thing to do was to avoid the subject of being Canadian. But I was always very proud of being Canadian. To me that was second nature."

The success accrued from *Mad Mad World* and its follow up, *Ragged Ass Road*, afforded Tom a few luxuries including his own recording studio north of Parry Sound, Ontario and, following in his father's footsteps, his own pontoon plane which he uses to fly back to Manitoba each summer to visit family. "I remember my mother brainwashing me saying 'People are friendly on the Prairies, don't you ever forget that. It's right on the license plate'. I always felt right at home in Manitoba, but I feel very strongly connected with every part of this country. There are not a lot of places in Canada where I don't feel at home, like I could kick my shoes off. I don't quite feel that way in the States."

In the spring of 2003, Tom was inducted into the Canadian Music Hall of Fame, joining early heroes like Neil Young, Ian & Sylvia and The Band. Unlike his 1992 triumph, the timing was better. "I had time to put things into perspective. I was a little older if not necessarily all that much wiser. So I'm very appreciative of it."

Despite his many accolades and successes, at heart Tom Cochrane remains true to his small town nature. "There are certain values that you find in a small town, things like caring neighbours, for example, that can really fuel the artistic spirit," he says. "It's influenced my music. And I also feel that playing these small towns has kept me grounded. Even though I don't live there any more I still feel that connection." ■

Born in Lynn Lake, Manitoba; moved to Ontario as a child

BAND: Red Rider

ALBUMS WITH RED RIDER: Don't Fight It (1980); As Far As Siam (1981); Neruda (1983); Breaking Curfew (1984); Tom Cochrane & Red Rider (1986); Victory Day (1988); The Symphony Sessions (1989); Hang On To Your Resistance (1987); as Tom Cochrane: Mad Mad World (1991); Ragged Ass Road (1995);

Songs Of A Circling Spirit (1997); X-Ray Sierra (1998)

HIT SINGLES: "White Hot", "Lunatic Fringe", "Boy Inside The Man", "Victory Day", Big League", "Good Times", "Life Is A Highway", "Sinking Like A Sunset", "Mad Mad World", "I Wish You Well"

Juno Awards for Group of the Year (1987), Composer of the Year (1989), Album, Single, Male Vocalist and

Songwriter of the Year (1992), Best Album Cover (1997), Inducted into the Canadian Music Hall of Fame (2003), plus multiple SOCAN awards

Early in his career Tom composed music for Happy Hooker Xaviera Hollander's soft porn movie *My Pleasure Is My Business*

His million selling "Life Is A Highway" was inspired by his World Vision sponsored trip to Mozambique

# CRASH TEST DUMMIES

**S**INGER/SONGWRITER AND FOUNDER Brad Roberts is realistic about the signature sound of Crash Test Dummies, his sub-basement baritone. "I ended up singing in the band by default," he admits, "because I couldn't get people to sing the songs the way I heard them. I didn't want to sing. I felt my low voice was a handicap. Ironically it became a positive because it was so different."

> "I REALLY DUG THE WINNIPEG FOLK FESTIVAL. THAT KIND OF COUNTERCULTURE ATMOSPHERE DEFINITELY INFLUENCED HOW I WANTED TO LIVE."

By the mid 1990s, the quirky Winnipeg-based quintet had sold 7 million albums worldwide, enjoyed several Top 10 hit singles, contributed to a platinum-selling soundtrack, and appeared on major television shows and concert hall stages across North America. Their celebrity status forced them to flee their own hometown in order to lead normal lives.

The story of Crash Test Dummies is almost as atypical as their distinctive

sound, emerging from a loose musical revolving door centred around Winnipeg's funkiest nightclub. St. James-raised Brad Roberts, an English literature and philosophy major at the University of Winnipeg, and neighbourhood friend Curtis Riddell formed a band to play Riddell's Blue Note Café on south Main Street in 1986. Bad Brad Roberts & the St. James Rhythm Pigs lasted only one performance, but the Blue Note remained the focal point for the aggregations Brad would assemble over the next few years that included George West, Danny Koulack, Megan Saunders, and Vince Lambert (who remained long enough to record their debut album). "Many people passed through on the premise that they were not going to be in a band," says Brad. By 1990, the familiar lineup of Brad, Ellen Reid, Ben Darvill, Dan Roberts and Mitch Dorge had coalesced.

Brad was a typical teenager obsessed with KISS, Alice Cooper and Aerosmith records. "Guitar and music were very much an escape for me from what I didn't like going on at school," he reveals. Picking up the guitar at age thirteen his tastes soon drifted toward folk music. "I really dug the Winnipeg Folk Festival. That kind of counterculture atmosphere definitely influenced how I wanted to live." But it wouldn't be until the Blue Note that he would begin taking music more seriously. "That was our gig every weekend. We really didn't play anywhere else. It grew very slowly, but I frankly had no intentions of making music my career. It was purely for fun."

When Selkirk-born keyboard player/vocalist Ellen Reid joined, the musicality of the Crash Test Dummies was elevated. Her oddball harmonies added another dimension to Brad's voice. The two had met at university. Harmonica/mandolinist Ben Darvill was the icing on the cake. "Ben came into the picture at the point when I was writing original material. He had that multi-tasking capability I felt the band needed to change up the sound."

From the get-go, the band's style defied categorization. "The thing I enjoyed was that we did a very eclectic set list," offers Brad, "everything from Alice Cooper to folk music. It was not meant to be taken seriously."

A five-song demo tape earned the group CIDO funding for a further two-song tape sent out to record labels in 1989. The group signed with BMG, who released their debut album *The Ghosts That Haunt Me* in 1991. Driven by the surprise hit single, the somber "Superman's Song", the album went on to sell 1.5 million copies, vaulting the group to the pop forefront.

Their follow-up album, *God Shuffled His Feet*, surpassed its predecessor by more than two million more copies with the unlikely single "Mmm Mmm Mmm" rising to #2 on the Billboard charts after a radio station in Georgia began playing it. The band toured relentlessly through 1994, capped by three appearances on *Late Night With David Letterman*. "Dave listened to 'Mmm Mmm Mmm' and said it would put viewers to sleep so we couldn't play it. Instead we played 'Afternoons And Coffeespoons'. A couple of months later we came back. 'Mmm Mmm Mmm' was #2 but Dave still wouldn't let us play it. We get booked a third time and still no way so we had to pull out an obscure track off the album. It was comical."

The group enjoyed an unexpected hit in 1995 with a cover of XTC's "The Ballad of Peter Pumpkinhead" sung by Ellen for the *Dumb And Dumber* soundtrack.

Despite the staggering success, Brad found touring an exhausting grind. "Some people thrive on that. I do not." He whiled away the countless hours jotting down ideas for songs. Retreating to London, England to avoid public scrutiny, Brad wrote *A Worm's Life*. "I'd made copious notes for songwriting on long bus rides."

When their fourth album, *Give Yourself A Hand,* failed to match the earlier sales, BMG began to have doubts. "I was pretty naïve about judging hit potential. I really did just write what I thought was the best thing I could write." Now residing in Harlem, New York, Brad reluctantly co-operated with the label's heavy-handed direction. "That was a long, painful record to make. I wrote thirty-five songs that were rejected by BMG before they were satisfied. That's the most urban-sounding record I ever made, which was inspired by where I was living." The album did not sell. "I was so tired of being micro-managed by the label that I negotiated to get out of my contract.

With BMG out of the picture, the group began unraveling. With less to contribute to the new sound, Ben Darvill opted for a solo career. Ellen Reid departed soon after to return to school. *I Don't Care If You Don't Mind* (2001) retained the Crash Test Dummies name but was released on Brad's own label. Conceived in Nova Scotia during his recovery from a serious car crash, Brad recruited local players for the album with Ellen Reid guesting.

Brad continues to release records and tour as Crash Test Dummies. "I would never get racked at retail if I used Brad Roberts. Crash Test Dummies is my brand." His voice remains the distinctive hallmark of the band. Brad plays solo acoustic versions of Dummies' classics on a live album, *Crash Test Dude Live* (2001). *Puss 'n' Boots* in 2003 again featured Ellen Reid. The two also teamed up to record *Songs For The Unforgiven* in an old church in Duluth, Minnesota.

And what of that voice? "I came out of the '80s where it was all screaming tenors and nobody had a low voice," he reflects. "It was good timing because it sure wouldn't have helped me a decade before." ∎

Formed in Winnipeg in 1987 at Main Street's Blue Note Café

Five-song demo tape (including "Superman's Song") recorded in Winnipeg lands contract with BMG Records

ALBUMS: The Ghosts That Haunt Me (1991); God Shuffled His Feet (1993); A Worm's Life (1995); Give Yourself A Hand (1997)

HIT SINGLES: "Superman's Song", "Mmm Mmm Mmm", "Afternoons and Coffeespoons", "The Ballad of Peter Pumpkin Head"

AWARDS: Over seven million records sold; Juno Group of the Year (1991)

Appeared three times on Late Night With David Letterman; band featured on Dumb and Dumber soundtrack

Founder/singer/songwriter Brad Roberts continues to record as Crash Test Dummies with Songs For The Unforgiven (2005), with Ellen Reid guesting

**T**O SUSTAIN A LIFELONG CAREER in the music industry you not only need talent and perseverance, but also adaptability. For former Winnipeggers Rick Johnson and Terry Thorne, change has become their hallmark over three decades on the Canadian music scene. Whether as Crawford, the Terry Crawford Band, Terri & Rick, or Terri Crawford & the Retro Rockets, they continue to entertain audiences of all ages. "We just found that to survive in this business you have to diversify," says Rick, from his home near Lindsay, Ontario. "And we've done that constantly."

**HEARING TERRY'S VOCAL PROWESS ROMPIN' RONNIE HAWKINS REMARKED, "MY GOD GIRL, YA'LL GOT PIPES STRONGER THAN A FORTY ACRE FIELD OF GARLIC!"**

Rick and Terry first met at Charleswood Collegiate in southwest Winnipeg, and formed Crawford with some classmates in 1971. The original lineup was Terry on vocals, Rick on guitar, plus drummer Birch Nero (later replaced by Dave MacKenzie), bassist Scott Gair, and Tony Ward on vocals and guitar. The group earned a name playing clubs and socials around Winnipeg, with teenage Terry's powerful vocals the major drawing card. Pianist Alan McDougall later replaced Tony.

Frequent forays into the lucrative southern Ontario market resulted in relocating to Toronto in 1977. "Back then there was a tremendous club circuit down here in Ontario," notes Rick. Guided by influential Montreal-based manager Allan Katz, the Crawford Avenue Band, as they were now known, signed with RCA Records, releasing their debut album in 1980. "They thought Crawford sounded like the Osmonds so when we signed with RCA they said, 'We want Terry's name out front.' Then when she got nominated for a Juno it was as Terry Crawford. So we just thought, 'Well, that's your name now.'"

Recorded in Montreal with producers Richard Blakin and Dixon Van Winkle, who had worked with Paul McCartney and Men Without Hats, the album yielded the single "Dreamer", featuring Terry's gritty vocals. "That raspy voice is a reflection of being on the road for ten years in smoky bars," says Rick. "She can do that Rod Stewart, Bonnie Tyler thing perfectly, then turn around and knock off a Céline Dion song." Hearing Terry's vocal prowess Rompin' Ronnie Hawkins remarked, "My God girl, ya'll got pipes stronger than a forty acre field of garlic!"

"Dreamer" was Pick of the Week in *Billboard* magazine in February 1981, and pegged to rise up the charts, but the group found themselves victims of corporate restructuring. "It got a lot of airplay across Canada," says Rick. "Then it just sat there. No one would authorize doing anything with it. But it opened a lot of doors for us. We still get requests for

Formed in Winnipeg in 1971

Original lineup consisted of class-mates from Charleswood Collegiate

ALBUMS: The Terry Crawford Band (1980); Good Girl Gone Bad (1982); Virgin Heart (1983); Total Loss of Control (1986)

HIT SINGLES: "Dreamer", "Running", "Get Away", "One Time for Old Times"

Relocated to Toronto in 1977

Toured three summers with the Beach Boys in the 1980s

"Dreamer" was Pick of the Week in *Billboard* in February 1981

Terry was the voice of Hanes' 'Wait'll we get our Hanes on you' jingle

Terry and Rick Johnson are currently working as children's entertainers in Ontario

it. We'd been on the road for ten years and it was a reflection on what we had come through."

Over the next seven years the Terry Crawford Band performed in concerts and clubs across eastern Canada. "We were in the Maritimes three or four times a year doing a college tour one time, clubs the next, then festivals." Their brand of hard rock never failed to ignite an audience. One memorable night Burton Cummings joined the band onstage. "Terry and Burton were doing 'Whole Lotta Shakin' Goin' On' and trying to out-sing each other."

The group toured three summers supporting the Beach Boys, appearing at the Edmonton Coliseum, Calgary's Saddledome, the Montreal Forum, and the CNE Grandstand. During this period, Winnipeg musicians Leonard Shaw and Sandy Chochinov joined the band. More albums appeared, including *Good Girl Gone Bad* and *Virgin Heart*, as record labels transformed Terry into an eighties rock 'n' roll diva in big hair, heavy make-up, and leather. She was nominated for a Most Promising Female Vocalist Juno in 1981 and 1982.

Further singles such as "Running", "Get Away", "Chocolate Candy" and "The Gunfighter" all received strong airplay across the country and even cracked the European market. *Total Loss of Control,* co-produced by ex-Winnipegger Tim Thorney, led to the group's debut video for "First Step". But the album proved to be their last. "As soon as the word got out that Terry was pregnant we no longer had a deal."

Undiscouraged, The Terry Crawford Band joined the resort circuit for the next few years while Rick and Terry raised their two young children. Terry also found work in the lucrative commercial jingles market. "She had a phenomenal run for about five years. She was the voice of Budweiser doing stuff like 'This Bud's for you'. She did Labatt's commercials, Hostess potato chips, Coast soap, Sprite, General Motors, Coca-Cola. She did all the 'Wait'll we get our Hanes on you' commercials. She was getting royalty cheques from as far away as Bahrain." Terry also appeared on the soundtrack for one of the *Friday the 13th* movies.

As the jingles market dried up in the mid nineties, Rick and Terri (changing the "y" to "i") once again proved their flexibility, moving into children's entertain-ment and releasing three popular children's albums and appearing at over 300 schools across Ontario. "The kid's stuff we're doing now is just a hoot. We've made more money from the kid's records than the band records. We're doing the same show we were doing for adults twenty years ago with the lights and effects only the audience is shorter and sober. We have a new audience every three years."

Rick and Terri continue to perform for rock audiences as Terri Crawford and the Retro Rockets. "We'll do a kid's show in the morning and an adult show in the evening. You have to hustle to make a living but we're booked far ahead and we're always busy."

As a longtime school trustee, Rick was recently elected President of the Ontario Public Schools Association. He also operates Ricter Scale Music which includes his own home recording studio.

In July 2000, Rick and Terry returned to Winnipeg for the Charleswood Collegiate reunion, reuniting with the original members of Crawford to play the gala dance.

"To be able to have had a career in this country for thirty-three years is really quite remarkable," muses Rick. "We've always said that we'd continue doing it until it's no longer fun. And we're still doing it." ■

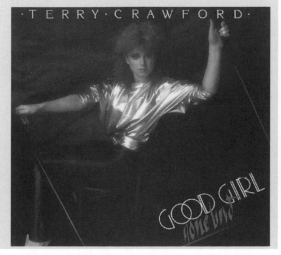

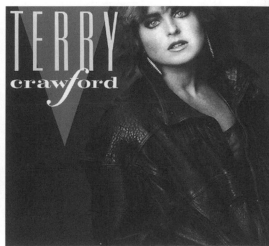

# THE CRESCENDOS/ 5 AM EVENT

**T**HEY NEVER TOURED NATIONALLY NOR APPEARED ON TELEVISION; they only recorded one obscure single. Yet while the name may not mean much to most Canadians, Winnipeg's Crescendos accomplished something no other Canadian artist can claim, and in doing so achieved an immortality that is the envy of every 1960s-era musician.

> "WE GOT TO A POINT WHERE WE FELT THE ONLY WAY TO MAKE IT WAS TO GET OUT OF WINNIPEG. WE DECIDED THAT THE BEST THING WAS TO GO TO ENGLAND. WE THOUGHT EVERYONE IN LIVERPOOL HAD A RECORDING CONTRACT."

Recently a commemorative wall was unveiled in Liverpool, England near the site of the original Cavern Club, the dingy cellar where the Beatles were discovered. The Cavern served as the launching pad for the entire Merseybeat scene and was ground zero for the British Invasion. Prominent bands associated with the Cavern in its heyday are inscribed on individual bricks surrounding a plaque. The list is impressive, a who's who of Merseybeat including the Beatles, Gerry & the Pacemakers, and the Searchers. Set amongst the bricks is the Crescendos. Further down is another brick with the inscription 'The 5 AM Event', the name the Winnipeg quartet took soon after their debut appearance at the legendary club.

In the summer of 1965 the Crescendos — vocalist/sax player Glenn MacRae, drummer Vance Masters, guitarist Terry Loeb, and bass player Dennis Penner — dared to live the dream of every North American teenager when they left Winnipeg bound for the Mecca of pop music: Liverpool. "We had seen the Beatles movies and *Ferry Cross The Mersey* and figured that's where it was at," says Glenn.

Formed in the Elmwood neighbourhood in 1963, the group became popular on the Winnipeg community club circuit, and also appeared often at the Twilight Zone, a trendy St. Vital teen club. "We got to a point where we felt the only way to make it was to get out of Winnipeg," Glenn recalls. "We decided that the best

thing was to go to England. We thought everyone in Liverpool had a recording contract."

In August 1965, the four received a royal send-off at the train station with dozens of fans and media on hand to bid them good luck. "We arrived in Liverpool by boat in the evening," Glenn remembers. "The immigration offices were closed so we stood by the rail and stared at the city all night. We couldn't sleep from excitement." Their first destination was the Cavern. "They were having an all-night session with a half-dozen bands. We met a group called The Easybeats that night who introduced us around. We had no idea that Britain had different electric circuits. They got our gear straightened out so our amps worked." The Crescendos soon discovered a similarity between the Winnipeg music community and Liverpool's. "There was a family feeling amongst the bands. We were never treated as outsiders."

The group found being Canadians was a novelty to Liverpudlian teens, and the locals considered their repertoire unusual. "We were playing all the British songs we used to do at the community clubs," laughs Glenn. "Musicians would ask, 'Why are you doing those tunes?' We were playing Merseybeat music in the middle of the Merseybeat scene. It would be like a band coming to Winnipeg and playing Guess Who songs." After a month of tough slogging, on September 26, 1965, the Crescendos played the Cavern.

"The first time we were so nervous," recalls Glenn. "That was the ultimate thrill

for us to stand on that stage. I was quite shocked at how tiny it was. We went down well but I felt we needed to get ourselves together more. When we came back the next time we were ready. By then we had Stuart McKernan in the band, a Liverpudlian." (Stuart replaced Dennis Penner, who had returned home.) The group played the Cavern several times over the next six months.

"In Liverpool you did an hour and then another band would do the next set," reveals Glenn. "So you had to line up several gigs a night because they didn't pay that much. You would play a set, pack up and head to another place, set up, play, then head to another gig."

Besides the Cavern, the Crescendos appeared at several popular Liverpool nightspots. "If you couldn't get a gig anywhere else, you'd go down to the Blue Angel and play there," Glenn explains, "where you played from eight in the evening until two a.m. with only two breaks. We played there a lot in the early months. We had some heavy-duty people

come in and play because they were gigging in the vicinity. Paul McCartney got up one night when we were playing. He and Freddy Starr, a popular singer and comedian, were doing Little Richard songs, trying to out-Little Richard each other. The Who came in and played one night."

"Another night John Lennon came in. He was drunk and I couldn't get over what a jerk he was. Peter Noone of Herman's Hermits came into the Blue one night. He was not viewed as a musician, and was from Manchester, so there was animosity. He announced, 'Drinks for everybody' and no one would drink them."

At a late night set at the Iron Door club, the Crescendos were spotted by Searchers' drummer Chris Curtis who renamed them the 5 AM Event and took them to London to record a single for Pye Records. Despite signing with music industry heavyweight Tito Burns, the single, a cover of Paul Revere and the Raiders' "Hungry", failed to chart. Today the single is one of the UK's most highly

collectible '60s-era artifacts, valued at £100.

With the failure of their single and still plying the Liverpool club circuit, the Crescendos decided to come home in early 1967. "We had no money and we used to steal coal from neighbour's bins," chuckles Glenn. "We had burned all the furniture in our flat for heat. We would follow the milkman, steal the bottles from doorsteps and turn them in for a couple of cigarettes and a little food." It was an ignominious return. The group resumed playing locally before going their separate ways, Vance to the Fifth and later Brother before joining a latter day Guess Who, while Glenn went on to manage Long & McQuade Music in Winnipeg. Terry was killed in a car accident in the 1980s.

"When I'm lying in bed sometimes and can't sleep, I often envision myself walking down the old streets in Liverpool, going to the Kardoma Café or Hessy's Music, the Cavern, and all my old haunts," Glenn reflects ∎

Formed in Winnipeg in 1963

Left Winnipeg in 1965 for Liverpool, England

September 26, 1965 played the Cavern Club, the only Canadian band to ever do so

SINGLE: "Hungry", produced by The Searchers' Chris Curtis in London (copies are highly-prized today)

Drummer Vance Masters briefly backed the Merseys, who enjoyed a hit with "Sorrow"

Played the Blue Angel club with Paul McCartney

The group is included in a Cavern Club commemorative wall in Liverpool

Bass player Stuart McKernan turned down an offer to join the Bee Gees

# CROWCUSS

## CROWCUSS

**W**INNIPEG IS PERHAPS BEST KNOWN for guitar-driven bands. But one local group enjoying a Top Ten hit single and prominence as far away as Guatemala without a guitar player. That band was Crowcuss.

Named for Manitoba's prairie flower, Crowcuss emerged phoenix-like from the ashes of much loved local quartet Mood Jga Jga in the spring of 1976. Guitarist Greg Leskiw and keyboard player Hermann Frühm found themselves without a rhythm section for a weeklong gig at the Norlander Hotel on Pembina Highway. A call was placed to bass player Bill Wallace and drummer/singer Marc LaFrance. Adding keyboardist Larry Pink, the five fulfilled the commitment as Mood Jga Jga. From that Crowcuss was born.

Each of the five had solid musical credentials. Greg and Bill were veterans of the Guess Who while Larry and Marc came from popular club act Musical Odyssey. "They were like the older guys and I was the young kid who was fortunate enough to be playing with Guess Who alumni," Marc says.

With an ear toward the free-flight sonic excursions of jazz-rock fusion artists like Herbie Hancock and the Mahavishnu Orchestra, Crowcuss became known as a musician's band. "Some songs would last twenty minutes and we'd go through a huge amount of complicated time changes," laughs Marc. "At rehearsals they were calling out chords and I didn't know what the hell they were talking about." As principal songwriter Greg found the complex arrangements daunting at times. "For me it was a real challenge keeping up with guys who, musically, were someplace else." he says. "Were we a jazz fusion band, a pop band, or a country rock band? We had all those things going on at once."

> ### NAMED FOR MANITOBA'S PRAIRIE FLOWER, CROWCUSS EMERGED PHOENIX-LIKE FROM THE ASHES OF MUCH LOVED LOCAL QUARTET MOOD JGA JGA IN THE SPRING OF 1976.

An instant attraction around Winnipeg, Crowcuss hit the road in a refitted school bus, working their way to Vancouver. At a gig in Powell River, BC, the five were surprised by the marquee billing them as the Guess Who. A demo tape cut at Roade studio under the auspices of arranger Jack Lenz led to a contract with Edmonton-based Stony Plain Records. Owner Holger Peterson mortgaged his Edmonton home to finance sessions.

But by the time Crowcuss booked into Mushroom Studios in Vancouver, Greg was gone, citing musical differences. "I went to pick him up one day," says Marc, "and I said to him, 'Wow, what a beautiful day,' and he said, 'Yeah, it's a great day to quit the band.' We had a lot of dominant people in that band who would argue for hours. I think Greg works better when he's more in control."

"It went from a jazz fusion group to pop R & B," states Greg. "I just wanted to get back to having my own band again."

Rather than spend time searching for a replacement, the four soldiered on, cutting their self-titled album with a unique twin synthesizer and electric piano sound and stellar vocals. Released in 1979, *Crowcuss* was an impressive debut, with the hit single "Running Start" penned by Larry Pink. Besides becoming a hit in western Canada, the bouncy, disco-flavoured single rose to #1 in Guatemala. "Apparently we had two #1 hits down there," chuckles Marc. Their success in Central America was the result of a local importer who cajoled radio stations into spinning the record. However, the group couldn't exactly afford to tour Guatemala.

Instead they relocated to Revelstoke, British Columbia where Bill and friend Tim Sewell purchased a restaurant. With Revelstoke as a base, Crowcuss worked throughout BC and Alberta, occasionally flying out to gigs across Canada. "We were on the road all the time," states

Formed by ex-Guess Who members Greg Leskiw and Bill Wallace in Winnipeg in 1976

Played first gig as Mood Jga Jga before changing name

Greg Leskiw left in 1978 to form LesQ (later Kilowatt)

ALBUMS: Crowcuss (1979); Starting To Show (1980)

HIT SINGLE: "Running Start"

Enjoyed a #1 single in Guatemala

Relocated to Revelstoke BC in 1980

Bill Wallace owned Timothy Eatin's Great Canadian Restaurant in Revelstoke

Drummer/vocalist Marc LaFrance has recorded with Bon Jovi, Motley Crue, David Lee Roth, Scorpions, the Cult, and Cher

Marc. "We played at the CNE in Toronto warming up Burton Cummings and a week later we were at the PNE in Vancouver. And in between we played festivals, concerts and club dates."

Sessions for a follow up album were held at Winnipeg's Century 21 Studios, but by now the group had once again retooled their sound. "When Greg left we just took a different direction," says Marc, "but we were a rock band so we went back to our rock 'n' roll roots. That album was more hard-edged than our first, which was a little more disco. The second one had more of that Winnipeg prairie rock guitar flavour." Crowcuss recruited Saskatchewan guitarist Bob Deutscher to give them the energy they sought. Tours and TV appearances (including 10:30 Live and Peter Gzowski) followed the 1980 release of Starting To Show, the title track a Greg Leskiw composition. "There were some of Greg's songs on both albums," notes

Marc, "because he was such a great writer." Despite not spawning another hit single, the album showcased the group's strong writing and skilled playing and drew even more fans. "A big moment for me," Marc remembers, "was when we played the CHED Bicycle Picnic in Edmonton. There were about 20,000 people and fifty or sixty girls were screaming and trying to rip my clothes off. Security had to help me get off the grounds."

By the following year Crowcuss found its wheels spinning. "We had all moved out to BC," states Marc, "and I started doing a ton of session work. When someone is paying you thousands of dollars you're not going to want to go make a hundred dollars with a band. Each of us just moved on and started doing other things."

The respect accorded Crowcuss by the music community carried considerable weight for the individual members

following dissolution. "I was able to walk into recording studios and get work singing on over a hundred albums," Marc says, "The band certainly kick-started my career." Marc's resumé includes working with Bon Jovi, Motley Crüe, David Lee Roth, Scorpions, the Cult, and Cher to name but a few. He released a solo album, Out of Nowhere, produced by Loverboy's Paul Dean. Larry Pink hooked up with Edmonton country rockers One Horse Blue. Hermann Frühm later founded and operates Megapro Tools in Vancouver. Back in Winnipeg, Bill Wallace teamed up again with Greg Leskiw to form Kilowatt.

"It was always fun," maintains Marc, who recalls his one brush with fame. "We were doing a CBC TV show and all these girls came up to me and wanted my autograph. So I'm signing away and then one of these girls looks at me and says, 'Hey, you're not from Cheap Trick!'" ∎

**B**URTON CUMMINGS IS UNQUESTIONABLY Winnipeg's favourite rock 'n' roll son, with a community centre and performing theatre named in his honour. He has rarely failed to acknowledge his debt of gratitude to his hometown in general, and his beloved North End in particular, and continues to reside in Winnipeg. "It's my home and always will be," he says.

Burton Lorne Cummings was raised on Bannerman Avenue east of Main Street. His gift for music emerged at an early age. "I started piano lessons at age four," he reveals. "I loved rock 'n' roll but I didn't much care for classical piano. I hadn't put the two together yet. But the minute I found out I could play 'Diana' by Paul Anka that was it. Next thing I knew, my mother couldn't tear me away from the piano." At St. John's High, Burton starred in several Gilbert and Sullivan operettas but it was a neighbourhood group of novice rock 'n' rollers that piqued his interest. At age fourteen he joined his buddy Edd Smith in the Deverons.

"It was mostly instrumentals," he recalls. "I would come out and do 'Wild Weekend' on sax, maybe 'Crossfire', and sing 'Walk Right In' or 'Come On Let's Go'. Then I'd have to leave the stage. I didn't like that. One night instead of leaving I started playing the piano along with their instrumentals and the kids went nuts! Now I didn't have to leave the stage. From that moment on, the band became mine."

As the Deverons' reputation spread beyond the North End the teenage group released two singles for the REO label. "Music was the only thing in my life," Burton says. "I couldn't care less about anything until four p.m. on a Friday, then it was, "We're on tonight!'" By late 1965 the group was among the top echelon of popular local groups. It was then that Burton was plucked to join the kingpins, the Guess Who. "I said 'Yes' right on the spot," he says. "They were the biggest band in the country. Gift horses are rare

animals and you shouldn't look them in the mouth."

Burton rode the Guess Who roller coaster for the next ten years, enduring the lean years of the latter '60s and the salad days of the early Æ70s, emerging as one of the finest vocalists in the music business and a talented songwriter in his own right, having penned or collaborated on the group's biggest hits. By late 1975, however, at odds with the other band members over musical direction, Burton

announced the end of the Guess Who and prepared to launch what was anticipated to be a successful solo career. He was twenty-seven years old.

Signing with Portrait Records, a division of CBS Records, Burton began recording his self-titled debut album the following year in Los Angeles under the direction of producer-to-the-superstars Richard Perry, whose previous clients included Barbra Streisand, Carly Simon and Ringo Starr. The choice of producer indicated Burton's star power potential. *Burton Cummings*, released in 1976, proved that potential, featuring the million-selling single "Stand Tall", a poignant, autobiographical ballad with lush orches-

**BURTON RODE THE GUESS WHO ROLLER COASTER FOR THE NEXT TEN YEARS, ENDURING THE LEAN YEARS OF THE LATTER '60S AND THE SALAD DAYS OF THE EARLY '70S, EMERGING AS ONE OF THE FINEST VOCALISTS IN THE MUSIC BUSINESS AND A TALENTED SONGWRITER...**

tration by Elton John's arranger Paul Buckmaster. Canadian hits "I'm Scared" and "Your Backyard" followed. The future looked rosy for Burton's solo career. With his neatly-coiffured do, trendy moustache, and well-tailored suits, Burton became every girl's dream date.

Sell-out tours across Canada, including his first solo appearance in Winnipeg November 8, 1976, at the Centennial Concert Hall, solidified Burton's position as the country's top solo attraction. "One of the most gratifying things has been touring under my own name," he reflected in an interview. "Sometimes when you leave a well-known band it's almost immediate death. I'm pleased there are still people who like me or my songs. It's amazing to me I'm still some people's favourite singer." He need not have worried.

*My Own Way To Rock* followed in 1977, once again produced by Richard Perry. Although boasting several more Canadian hits including the title track and

Born in Winnipeg

BANDS: the Deverons, the Guess Who, solo artist

DEBUT SOLO ALBUM: Burton Cummings (1976); BIGGEST SELLING ALBUM: Dream Of A Child (1979)

HIT SINGLES: "Stand Tall", "My Own Way To Rock", "Break It To Them Gently", "You Saved My Soul"

Juno Male Vocalist of the Year and Best New Male Vocalist (1977, 1980); Best Selling Album award (1979)

Starred in movie *Melanie* (1980) with Don Johnson; toured with Ringo Starr (1994); Burton Cummings Community Club (1990) and Burton Cummings Theatre (2001) named for him

"Timeless Love", the album did not fare as well in the States. His label wanted Burton the piano crooner, not Burton the hard rocker. The album marked a reconciliation with former Guess Who collaborator Randy Bachman, who guested on several tracks. Burton's own "Never Had A Lady Before" became a surprise hit for Tom Jones. Meantime Burton starred in his first national television special for CBC, beginning a run of several top-rated shows over the next five years that included *Burton Cummings West, My Own Way To Rock, Going For Gold*, and *Burton Cummings: Portage and Main*. The last one featured a Deverons reunion at St.

John's High School and Burton in goal taking slap shots from the Winnipeg Jets' star player, Bobby Hull.

At the 1977 Juno Awards, Burton scooped up Male Vocalist of the Year and Best New Male Vocalist for his debut album. He returned to the Juno podium in 1979, 1980, 1982 and 1983 to host the annual Canadian music fête, walking off with the Best Selling Album award in 1979 for his third solo album *Dream Of A Child*, and another Best Male Vocalist award in 1980. The self-produced album sold triple-platinum (over 300,000 sales) in Canada alone, the first Canadian album to do so, and again included hit singles like perennial crowd-pleaser "Break It To

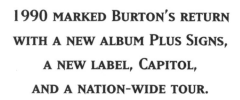

**1990 MARKED BURTON'S RETURN WITH A NEW ALBUM PLUS SIGNS, A NEW LABEL, CAPITOL, AND A NATION-WIDE TOUR.**

Them Gently", inspired by a TV cop show, and the elegant "I Will Play A Rhapsody". Settled in the well-heeled LA suburb of Sherman Oaks, it looked like there was no stopping Burton's train.

However, the release of his next self-produced album *Woman Love* pointed to some problems. Portrait Records in the US refused to release the album, worried that it lacked commercial appeal despite notching up a further Canadian hit with "Fine State Of Affairs" that sold over 100,000 copies. When they requested "additional sweetening" to the album Burton resisted and the label dropped him. In the end he was vindicated. *Woman Love* proved to be a cohesive album that found the singer in a mellower, more reflective mood. "I ended up walking away from a multi-million dollar deal," he later remarked, "and to this day I have never been sorry. Integrity comes at an extremely high price." A starring role in the feature film *Melanie* alongside *Miami Vice* star Don Johnson in 1980, while impressive for a newcomer with no acting experience, did poorly at the box office,

scuttling his dream of a film career.

Burton's next album, *Sweet Sweet*, released on Epic in Canada in 1981, was well-received and again Burton found his way to the top of the charts with the anthem "You Saved My Soul". He continued to tour Canada to sold out houses and appeared on several television shows.

A three-year hiatus ended in 1984 with *Heart*, released in Canada only. "Love Dreams" was another Canadian hit but the album disappeared quickly, a blow that left Burton reeling. There would be no new Burton Cummings records for the next six years. Married to Cheryl DeLuca, he remained somewhat reclusive and even entered a rehab facility to deal with substance abuse. Former glories marked those interim years as Burton took part in a 1983 Guess Who reunion tour as well as a tour alongside former Guess Who mate Randy Bachman in 1987. Both tours proved Burton still had immense drawing power. He also supported buddies Blair and Garry MacLean, appearing with them in taverns and clubs as MacLean, MacLean & Cummings. In 1992 he realized a teenage dream by joining Beatles drummer Ringo Starr's All Starr Band for a world tour where Burton stole the show each night.

1990 marked Burton's return with a new album *Plus Signs*, a new label, Capitol, and a nation-wide tour. The album yielded a television concert special and went gold. "I wouldn't have written those songs when I was in my twenties or even my thirties," he revealed. "Turning

forty was a milestone." The single "Take One Away", written with former Winnipegger Bill Ivaniuk, remained in heavy rotation across the country for several months.

In 1995 Burton launched his Up Close and Alone concept, featuring the singer alone at a keyboard onstage telling the stories behind his best-known songs and sharing personal moments from his career. The tour proved so successful that he extended it over the next four years,

releasing a live album for MCA Canada, and in the process moving back to his hometown.

In 1999 the Guess Who reunited for the closing of the Pan American Games. The event became the catalyst for a three-year reunion that found Canada's greatest band reliving old glories. Since then Burton has been recording new songs and plans to release another solo album in the future. His legion of fans wait in anticipation. ∎

# DW ACKER
## DOC WALKER

**F**OR PORTAGE LA PRAIRIE COUNTRY ROCK artists Doc Walker, slow and steady wins the race. In the last couple of years the multi-award winning quintet have wowed audiences with their high-energy blend of modern country and good old rock 'n' roll. But the group, led by Westbourne, Manitoba singer/songwriter Chris Thorsteinson, is hardly an overnight sensation, nor do they intend to be a flash in the pan.

**"BY PLAYING FIVE SETS A NIGHT YOU GET TO SEE WHAT IT IS THAT MAKES A PARTICULAR SONG AFFECT PEOPLE A CERTAIN WAY, OR GETS THEM JUMPING OUT OF THEIR SEATS AND DANCING."**

"We spent a lot of time going out on the road," says Chris, speaking from the band's tour bus. "That was really important. You've got to get out there and play the bars and play 'Takin' Care of Business' 500 times to understand why it's a hit. By playing five sets a night you get to see what it is that makes a particular song affect people a certain way, or gets them jumping out of their seats and dancing. After five years on the road you have that background. It's really all about knowing your audience and trying to connect with them."

The catalyst for the formation of the original lineup of the band in the Westbourne area was an unlikely event. "The first gig I ever did was for the Johnson family reunion. When they were talking about entertainment my mom said, 'My son plays in a band.' So she told us we had to learn forty country songs. We pulled it off." The group settled on calling themselves Doc Walker, named for a friend of Chris's. "Doc Thorsteinson was a little too much to handle."

Formed in Westbourne, Manitoba in 1991

Toured for five years before debut album released

ALBUMS: A Good To Ride (1995); Curve (2001); Everyone Aboard (2003)

HIT SINGLES: "She Hasn't Always Been This Way", "Whoever Made Those Rules", "Rocket Girl", "Get Up", "The Show is Free", "North Dakota Boy"

AWARDS: Fourteen MCMA Awards including Entertainer of the Year (1998); CCMAs for Independent Group of the Year and SOCAN Song of the Year (2003) and Group of the Year (2004); Prairie Music Awards' Country Recording of the Year (2002); Western Canada Music Awards' Entertainer of the Year (2004); five Top 5 video hits on CMT

Recently wrote and recorded with Guess Who/BTO legend Randy Bachman

Guitarist Murray Pulver used to be with Crash Test Dummies and Amanda Stott

Beat out Nickelback and Nelly Furtado for Entertainer of the Year at 2004 Western Canada Music Awards

Chris's parents, unlike those of many young musicians, were supportive of his decision to pursue a music career. "They've always been one hundred percent behind the band. They're not rich but if our Suburban broke down they would send us the money to get it fixed. We've been fortunate to have that support team early in our career."

The group followed up with local gigs, but the focus for Chris was on cutting a record. The addition of Portage la Prairie guitarist Dave Wasyliw had a major impact on the direction of Doc Walker. "I had written most of the first album myself and it was really very country, with fiddle and steel guitar. But Dave was a real rock 'n' roll guy. We realized we had something special onstage and singing together, so we started writing together. We have a mutual respect for each other's influences. I started to experiment more when Dave joined."

Released in 1995, *A Good Day To Ride* garnered solid reviews and yielded four singles. "The first album it was basically my mom Betty and I promoting it." It would be more than five years before the band's sophomore album, during which time drummer Mark Branconnier and bassist Blake Manley joined (Manley was recently replaced by Winnipegger Paul Yee). Hooking up with Toronto-based manager Ron Kitchener, the group secured a contract with Universal Music Canada and recruited Canadian country star Joel Feeney to produce the next album, *Curve*. "Being from Manitoba, our attitude was 'We don't want any Toronto producers' because we didn't want it to sound like a Toronto country album. But Joel said right off the bat, 'This is *your*

record. You've got to live with it, not me.' So that really caught our attention and he's been very supportive of what we wanted to do."

*Curve* was the breakthrough the band had worked so long to achieve. Sporting a rockier approach, the band scored four Top 10 hits. "When 'She Hasn't Always Been This Way' went Top 10, I went, 'Whoa, this is pretty cool!' Then every single went Top 10 other than 'Call Me A Fool' and it went to #11 so that was a pretty exciting time for the band." A throwaway song by country recording artist Jason McCoy and Denny Carr, "Rocket Girl", gave Doc Walker their biggest hit. "Jason didn't like it. Ron thought it was a hit and sent us a CD with just Jason singing with acoustic guitar. Dave and I thought it was fantastic. We couldn't believe Jason didn't want it. I never imagined that it would connect nationally like it did."

The album earned Doc Walker Juno nominations for Best New Country Artist/Group and Best Country Recording in 2003. They picked up Canadian Country Music Awards for Independent Group of the Year and SOCAN Song of the Year. They walked off with Country Recording of the Year at the 2002 Prairie Music Awards and hauled away six Manitoba Country Music Association Awards including Entertainer, Song, Male Vocalist, Group, Recording Artist and Video of the Year Awards.

The success was validation for the path Doc Walker chose. "From the get-go country music kept saying, 'You're too rock,' but we always kept that rock 'n' roll flair. Two years ago we went to Nashville and they looked at us like we were insane.

Now country is as rock 'n' roll as it gets. We just figured it's better to play our own stuff and our own sound and wait around for everyone else to catch up."

Their third album, *Everyone Aboard*, recorded at Winnipeg's Mid-Canada Productions, earned the group further accolades and singles success with "The Show is Free", "North Dakota Boy", and "Get Up", the latter one of three songs on the album co-written by Chris and ex-Northern Pikes guitarist Bryan Potvin. The album breached the Top 10, earned the band five CCMA nominations, and won them Country Group of the Year. In 2004 the group expanded to a quintet with the addition of former Amanda Stott and Crash Test Dummies guitarist Murray Pulver. At the Western Canada Music Awards in 2004, they won Entertainer of the Year, beating out Nickelback and Nelly Furtado.

Chris sees the band's future in Nashville. "We had to prove ourselves in Canada, so we're not frightened at all about going down to Nashville and plugging it out as long as it takes. That's the way that we do things. We always wanted to be thought of as a working, touring band."

Wherever they are based, Doc Walker will never lose touch with its fans. "We've always been writing and playing our music for the fans," declares Chris, who continues to reside in Westbourne. "We'll just keep playing as much as we can, trying to keep up with what the fans want and try to write the best we can.

"I think us doing it the slowpoke way has definitely made a difference and helped us out." ∎

THE DUHKS EMERGED FROM THE ASHES OF LEONARD'S PREVIOUS ECLECTIC ENSEMBLE SCRUJ MACDUHK, A MUCH-LOVED WINNIPEG FOLK GROUP

**W**HEN YOUR PARENTS are the first family of Winnipeg folk music it's inevitable that you're going to grow up with that music in your blood. For Leonard Podolak, son of legendary Winnipeg Folk Festival and West End Cultural Centre founders Mitch Podolak and Ava Kobrinsky, his music career with popular Celtic/traditional band the Duhks was almost predestined.

"It's funny because when I was growing up I took all that music for granted," says Leonard, taking a break from recording sessions in Nashville. "In fact I resented it. 'That was the thing that kept Daddy busy all the time.' Then, all of a sudden I was a big fan of Celtic and old time music and I didn't even know what they were if you asked me. It was, 'Oh, I know that song. I've been listening to that jig since I was three.' When it all came together in my head I realized, 'Oh shit, this really is a part of me.' I knew then that this was my calling."

The Duhks — Leonard, singer Jessica Havey, Tania Elizabeth on fiddle, guitarist Jordan McConnell, and percussionist Scott Senior — are currently riding an incredible tide of acclaim for their unique fusion of musical genres — from traditional Appalachian Mountain bluegrass to folk, Celtic reels and French jigs. Their debut album *Your Daughters & Your Sons* led to a contract with prestigious US-based Americana/roots label Sugar Hill Records, as well as a contract with the Creative Artist Agency in Nashville, pointing to a high-flying future for the Winnipeg-based group.

The Duhks emerged from the ashes of Leonard's previous eclectic ensemble Scruj MacDuhk, a much-loved Winnipeg folk group. Formed in 1997, Scruj recorded two albums, was nominated for a Juno Award, and won two Prairie Music Awards in 1999 for their album *Road To Canso*. "That was quite a pat on the back for us to be regarded on the same level as Great Big Sea and the Barra McNeil's."

Scruj featured singer Ruth Moody, who went on to form The Wailin' Jennys, along with a long list of personnel including fiddler Jeremy Penner, Jeremy Walsh on guitar, bassist Oliver Swain, percussionist Christian Dugas, and Leonard playing five-string clawhammer banjo. When the band split up in 2001, Leonard decided to carry on.

"It was our first band that we all really cared about and started to succeed in. I wanted to keep the party going with the blend of traditional influences." Having toured with a later version of Scruj, Jordan was enlisted for the new band. "This lineup was sort of an arranged marriage," laughs Leonard. "I called all these people and kind of forced them together. I was looking for people who were willing to not make any money for two years to get this thing off the ground. Jordan is a monster guitar player and I knew I could work with him. Jessica and I sort of grew up at the Winnipeg Folk Festival. Her mom was a longtime volunteer and friend of my family. Her uncle was living in my basement and he recommended Jessica. We got together and she sang and it was very cool."

Tania was first spotted at a Scruj gig in Vancouver. "She showed up with her fiddle and jammed, she was only fourteen years old, and she blew the roof off the joint. So she was in the back of my mind for the new lineup." Tania has released two solo albums and served as Celtic instructor at Nashville legend Mark O'Connor's fiddle camp.

Reconstituted and renamed ("We wanted to keep the connection with the old name"), the Duhks began their journey recording an independent album with help from Manitoba Film and Sound. "We are so lucky in Canada to have something like this. American musicians can't believe it: a government agency that provides money to artists to make records. There's nothing like that there. They've supported every project I've gone to them with." Appearances at festivals across North America brought the group to the attention of Sugar Hill Records.

"I have so many Sugar Hill albums in my own record collection but I never thought they would go for us. But they called us up after seeing us at a festival and picking up our CD. A couple of weeks later they signed us." The label sent the group to Nashville to record their second album under the direction of renowned banjo player Bela Fleck. "Our new album has branched out even further with gospel and even some rock 'n' roll! But we're still keeping it acoustic and not changing who we are." The album will be released in early 2005.

While in Nashville, they were approached by the powerful Creative Artist Agencies. "We played our stuff for them and they went nuts. The dude that signed us said, 'Don't let them out of here without a contract!' For this to happen for a band that plays the kind of music we play is incredible. That was such a huge affirmation of what we're doing."

Leonard sees the group's immediate future south of the border. "In the States there are far more festivals, folk clubs and gigs. It's on a bigger scale. And they really get our music down there. They really appreciate the diversity of what we're trying to do. That's certainly one of the

things that grabbed Sugar Hill. So I think the States is definitely where it's at for us right now."

Despite their growing reputation in the US, Leonard regards Winnipeg as the group's spiritual base and his own personal roots as inspirational. "There are a lot of songwriters in Winnipeg and a lot of really interesting musicians, too. And a lot of it has to do with the Winnipeg Folk Festival. People go to the festival and their world gets transformed. I can't really think of any folk musicians who would be playing that kind of music if it weren't for

the Folk Festival. Where would they get exposure to that kind of music or get to play or find like-minded people? I think the Folk Festival has been a huge catalyst for so many people.

"When I started doing this I wasn't thinking I was going to be signed to a huge agency and sell a pile of records. It was just because I wanted to play banjo with my buddies. It comes from the heart, what's inside you. Success isn't measured for me in career terms, but in doing something heartfelt that's what you enjoy." ■

Formed in Winnipeg in 2001

Originally Scruj MacDuhk

ALBUM: Your Daughters & Your Sons (2003), The Duhks (2005)

Recorded 2 albums as Scruj MacDuhk: Live At The West End (1997); Road To Canso (1999 — won two Prairie Music Awards)

Recently signed to US-based roots label Sugar Hill Records

Leader Leonard Podolak is the son of Winnipeg Folk Festival and West End Cultural Centre founder Mitch Podolak

Wailin' Jennys singer Ruth Moody began her career with Scruj MacDuhk

Teen fiddler Tania Elizabeth served as Celtic instructor at Mark O'Connor's Nashville fiddle camp

THE TENSE STANDOFF AT OKA, QUEBEC in the summer of 1990 was a flashpoint for Canadian Aboriginal people, but also a personal epiphany for Winnipeg musician Vince Fontaine.

"I hadn't embraced my Native culture then because you don't embrace things that bring you despair," says Vince, born Ojibway. "A lot of my upbringing was tough — poor and with a single parent. You didn't go around saying you were Native in the 1980s. But I saw a new pride in Native culture. Oka was part of that."

Born and raised in North Winnipeg, Vince began playing guitar in his early teens. Relocating to Fort Rouge in 1979, he hooked up with a group of young players who met at St. Ignatius Church. "We were trying to get into some Christian rock and original stuff," he recalls. Musician Steve Bell offered Vince encouragement, and Steve's partner Dave Zeglinski introduced Vince to local guitar legend and ex-Streetheart member John Hannah. Together the two formed Working Class in the early '80s. Vince says, "So much of

what I know about rock 'n' roll guitar I learned from John. He taught me to slow down and make my guitar solos sound *signature*."

After Working Class split up, Vince took time off to marry Dodi Bell, Steve Bell's sister, and to sort out his goals. Over the next four years Vince honed his guitar chops in a variety of local acts, including the Throbtones and Blackjacket, while earning his BA in psychology from the University of Winnipeg. Then Oka happened.

"That kind of shook me," he recalls. "To this point, I was just 'Vince Fontaine the rocker,' not 'Vince Fontaine the Native guy.' But Steve Bell, Dave Zeglinski and John Hannah had always told me, 'You're a great player, Vince, but you're also Native. If other Native people saw you making a go of it you could be a role model.' And that stuck in my mind. After Oka we were going across Western Canada with Blackjacket and seeing tipis set up in front of legislatures and protests going on. I had it in my head to start a Native band."

In late 1992, Vince hooked up with Blue Bombers kicker and singer Troy Westwood and embarked on a Native-inspired songwriting partnership. "We didn't even have a name for our group but the first song we wrote was called 'Eagle and Hawk'. So when we applied for a grant to record a cassette, Kevin Wynne at the granting agency just called it the Eagle & Hawk project. That's how the name came about." Their debut appeared in 1994. "I wanted to come up with something new, a vehicle to express myself," explains Vince, who immersed himself in Native music.

> "I DIDN'T MAKE THE BAND FOR CANADA, I BUILT IT FOR EUROPEAN AUDIENCES. THEY UNDERSTOOD IT FROM AN OUTSIDER POINT OF VIEW."

That same year Vince was invited to serve as musical director for an American Native dance troupe touring Russia and Scandinavia for the opening of the Goodwill Games. The twenty-four-day tour opened his eyes to European audiences' response to Aboriginal music. On his return he joined the leading American Aboriginal fusion band, Keith Secola and the Wild Band of Indians, touring Europe several times. "I saw that Europeans and the rest of the world really embraced Native American culture," he remarks. "I grew up with little appreciation for our roots. But in Europe people were freaking out over us. I knew I had to come up with my own version."

Over the winter of 1996 to '97 Vince and Troy, along with singer Jody Gaskin, recorded *The Dream* at Ambience Studios in Winnipeg. The album captured a strong Native vibe integrated with contemporary pop sounds. That February, the first international Eagle & Hawk tour was launched in Europe with traditional hoop dancers and a special guest: C-Weed's Errol Ranville. "Troy was doing his Jim Morrison Native thing big time," notes Vince. The group played the gala anniversary of the Indigenous Peoples' induction into the UN in Geneva.

With Eagle & Hawk, Vince set his sights on Europe. "I didn't make the band for Canada, I built it for European audiences. They understood it from an outsider point of view." In fall 1997 the group went on tour to Paris, Munich, Berlin, Warsaw, and Prague, bringing along drummer Steve Broadhurst and bassist Blair DePape. "We always like saying we're from Winnipeg, Manitoba, Canada," says Vince. By then Troy Westwood had bowed out, the band's growing tour schedule conflicting with his

football career. The next year, Jay Bodner replaced Jody Gaskin.

*Indian City*, a marriage of Native writing and mainstream rock recorded in 1999, was inspired by Vince's experiences in Europe. "On the train from Munich to Zurich I came up with the idea of a dance groove with a chant *and* a rap in it. Jay and Gerry Atwell brought in the rap part of it. That became our signature song and the album theme." An emphasis on songs and structure found Vince eschewing his lead guitar soloing. "I got away from the blues in my writing. I knew that if I wanted international appeal I had to have something new." The band did not court North American label interest.

The group's most Native-influenced album *On and On* (2001), earned the Juno Award for Best Music of Aboriginal Canada the following year. In 2002 Vince took on the role of cultural manager for the Indigenous Games, leaving less time for the band. A further personnel change saw Lawrence 'Spatch' Mulhall joining on bass and vocals.

In 2003 Eagle & Hawk released *Mother Earth* on Arbor Records, with vocals by Jay and Spatch. "I wasn't satisfied that *On and On* was our best CD," Vince concedes, "even though it won a Juno. *Mother Earth* was the hardest CD to write but it's the best one." Cathy St. Germain, daughter of entertainer Ray St. Germain, guested on vocals on the album. *Mother Earth* went on to receive a Juno nomination in 2004 and earn the group Best Rock Album and Best Song Single at the 2004 Canadian Aboriginal Music Awards. They also picked up Best Songwriter honours.

After more than ten European tours and praise throughout the European media, Eagle & Hawk are now focusing on

establishing themselves in North America with showcase performances in several cities including recently in San Francisco. Vince is writing a new album entitled *Indian Summer* which he plans to record in 2005. He also works for Grand Chief Phil Fontaine of the Assembly of First Nations as cultural adviser. In addition, he operates Rising Sun Productions, a management, promotion and festival event coordinator for Native American artists.

Eagle & Hawk is still his first priority. "I'm approaching my mid-forties and there's still a place for guys like me in this business," he laughs. ■

Formed in Winnipeg in 1994

Vince Fontaine played with Working Class, Black Jacket, Keith Secola and the Wild Band of Indians

ALBUMS: The Dream (1997); Indian City (1999); Eagle & Hawk (2000); On and On (2001); Mother Earth (2003); The Red (2004)

AWARDS: Juno Award for Best Music of Aboriginal Canada (2002); Best Rock Album at Canadian Aboriginal Music Awards (1999); Best Rock Album, Best Single and Best Songwriter at the 2004 Canadian Aboriginal Music Awards

Toured Europe ten times

Winnipeg Blue Bomber kicker Troy Westwood formed group with Vince Fontaine

Vince Fontaine works as cultural adviser for Grand Chief of the Assembly of First Nations' Phil Fontaine (no relation)

**W**HEN OAKBANK REAL ESTATE AGENT and drummer Lyle Foster sold Ray Martin a house across the street from his own, he had no inkling the two would forge a successful twenty-year songwriting partnership yielding a dozen hit records both here and in Europe. "About a year after he moved in Ray spied my drums in the basement," remembers Lyle. "I hadn't been playing since high school. He told me he was a songwriter and had written songs like 'What's It Like To Live In Texas' and 'Manitoba Sunshine' for other local artists. So one day I wrote some lyrics and gave them to him. He liked them and we began co-writing songs. I had a never-ending flow of ideas for songs and Ray had this incredible gift for writing." From that fortuitous alliance would emerge the Foster Martin Band, one of Manitoba's most celebrated country groups.

While Ray Martin's background was steeped in country music, Lyle grew up on a steady diet of rock 'n' roll, and that combination of influences informed their songwriting, giving the Foster Martin Band a distinctive country-rock style. "Country music was really starting to rock," notes Lyle of the band's emergence in the early 1990s. "Everybody wanted to dance. That's kind of what our music's all about, the 1960s rock 'n' roll influence. I leaned more towards that than Ray did. I kept coming up with ideas that rocked.

"We're pretty high energy. Wherever we play the floor is always packed with dancers and instantly there's a party going on. When you look out you can't see a seat for people, which is pretty nice."

The band grew from an informal group of players getting together once or twice a month over beers to play songs. Among the musicians were Alan Popowich on lead guitar and Ray Grenier on bass and harmony vocals. A Saturday afternoon matinee appearance at the Oakbank Hotel, east of Winnipeg, packed the pub and the band was on its way. "The first formal gig we played was the Oakbank Chicken Derby," chuckles Lyle, "and we didn't have a name. So Ray told them we were the Foster

Martin Band. That was a one-gig name but it stuck."

**DESPITE THEIR INTERNATIONAL SUCCESS, LOCAL ROOTS REMAIN ESSENTIAL FOR THE FOSTER MARTIN BAND.**

In 1993, the Foster Martin Band recorded *Willy's Bar & Grill* produced by local country music wonder-kid Craig Fotheringham and guitarist Randy Hiebert. Released independently, the album featured all original songs by Lyle and Ray and spawned an amazing six hit singles including the title track, "You Can't 2-Step", and "Rodeo Queen". "We were about to release our debut single, "I May Never Get To Heaven (But What A Way To Go)", when we got a call from Gary Buck in Nashville, who said he had someone pretty big who wanted to record the song down there and we said no. How dumb was that? But we wanted to have the hit for ourselves." Canadian performer Chris Bigfoot enjoyed a #10 hit with a cover of Lyle and Ray's "Just Like You".

"That album really opened up doors for us," states Lyle. "We had the biggest

radio station in Calgary playing us like crazy there. It gave us the opportunity to hurdle over the bar circuit and go right to festivals. We ended up playing every major festival in Canada over the years. Dauphin Countryfest we played six times." Despite the success, each of the members kept their day jobs. "We're sort of like the outcasts of the country music industry because we didn't follow the same road that others did. We didn't dedicate our lives to it, but I think that's allowed us to have a longer lifespan."

For *Ragtop Chevy*, along with production duties at his home studio, Craig Fotheringham joined the group officially on keyboards and guitar. Once again the band enjoyed singles success across Canada with the title track, "I'm The One" and "Rockin' Rodeo". "We had people in Nashville tell us they couldn't believe the sound we had on our album," boasts Lyle. "They said it was as good as what was coming out of Nashville and we didn't dare tell them it was made in a Winnipeg basement." The group was named Manitoba Country Music Association Entertainer of the Year in 1996 and '97, Band of the Year in 1995, '96 and '97, with Lyle and Ray five-time recipients of Songwriters of the Year honours.

By the time of *Moonshine N'
Moonlight*, Sean Borton replaced Alan,
with the band expanding further after the
addition of multi-instrumentalist Lyle
Baldwin from Louisiana Hot Sauce. "They
were a great band and when they split up
I said to Ray, 'You've always wanted a fiddle player. Why don't we give Lyle a call?'
'Oh, he won't play with us. He's too serious a musician.' But he jumped at the
chance." The album gave the Foster
Martin Band its biggest hit to date with
"Forever" reaching #14. "'Forever' did
well here but in Europe what happened
with that song was incredible. It was the
top independent song among 250 radio
stations and we won an award for it. They
really like that kind of country over there.

They stand in line for our CDs and we stay
there for two hours signing them." The
band has toured in Europe several times,
playing festivals in Spain, France and
Switzerland. "There's a great market over
there for Canadian country acts. We're
going back next year to play in Cannes,
France. We had to promise our wives that
we'd take them this time."

Prior to the fourth album, Ray Martin
left to pursue his own songwriting career.
"It was like losing a family member,"
says Lyle, who continues to collaborate
with Ray. "But it was a very friendly
split. He just couldn't do it anymore."
Lyle Baldwin stepped up to fill the lead
vocal role for 2004's *On A Roller Coaster
Ride*, and the band never missed a beat

earning a CCMA nomination as well as a
Western Canada Music Award nomination
for the album.

Despite their international success,
local roots remain essential for the Foster
Martin Band. "There are a lot of local
places mentioned in our songs, like the
Red Top. Those places are important to us.

"You couldn't ask for a better place
in Canada to play music than right here.
There were so many places to see live
music. If you go to Nashville or Calgary,
good luck finding the same level of
live music. That's why bands from
Calgary come here. There's so much
happening." ■

Formed in Oak Bank, Manitoba in
1985

First formal gig: Oakbank Chicken
Derby

ALBUMS: Willy's Bar & Grill (1993);
Ragtop Chevy (1996); Moonshine N'
Moonlight (1999); On A Roller
Coaster Ride (2004)

HIT SINGLES: "I May Never Get To
Heaven", "You Can't Two-Step",
Willy's Bar & Grill", "Forever"

AWARDS: Numerous Manitoba
Country Music Association awards
including Entertainer of the Year
(1997), Country Band of the Year
(1995, 1996, 1997), Recording Artists
of the Year (1995, 1997, 2000),

Songwriters of the Year (Ray Martin
and Lyle Foster (1995, 1996, 1997,
200, 2002)

Ray Martin left in 2002 and fiddler
Lyle Baldwin assumed lead vocals

Real estate agent Lyle Foster first met
partner Ray Martin when he sold him
a house

# FRESH I.E.

FRESH I.E.

"I WANT TO START A MUSICAL ARTS CENTRE WITH A STUDIO HERE FOR URBAN KIDS WHO WANT TO LEARN HOW TO USE THEIR MUSICAL GIFTS."

HIP-HOP MUSIC IS OFTEN ASSOCIATED with tough urban street life and gang-related violence. But Winnipeg-based hip-hop artist Fresh I.E. managed to break that cycle in his own life, and now uses those experiences through his music to inspire young people to live positive lives. His message is getting through. In 2003 he was nominated for a Grammy Award in the US, and he has won Vibe and Western Canada Music Awards for his groundbreaking gospel hip-hop recordings.

"We try to do it in a way that people can relate to," he explains. "We go out there in our track suits and our Bibles and microphones and share our truths on beats."

Born Robert Wilson in Winnipeg's rough-and-tumble North End, he adopted the handle Fresh E working as a dancer both in Winnipeg and Vancouver. As a young man he attended Shaughnessy Park School, St. John's High and R. B. Russell Vocational School, but found himself on the streets in Vancouver at age eighteen. "I was taking from what I learned in the streets and trying to make a living from it. I was performing in hip-hop clubs. I had a group called Sphere with two later members of Swollen Members. We performed in bars in Vancouver and on the island in the underground scene. Then they went off and did their thing and I continued to do my thing."

For Fresh, his thing was crime. "I was too involved with the drinking and the hustling to take my music seriously. I got caught up in that and had some life and death experiences there and in Toronto that brought me back to Winnipeg. I witnessed a murder and that was too close to home for me. It caused me to slow down a little bit. But I couldn't get away from the alcohol and because of that I got into a bad car accident in 1996, which almost ended a young woman's life. I was looking at fourteen years, but then I got off those charges after the girl lived. So I left Toronto and returned to Winnipeg. That's when I gave my life to God. I met an old friend who invited me to come to his church, and I did. Now I'm back in the neighbourhood in the North End counseling young kids to stay away from that lifestyle."

His acceptance of God in his life allowed Fresh to once again pursue his music. "In the States there are thousands doing gospel hip-hop but in Canada there are only a handful. For me it wasn't 'Hey, there's no gospel rap, maybe I'll do that.' It was just that I had something to say."

The new direction required a name change. "I didn't want anyone to know me by that old person because I was a bad person then. I had to find a new meaning for this name so I used Fresh I.E., which stands for 'Fresh In Eternity', meaning old things are passed away and become brand new. I'm not that old person anymore."

His debut album, *The Revelation*, released on local Sunshine Records in 2000, earned attention for its message and compelling music. *28:3* followed the next year on Verb Records. In 2002, the double CD *Tha Blacksmith & Tha Blade — Tha Worship & Tha Praise* received a Vibe award nomination. But it was his fourth album *Red Letterz* that broke Fresh I.E. internationally, with a release in the US, Australia and in Africa, earning a Grammy nomination for Best Gospel Hip-Hop recording. "Imagine that — doing what God called me to do and getting nominated for a Grammy!" he told the media. Fresh travelled to Los Angeles for the ceremony. "CTV actually followed me and made a documentary. I ran into Puff Daddy and Snoop Dog, Reuben Studdard and Prince. It was an amazing experience." The album also produced two hit singles on Canadian Christian radio. He guested on CDs by G-Side, Jon Buller, Freeman and Sandra Park as well as appearing onstage with P.O.D., L.G. Wise and Knights of the Realm.

At last year's Juno Awards in Edmonton, Fresh was invited to perform a showcase alongside the Canadian hip-hop community. "It was well-received. All the artists came offstage with me afterwards. I told them that we needed to bring them back with love to the music. We don't need to follow those stereotypes. We have to move forward and not bask in what the media has created about this music." He believes that the violent image must be changed. "You've got rich kids walking around in hip-hop clothes looking to do something bad just to be accepted by someone in those circles."

Fresh continues to use his music as a youth leader with Living Bible Explorers, an inner city ministry in downtown Winnipeg. "I try to share my life experiences so that when they go back out on the streets they'll recognize those things that are out there waiting for them, and to get them out of the gang cycle. I don't like to push religion on people, I just share my life and share the love. I believe that music is a powerful tool in society itself. Every time the music changed, society changed. Right back to Elvis through the Beatles, Jimi Hendrix, and with hip-hop, it all changed society."

While Winnipeg is best known as a rock 'n' roll city, Fresh insists there is change in the wind. "The hip-hop scene is on the rise here. There are other artists like Shades of Black and Mood Ruff. I have about nine artists, young men from across Canada who, because of the Grammys, want to come and do gospel hip-hop here in my studio. There's going to be an explosion of urban music in Winnipeg, not just secular but in the genre that I'm doing too." Currently completing his next album *Truth Has Fallen In The Streets*, Fresh toured western Canada in the fall of 2004, with a foray into the US in the spring.

In spite of his acclaim, Fresh remains focused on inner city youth. "I want to start a musical arts centre with a studio here for urban kids who want to learn how to use their musical gifts. I want to be able to teach them without the burden of charging big money and maybe have some government program to teach our urban youth." ∎

FRESH.I.E

Born Robert Wilson in Winnipeg

Performed in clubs in Vancouver and Toronto before returning to Winnipeg

ALBUMS: The Revelation (2000); 28:3 (2001); Tha Blacksmith & Tha Blade - Tha Worship & Tha Praise (2002); Red Letterz (2003); Truth Has Fallen In The Streets (2005)

AWARDS: Vibe Award (2002); nominated for Grammy for Best Gospel Rock Album (2003)

Early in his career worked with members of Rascalz and Swollen Members

Fresh I.E. means Fresh In Eternity

Red Letterz nominated for 2005 Juno for best contemporary Christian/gospel album

# JOEY GREGORASH

**JOEY'S SONG PARODIES WERE ALWAYS CLEVER AND HIS GUESTS OFTEN FOUND THEMSELVES TRYING TO KEEP UP WITH THEIR HOST.**

**W**HO WAS THE FIRST SOLO ARTIST FROM MANITOBA to win a Juno award? Answer: Joey Gregorash. At the second ever Juno Awards ceremony on February 28, 1972 in Toronto, Joey received the Outstanding Male Performance of the Year Juno. He was only the second Manitoban to win a Juno, the first being the Guess Who. Joey would go on to enjoy a multi-faceted career, earning the title Winnipeg's Mr. Entertainment.

Joey's music career began behind the drums in rock band The Wellingtons, who eventually became the Mongrels, with Joey becoming lead vocalist as the group became one of the city's top bands on the community club circuit.

In 1968, the Mongrels released their debut single on the local Franklin label, "Death Of A Salesman", written and produced by Guess Who guitarist Randy Bachman. Follow-up singles included "My Woman" and another Bachman number, "Funny Day", which was reviewed on *American Bandstand's* 'Rate-The-Record' segment. This segment famously used the sound of a bomb dropping to signify that the reviewers, usually a couple of pimply teens, thought the record was a bomb. The American chances for "Funny Day" ended with that fateful sound effect.

After throat problems forced Joey to leave the Mongrels in 1969, he landed a two-year stint as host of the weekly CJAY TV series *Young As You Are,* an *American Bandstand*-style showcase featuring records and live bands. He also embarked on a solo career, signing with Polydor Records at the tender age of twenty. Joey's first two singles, "Stay" and "Tomorrow Tomorrow", penned with local songwriter Norman Lampe, garnered sufficient interest for Polydor to send Joey to the legendary Stax studio in Memphis in 1971. There he recorded *North Country Funk* which yielded two of his biggest hits, the upbeat self-composed "Jody", and a funky cover of Neil Young's "Down By The River".

"We needed one more song to complete the album," Joey recalls. "We were sitting in the hotel room the night before we had to leave, and I started fooling around on acoustic guitar doing José Feliciano does Neil Young on 'Down By The River'. My producer, Ron Capone, said, 'Hey, I like that rhythm. Let's lay that down.' So we went to the studio and laid down the backing track. I sang it live in the studio. They finished it after we left. Bobby Manuel, Isaac Hayes' guitarist, played the lead guitar.

"After 'Jody' was a hit, Polydor, released 'Don't Let Your Pride Get You

Girl', which started tanking. I told them not to release it. Someone in the Maritimes started playing 'Down By The River' off the album, the full-length version, so Polydor edited it as a single." The song went Top 10 nationally. The success earned Joey the Juno nod.

A second album, *Tell The People*, recorded at Steve Cropper's Trans Maximus studio in Memphis, included the hits "My Love Sings" and "Take The Blindness", however Joey was unable to capitalize on his earlier success with a national tour. "Liza" failed to stem a downward slide. "I don't think the songs were strong enough," he reflects. "And I never had strong management behind me." While recording at Trans Maximus, Joey wrote a song for R & B legend Roy Head called "Hit The Road".

In 1975 Joey set his sights on eastern Canada. A two-week stand at Toronto's Friars Club led to further engagements in the Maritimes on the heels of the single "I Know We'll Make It Together". "It was tough to be on the road in the '70s. We pulled into this club in Galt, Ontario and the owner came up and said, 'the last group had a trapeze.' That was it for me."

Returning to Winnipeg, Joey entered the world of radio, working his way up to morning man at CKY 58 AM and CKIS-97 FM. A dual career as a commercials writer brought him further acclaim, winning fourteen national awards and a Gold Medal from New York's International Radio Festival for creative excellence. In 2003, he captured radio's prestigious Crystal Award Gold Medal for commercial writing and voicing. Returning to CKY TV in 1986, Joey starred in the daily children's program *S'kiddle Bits* which ran for seven successful years. Joey's song

parodies were always clever and his guests often found themselves trying to keep up with their host. He followed *S'kiddle Bits* with *Hi Noon*, another daily show that featured guests like Jann Arden, Spirit of the West and Garth Brooks.

Despite the shift into other media, Joey kept up his singing career. His song "Together (The New Wedding Song)" earned him a gold record in 1987. "'Together' was written for Brian McMillan's wedding. His fiancé wanted something special for me to sing at the church service so I thought of 'Tomorrow Tomorrow' and came up with new words. People came up afterwards saying how much they loved that song. Years later, I was working at CHMM FM radio. Program director Peter Grant suggested recording a single for a fundraiser. I played 'Together (The New Wedding Song)' for producer Craig Fotheringham. Afterwards he drawled, 'That's a hit, man.'"

"Together (The Wedding Song)" quickly sold out all copies in Winnipeg. A month later Joey received a call from an Ottawa record shop looking for copies. "We sent them copies and it sold out. We did that a few more times and it kept selling out." But it took four years to convince a record label to release the single nationally. Attic Records finally put it out, and it sold over 50,000 copies reaching #1 in several markets across Canada. "I was one of only four Canadians to earn a gold record that year."

Attempts to record a follow up, however, were met with indifference. "That's when the music business started to change. Instead of demo tapes, labels wanted 8 x 10s."

"Together (The New Wedding Song)" received the prestigious Canadian Music

Publishers' Association Award and a PROCAN Award for Outstanding Air Play. It remains a perennial favourite at weddings and anniversaries and, along with "Jody" and "Down By The River," is still heard regularly on Canadian radio. In 1988 Joey penned "Golden Boy", for another fundraising event, this one initiated by local boxing celebrity Donnie Lalonde, for victims of child abuse.

In the '90s, Joey became master of ceremonies for McPhillips Street Station casino's weekly concert series in Winnipeg, a position he held for four years. He continued writing commercials as well as appearing on local radio. In 2002 he resumed his singing career with a spectacular set at the Spirit Fest concert, held at Winnipeg's Forks outdoor concert bowl. He followed this with a return to McPhillips Street Station, only this time as a performer to a sold-out crowd, proving once again that Joey Gregorash is a Winnipeg entertainment institution. ■

Born in Winnipeg

BANDS: The Wellingtons, Mongrels, Walrus, solo artist

ALBUMS: North Country Funk (1971); Tell The People (1972)

HIT SINGLES: "Funny Day" (with The Mongrels); "Sitting In The Station" (with The Mongrels); "Jodie", "Down By The River", "My Love Sings",

"Take The Blindness", "Liza", "Together (The New Wedding Song)"

AWARDS: Juno award for Outstanding Performance of the Year, Male (1971); Canadian Music Publishers' Association Award and a PROCAN Award for Outstanding Air Play and gold record for "Together (The New Wedding Song)" (1987); Crystal Award Gold Medal for commercial writing;

14 national awards and a Gold Medal from New York's International Radio Festival

Created and hosted CTV's *S'kiddlebits* and *Hi Noon*

Wrote "Golden Boy" for boxer Donny Lalonde charity fundraiser and "Hit The Road" for R & B singer Roy Head

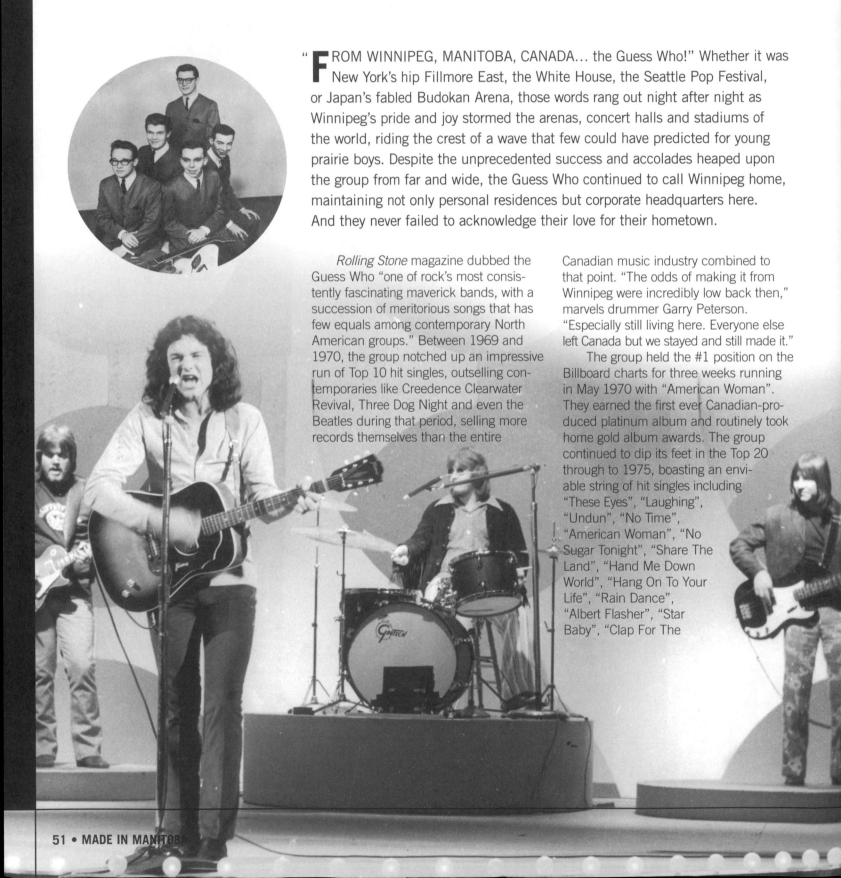

# THE GUESS WHO

THE GUESS WHO

"**F**ROM WINNIPEG, MANITOBA, CANADA… the Guess Who!" Whether it was New York's hip Fillmore East, the White House, the Seattle Pop Festival, or Japan's fabled Budokan Arena, those words rang out night after night as Winnipeg's pride and joy stormed the arenas, concert halls and stadiums of the world, riding the crest of a wave that few could have predicted for young prairie boys. Despite the unprecedented success and accolades heaped upon the group from far and wide, the Guess Who continued to call Winnipeg home, maintaining not only personal residences but corporate headquarters here. And they never failed to acknowledge their love for their hometown.

*Rolling Stone* magazine dubbed the Guess Who "one of rock's most consistently fascinating maverick bands, with a succession of meritorious songs that has few equals among contemporary North American groups." Between 1969 and 1970, the group notched up an impressive run of Top 10 hit singles, outselling contemporaries like Creedence Clearwater Revival, Three Dog Night and even the Beatles during that period, selling more records themselves than the entire

Canadian music industry combined to that point. "The odds of making it from Winnipeg were incredibly low back then," marvels drummer Garry Peterson. "Especially still living here. Everyone else left Canada but we stayed and still made it."

The group held the #1 position on the Billboard charts for three weeks running in May 1970 with "American Woman". They earned the first ever Canadian-produced platinum album and routinely took home gold album awards. The group continued to dip its feet in the Top 20 through to 1975, boasting an enviable string of hit singles including "These Eyes", "Laughing", "Undun", "No Time", "American Woman", "No Sugar Tonight", "Share The Land", "Hand Me Down World", "Hang On To Your Life", "Rain Dance", "Albert Flasher", "Star Baby", "Clap For The

Wolfman", and "Dancin' Fool". Notes rock journalist Lenny Kaye, "Their songs all contain the one thing that any hit single needs to make it a hit single. Once you've heard it, you never stop hearing it. It's all amazingly accessible, a bit familiar, nearly an entire history of post-Beatles rock 'n' roll. The touch, as those little gold disks always prove, of genius."

The Guess Who's songs have been featured in hit movies including *Almost Famous*, *The Cable Guy*, *Austin Powers: The Spy Who Shagged Me*, *Jackie Brown* and Academy Award winner *American Beauty*, and continue to be radio staples. Several earned prestigious BMI awards for over 1 million airplays. And twenty-nine years after it first held the #1 position on *Billboard's* pop charts, "American Woman" once again topped those charts in 1999, recorded by longtime Guess Who admirer Lenny Kravitz.

The group has been inducted into the Canadian Music Hall of Fame, the Canadian Walk of Fame, the Canadian Broadcasters Hall of Fame, the first ever recipients of the Prairie Music Hall of Fame Award, and the coveted Governor-General's Performing Arts Award.

Formed by East Kildonan-raised singer/guitarist Allan Kowbel (aka Chad Allan), the first incarnation of the group went under the title Allan's Silvertones. As various members fell by the wayside, Allan recruited bass guitarist Jim Kale and piano player Bob Ashley from St. Vital before snagging budding guitar hero Randy Bachman and child prodigy Garry Peterson on drums from West Kildonan. Switching their name to Chad Allan & the Reflections, the quintet played

community clubs and church basements throughout Winnipeg.

Their debut single, "Tribute To Buddy Holly", was among a cache of songs drawn from the pre-Beatles British hit parade that comprised the group's repertoire. "We became influential," states Jim, "because we were doing unfamiliar material which gave people something different to listen to." The Reflections were first to pick up on the Beatles, performing their songs months before the Fab Four stormed our shores. Further singles established the group's credentials as serious recording artists.

In 1964 the group altered their name to the Expressions after Detroit combo the Reflections scored a hit with "Just Like Romeo and Juliet".

At a makeshift recording session at CJAY TV studio in December 1964, the Expressions cut their own rendition of the British hit "Shakin' All Over", a raunchy song complete with clink-clink piano and

raspy vocals from Chad, who was nursing a sore throat. "There was just one microphone in the middle of the room and the entire band plugged into Jim Kale's Fender Concert amp, all the instruments," recalls Randy. On one take the recording engineer inadvertently patched the mikes into the speaker jacks. "It had this slap-back echo on it, the instruments, drums and voice, everything. We heard it and yelled, 'That's like Elvis!'"

Quality Records released the single with "Guess Who" on the label hoping to attract curious radio programmers. The trick worked. By March 1965, "Shakin' All Over" was #1 across Canada. "We received a phone call," Randy recalls, "and the voice said 'We've got your new name. It's Guess Who!' And we said, 'We hate it!' So we had become the Guess Who."

Licensed to New York-based Scepter Records, the single peaked at #22 on the Billboard charts by the summer of 1965,

Formed in Winnipeg in 1963

Members of the band were also in Allan's Silvertones and Chad Allan & the Reflections (later Expressions)

ALBUMS: Wheatfield Soul (1969); American Woman (1970); Share The Land (1970); The Best of the Guess Who (1971); So Long Bannatyne (1971); Artificial Paradise (1973); Road Food (1974); Running Back Thru Canada (2000)

HIT SINGLES: "Shakin' All Over", "His Girl", These Eyes", "Laughing", "Undun", "No Time", "American

Woman", "Hand Me Down World", "Share The Land", "Albert Flasher", "Rain Dance", "Glamour Boy", "Clap For The Wolfman", "Star Baby"

Juno Vocal/Instrumental Group of the Year (1971 - several RPM awards previously); Canadian Music Hall of Fame (1987); first recipients of the Prairie Music Hall of Fame Award (1999), Canadian Walk of Fame (2001), the Canadian Broadcasters Hall of Fame (2002), Governor-General's Performing Arts Award (2002); several SOCAN and BMI song awards

In 1970 sold more records than the entire Canadian music industry combined to that point

Performed at the White House by invitation of Tricia Nixon in 1970

Earned Canada's first platinum album in 1971 (Best of the Guess Who)

"American Woman" topped the charts twice: in 1970 and again in 1999 with a Lenny Kravitz cover

Re-formed to play the closing of the Pan American Games in 1999 — embarked on a successful cross-Canada tour in 2000 and 2001

an astonishing achievement for a group yet to cross the border. The group toured the eastern US with the Kingsmen, Crystals, Sam the Sham, Dion, and the Shirelles. Scepter paired the group with young black songwriting team Ashford and Simpson, who composed "Hey Ho (What You Do To Me)." Despite notching up another Canadian hit, the single failed to crack Billboard's Hot 100. "Hurting Each Other" (later a hit for the Carpenters), also failed to emulate the success of "Shakin' All Over".

In December 1965 Bob Ashley left the group and was replaced by up-and-comer Burton Cummings who brought with him both an infusion of much needed energy and a harder-edged sound. "He was young, hungry, aggressive, and wasn't afraid to shake things up," offers Randy. Burton Cummings remembers it this way: "I think I said, 'Gee fellows, I'd love to but the Beatles just asked me to join last week' and I walked out the door. Then I realized they weren't kidding and I said 'Yes' right on the spot." Chad Allan bowed out soon after and the group carried on as a quartet.

In February 1967 "His Girl" eked into the British charts and the group hastily booked a flight to London only to discover no bookings. Returning $25,000 in debt, an offer to host CBC TV's Winnipeg edition

of *Let's Go* saved their necks. *Let's Go* producer Larry Brown encouraged Randy and Burton to write their own material. "Randy would write half finished songs and I would write half finished songs and nine times out of ten we'd put them together and they would work," says Burton. Toronto record producer Jack Richardson saw potential in the group and signed them to his Nimbus 9 Production Company. The association produced the promotional album *A Wild Pair* featuring original songs by the Guess Who and Ottawa's Staccatos. Jack then took the Guess Who to New York to record *Wheatfield Soul*, which included a Bachman-Cummings composition "These Eyes".

"Our first goal had been to get a record in the Billboard Top 100," recalls Randy. "When 'These Eyes' entered the charts, we screamed and yelled and hugged each other." The group was presented with their first gold record by Dick Clark on *American Bandstand*. "Laughing" followed, peaking at #10. As it began slipping from the charts, deejays flipped it over to discover the jazzy "Undun" and the group enjoyed another hit. "No Time" broke the soft rock formula in early 1970, reaching #5 on Billboard. "'No Time' is probably my favourite Guess Who song because it proved that we

could rock 'n' roll and gained us a whole new respect and credibility," stresses Burton. In May of that year, "American Woman", inspired by an impromptu onstage jam in southern Ontario, hit #1 where it stayed for three weeks. The Guess Who had the biggest hit in the world. Gushed rock critic Lester Bangs, "Not only do the Guess Who sing about America a lot, they've managed to catch the essence of American rock 'n' roll."

Replacing guitarist/songwriter Randy Bachman with Winnipeggers Kurt Winter and Greg Leskiw in June 1970, the momentum continued unabated with "Hand Me Down World" and "Share The Land", earning a whole new audience with their harder-edged sound. Burton found a willing collaborator in Kurt and a new prolific partnership fuelled the group, who appeared that summer at the White House by special invitation of Tricia Nixon. *So Long Bannatyne, Rockin'* and *Artificial Paradise* proved that the group was capable of a more eclectic range of styles while still notching up hit singles like "Rain Dance", "Guns Guns Guns" and "Orly". Greg Leskiw and Jim Kale left, replaced by more Winnipeggers, Don McDougall and Bill Wallace, as the group carried on touring as far afield as Australia, New Zealand and Japan. "Clap For The Wolfman" brought them back into the Top 10 in 1974 as the group hosted NBC TV's *Midnight Special*. That same year Kurt and Don were replaced by Toronto guitarist Domenic Troiano, the only non-Winnipegger to join their ranks, as the group again hit the charts with "Dancin' Fool".

But by 1975 the relentless pace of the past six years had become too much. Following a September concert at the Montreal Forum, the Guess Who called

it quits. Burton immediately launched a successful solo career. Randy Bachman was already topping the charts with Bachman-Turner Overdrive. Garry Peterson later joined Burton's backing band, as well as BTO, before touring with Jim Kale under the Guess Who banner in the '90s. Various Guess Who alumni pursued other musical endeavours. Tragically, Kurt Winter died in December 1997.

Bachman, Cummings, Kale and Peterson reunited for a successful 1983 Canadian tour but old wounds resurfaced and the group split acrimoniously soon after. In the latter '80s Randy sued Burton over the still lucrative Guess Who song catalogue, which Burton had purchased years earlier. The lawsuit, predicated on a handshake agreement back in the '60s to share their song publishing, was tipped to become the biggest of its kind in Canadian music history with millions at stake but the two settled out of court. Nonetheless the bitterness remained between the two former partners for several years. Compounding the ill will in the Guess Who camp was Jim Kale's trademarking of the band name and mounting touring units for more than a decade. The four original members managed to briefly bury the hatched for their induction into the Canadian Music Hall of Fame in 1987 but a gaff by CBC found them cut off as

they approached the podium to accept the honour. A hastily-produced tribute failed to redress the snub.

It was not until 1999's Pan American Games in Winnipeg that the four-man lineup came together at the behest of Premier Gary Filmon to close the event, performing for a sold-out stadium crowd and a worldwide audience of over 100 million. Many in the audience thought they would never see the group together again and from the opening notes of "No Time" stood through the rain to cheer them on. With Bill Wallace again replacing Jim Kale, who bowed out citing health problems, the reunited Guess Who embarked on their Running Back Thru Canada tour the following year, netting over $6 million. Every stop coast to coast was a joyous outpouring of genuine Canuck pride for Canada's first rock 'n' roll heroes. In 2003 the reunited Guess Who performed before over 200,000 at Toronto's SARS concert, opening for the Rolling Stones. A concert DVD of their triumphant 2000 Canadian tour was released in 2004.

Reflecting on the Guess Who legacy, Burton says, "The magnitude of our success escaped all of us. When 'American Woman' reached #1 in Billboard the stigma of Canada being inferior died forever. Someone had to do it first and I'm proud that it was us." The Guess Who made Canadian rock international. ∎

# H A R L E Q U I N

## *H A R L E Q U I N*

**F**OR HARLEQUIN VOCALIST/SONGWRITER George Belanger, the words of Henry David Thoreau, read one day on a bus en route to a dead-end job, set the course for his life: "Most men lead lives of quiet desperation because they hate the work they do." George says, "I was seventeen years old. I got off that bus, went home and called a band rehearsal." And he has never regretted a day since.

In the early 1980s you could not turn on a radio station anywhere in Canada without hearing at least one of Harlequin's many hits. "Sweet Things In Life," "You Are The Light," "Innocence," "Thinking Of You," "I Did It For Love" are all staples of Canadian classic rock radio.

Formed in Winnipeg in the mid '70s, the band actually took its name from a Toronto outfit that included Winnipeggers John Hannah on guitar and bass player Ralph James, both veterans of local bands like Blakewood Castle and Chopping Block. Returning home, John went AWOL (later surfacing in Streetheart), so Ralph hooked up with guitarist Leroy Hawk (Laurie Koyle), keyboard/guitarist Gary Golden and drummer Dave Budzak under the Harlequin banner, playing clubs and socials. Believing they needed a front man, the group recruited George Belanger, one of the city's most respected singers after having done stints in the Fifth, Next, and Chopping Block. George flew out to join the group at a gig in Kirkland Lake, Ontario. Not long after, Leroy left and was replaced by Glen Willows. Together, George and Glen became the writing team, steering Harlequin towards all-original material.

The turning point came at Toronto's Chimney club, where a talent representative there to check out Goddo ended up approaching Harlequin. The rep was associated with New York record producer Jack Douglas, whose resumé included Jimi Hendrix and John Lennon. Douglas

flew the band to New York to record demo tracks that ultimately led to a contract with Epic Records, who released *Victim Of A Song* in 1979. The album had a commercially appealing hard rock sound and went gold, spawning two hit singles, "Sweet Things In Life" and "You Are The Light".

Over the next five years Harlequin gigged relentlessly, as much as forty-five out of fifty-two weeks a year, supporting such major artists as Triumph, April Wine, Chilliwack, Saga, Streetheart, and Max Webster, with forays into the United States. The group even headlined in

Puerto Rico and Venezuela where they were surprised to discover Harlequin records in the Top 10. "They loved Canadian music down there," marvels George. "They were screaming and yelling, and the stage was surrounded by policemen with nightsticks and Uzis. It was crazy." In Puerto Rico, the band had to bribe customs officials to get their equipment out of the country. Back home, the group's popularity extended to the most unlikely places, including an ecstatic reception from inmates at Stony Mountain Penitentiary.

*Love Crimes* went platinum in Canada, producing the group's biggest hit, "Innocence", as well as "Thinking Of You". A controversy surrounded the title of the album after their original choice, *Crimes Of Passion*, was pinched by singer Pat Benatar, who was recording in a near-by studio. The group toured in the US, supporting John Waite and Survivor but, despite favourable response from audiences and radio programmers, distribution of their albums was spotty. "Epic was more interested in pushing Michael Jackson than a little Canadian band, so all that touring in the States was for nought."

Their third album, *One False Move*, earned another gold disk and boasted the hits "I Did It For Love" and "Heart Gone Cold". But despite enjoying several Canadian hits, financial problems continued to plague the group. "We had a manager who believed we had to have the best in order to get results. We weren't putting any money in our jeans. We were spending more than we had." With album covers designed by British company Hipnosis, responsible for Pink Floyd's elaborate album sleeves, and paying a US song plugger $50,000 to get their songs on radio, the band was in the hole on each release and ultimately declared bankruptcy. The band folded after the release of their fourth album, titled *Harlequin*. It was produced by Alfie Agius from British band The Fixx. "Alfie flew from England to meet us at a gig in Thompson, Manitoba and immediately froze his feet in these little Italian leather shoes," laughs George. "He couldn't believe the cold!" George spent several months in New York recording and mixing the album with Alfie, but sluggish sales hastened the demise of the group.

In 1986 Epic Records contacted George, who had bought the other members out of their ownership of the Harlequin name, with the proposition to record a new Harlequin song to be included on a greatest hits compilation. Recruiting drummer Jörn Anderson, Randy Hiebert on guitar and Randy Booth on bass, plus keyboard player Lou Pomanti, George cut Tom Cochrane's "It's No Mystery".

George continues to perform and tour as Harlequin, albeit at a more sedate pace, in the company of original guitarist Glen Willows and Gary Golden, plus various local players. He also owns Pasta & More on Pembina Highway in Winnipeg. Ralph James has become one of the most powerful booking agents in the Canadian music industry with a roster of A-list Canadian artists. Dave Budzak operates Q1 sound production company, Gary Golden went into financial planning, and Glen Willows is in artist management with Burning Circus Media.

Reflecting on Harlequin's heyday, George remains philosophical. "It was really hard work, but we had a lot of fun and many great experiences. We may not have made a lot of money but you couldn't buy that kind of experience anywhere. We were doing what we loved. We gambled and went for it. Sure, we didn't make it big but I'm not one to cry over spilt milk." Remembering Thoreau's famous line, he concludes, "Money isn't going to make you happy." ■

Formed in Winnipeg in 1975

Members from The Fifth/Next, Chopping Block, Blakewood Castle, Bentwood Rocker

ALBUMS: Victim of a Song (1979); Love Crimes (1980); One False Move (1982); Harlequin (1985); Radio Romances (1986)

HIT SINGLES: "Sweet Things In Life", "You Are The Light", "Innocence", "Thinking Of You", "I Did It For Love", "Take This Heart"

Headlined pop festivals in Puerto Rico and Venezuela

Album covers designed by Hipgnosis in the UK, who also designed Pink Floyd's covers

Producer Jack Douglas had worked with Jimi Hendrix

Singer George Belanger and guitarist Glen Willows still tour as Harlequin

**PRESERVING THEIR LANGUAGE AND CULTURE WAS PARAMOUNT TO GRAIN FARMER EMILE CAMPAGNE AND HIS WIFE MARGUERITE, AND FAMILY SING-ALONGS WERE CONDUCTED WITH A TRADITIONAL FRENCH SONGBOOK.**

**T**HEIR ALLURING VOCAL BLEND PROMPTED one reviewer to write about Hart-Rouge's "jaw-dropping harmonies". Critics worldwide — from across North America to as far east as Estonia and west to Vietnam — gush superlatives about the band's recordings and live performances. *Acoustic Guitar* magazine declared, "in a perfect world, Hart-Rouge would be on a short list for a Grammy," while the *Boston Herald* proclaimed them "one of the most vibrant sounds in modern folk." Hart-Rouge have found their niche, an exciting and distinctive mix of traditional French music, Cajun, world music rhythms, and acoustic folk, all delivered with those dazzling voices.

"There are not many people who can harmonize the way we do," says Suzanne Campagne, one of three Campagne siblings that comprise Hart-Rouge. "Being family has a lot to do with it, the timbre of the voices that have a genetic blend, and also having sung so often together when young."

Hailing from the tiny Anglophone farming community of Willow Bunch, Saskatchewan, the Francophone Campagne family — six girls and one boy — was in the minority. Preserving their language and culture was paramount to grain farmer Émile Campagne and his wife Marguerite, and family sing-alongs were conducted with a traditional French songbook.

By the mid 1970s La Famille Campagne was performing throughout southern Saskatchewan. From that came Folle Avoine (Wild Oats), comprised of six siblings — Aline, Suzanne, Solange, Paul, Annette, and the youngest, Michelle (middle sister Carmen bowed out early on to become a teacher) — performing traditional Francophone songs at folk festivals and cultural events. "We were great for the folk festivals," laughs Suzanne, "because they needed to have more women, minorities and Francophones on the bill and we were all of those."

Formed in Winnipeg in 1986 by members of the Campagne family who were attending St. Boniface College

Hail from Willow Bunch, Saskatchewan

ALBUMS: Hart-Rouge (1988); Inconditionnel (1990); Blue Blue Windows (1992); La Fabrique (1994); Beaupré's Home (1997); Live At The Mountain (2002)

HIT SINGLE: "Inconditionnel"

AWARDS: SOCAN Award for "Inconditionnel" (1990); International Sponsor Award in Poland at the Sopot festival (1987); Two Parents' Choice Awards for children's albums

Originally sang together as La Famille Campagne and Folle Avoine (Wild Oats)

First discovered by Daniel Lavoie and signed to his Trafic recording label

Sister Carmen Campagne is Quebec's leading children's recording artist

Recorded a French language version of "With God On Our Side" for a Bob Dylan tribute album (2001)

After Aline, Paul and Annette enrolled in St. Boniface College, Folle Avoine relocated to Winnipeg from 1981 to 1987. "We had to centralize somewhere and so Winnipeg was it. We were getting a following in St. Boniface with Folklorama and the Festival du Voyageur and had a great partnership with Les Danseurs de la Rivière-Rouge. The Francophone community was more cohesive, centralized and bigger than in Saskatchewan. Those were great years for us." Touring continued, including several months at Vancouver's Expo '86. Following that extended engagement, Aline and Solange left and the four remaining Campagnes retooled the group's sound and image.

"We had already started to veer toward more pop music but it was never really a big hit with Folle Avoine audiences," recalls Suzanne. "I remember Mitch Podolak [founder of the Winnipeg Folk Festival] being disappointed with our show because it had pop music in it. Aline and Solange didn't agree so it was down to the four of us." Hart-Rouge, conceived in manager Roland Stringer's Wellington Crescent living room, emerged in 1986 in Winnipeg, named for the original Francophone community at Willow Bend.

"Roland's plan was more of our own writing, try to go with what radio wanted, and really play in the big league," notes Suzanne. "And that meant moving to Montreal." Quebec singing sensation Daniel Lavoie, another ex-Manitoban, signed the group to his Trafic record label. Hart-Rouge was recorded in Winnipeg with musical arrangements by Norman Dugas, and production by Dan Donahue. With a definite '80s pop sound surrounding the familiar harmonies, Hart-Rouge attracted enough attention to warrant the move to Montreal in 1988. Inconditionnel, another pop album, followed in 1990, earning three Top 10 hit singles in Quebec and a SOCAN award for top song played on radio that year.

Le Derniere Mois de L'Année, an album of French Christmas songs, sold well, but the following year the group released their first English-language album, Blue Blue Windows, named for a line from Neil Young's "Helpless," a song performed a cappella on the album. "We worked for about three days on it," recalls Suzanne. "We really wanted to take that song somewhere else." La Fabrique, another pop-oriented album, bridged the two languages by including a bilingual version of James Taylor's "The Millworker".

Despite chart success, some members of the group remained unconvinced that pop was the right direction, preferring a return to traditional roots. Annette left the group, who then added guitarist/mandolin player Davy Gallant and percussionist Michel Dupire (with Paul on bass, Michelle on acoustic guitar and accordion, and Suzanne on percussion). Beaupré's Home, a bilingual album targeted more at the American market, completed a transition period and marked the realization of their true musical identity. "I consider that our most successful album," says Suzanne. "It was just getting back to our comfort zone. Red House Records picked it up and we toured a lot with that show." Besides original songs and traditional French and MicMac tunes, the album includes covers of tunes by Roy Forbes, Nanci Griffith, and Connie Kaldor, wife of Paul Campagne. "We had a lot of airplay with stations that play folk roots music and world beat." The group appeared at the prestigious Newport Folk Festival and the Strawberry Festival in California.

Nouvelle-France and j'ai fait un rêve continued in the same vein as Beaupré's Home, earning Hart-Rouge further accolades both in Quebec and the US. Sound system manufacturer Bose invited the group to record a live album using their cutting-edge equipment. The result is the impressive Live At The Mountain in 2002.

Back in the early '90s, Carmen Campagne followed her siblings to Quebec, quickly earning a reputation as the premiere children's recording artist there. Working with Hart-Rouge she has released six albums and earned gold and platinum sales in Quebec. The band followed Carmen's lead with a series of international lullabies on their own label La Montagne Secrète. "We figured out very fast that we can't put all our eggs in one basket," says Suzanne. The albums, Dodo la planète do 1 and 2, have been successful, winning two gold Parent's Choice Awards and earning Juno nominations. Another recent project was the recording of two albums of traditional French songs by their father, Émile.

Hart-Rouge recently took an eighteen-month sabbatical after the birth of Michelle's second child (she is married to guitarist Davy Gallant). Paul is producing a Connie Kaldor album, while Suzanne is involved in another children's project. Plans call for the group to tour again in 2005. ∎

# TARA LYN HART

THARRATLYN

> "I WAS SCARED TO STAND UP TO
> THE RECORD COMPANY IN CASE I
> MIGHT LOSE WHAT I HAD WORKED
> SO HARD FOR. SO I PUT ON THIS
> HUGE FRONT, BUT EVENTUALLY
> I GOT TO THE POINT WHERE
> I SIMPLY SAID, 'I DON'T
> WANT THIS ANYMORE.'"

**C**AREFUL WHAT YOU WISH FOR. Country singer/songwriter Tara Lyn Hart's dreams came true all at the same moment. "Everything happened so fast for me," she reflects on the whirlwind that engulfed her shortly after her eighteenth birthday. "Getting married was something I always wanted to do. Having children was something I always wanted to do. Getting a record deal was something I worked really hard since age five to get. But I didn't expect to get them all at once." Coming to terms with the fulfillment of all her dreams simultaneously would be more than most people could cope with.

Born in 1978 and raised on a farm near Roblin, northwest of Winnipeg, Tara Lyn Mohr began singing in school. "As I got older people started saying, 'Wow, she has a really nice voice,' so I started singing at everything that I could get into: fairs, festivals, lots of weddings and even some funerals. Funerals were odd gigs for a nine-year old." Her music of choice was country. "Where I grew up, the only radio stations we could pick up were country stations. Until I was ten or eleven I didn't even really know there was anything else out there."

By age fifteen, Tara Lyn was performing each summer at the Calgary Stampede. "People kept asking me, 'Don't you have anything we can purchase?' So we decided to put together an album that we could sell from the stage where I appeared." Working with Winnipeg-based producer Craig Fotheringham, she recorded ten tracks, written or co-written by her and Craig. "He was so much of a mentor to me. My mother used to drive me into the city to work with him. He would make me practise piano until I cried, saying, 'You can't write songs if you can't play.'" The album yielded five singles that received airplay across Manitoba.

By high school, Tara Lyn had set her sights on university. "I came to the conclusion that the reality of a farm girl from Roblin, Manitoba getting a recording contract was pretty remote." However, win-

ning Dauphin's CKDM talent contest changed all that. The prize was a recording session at Sunshine Studios in Winnipeg with Danny Schur, who was working with budding singer/songwriter Chantal Kreviazuk.

Danny and Tara Lyn cut two of her songs that came to the attention of Sony Music A&R head Mike Roth. "Chantal was stuck in traffic, so Mike asked Danny what else he was working on. Danny played my two songs." Mike later tracked Tara Lyn down after phoning all the Mohrs in the Roblin phone book. However, the opportunity was almost lost in preparations for her impending wedding to Brandon deejay Perry Hart. "I told Mike, 'This is a really bad time. Can I call you back?' not realizing who he was or what it might possibly be about. Perry was in the background going, 'No! Talk to him now!'" Three days later the couple were on a plane to Toronto to meet with Sony officials; two weeks after the wedding Tara returned to ink her deal. "That was the best wedding present ever."

Six weeks later she discovered she was pregnant. "I was petrified that the recording deal would be over. I was only eighteen and this had been my dream for so many years. I felt sick to my stomach having to sit everyone from Sony down and tell them, but they were amazing about it." Unruffled, Sony adjusted the timeline to accommodate her pregnancy.

Sessions resumed following the birth of daughter Teal, but were again interrupted when son Davian arrived. In the end, Tara Lyn's album involved six different producers, all top names in the business including Peter Asher, Barry Beckett, and Josh Leo.

Released in 1999, *Stuff That Matters* earned rave reviews and spawned four hit singles — the title track, "Save Me", "I Will Be Loving You", and "What He Used To Be" — receiving six CCMA nominations with Tara Lyn picking up the Rising Star award.

But Tara Lyn found herself torn between the demands of the music business and her desire to be a good mother and wife. "As much as I wanted to enjoy the success, there was a part of me that felt guilty for not being home with my husband and children. It was difficult to be gone for so long. My husband didn't get married so he could be alone and I didn't want to drag my baby around with me."

A move to Nashville only deepened the pain. "I was scared to stand up to the record company in case I might lose what I had worked so hard for. So I put on this huge front, but eventually I got to the point where I simply said, 'I don't want this anymore.'"

Despite a career that was pointing directly upward and with follow-up sessions planned, Tara Lyn negotiated a release from her contract. "That's the one thing I had been working for my whole life and then to say, 'No thanks,' was a scary decision even though in my heart I knew I didn't want it any more. I think I was scared of letting go of 'Tara Lyn Hart the Artist'. If I wasn't that then who was I? But Sony understood. I went out with a bunch of my girlfriends and celebrated the

beginning of my new life. I have this incredible sense of peace."

Relocating to Port Hope, Ontario, Tara Lyn has chosen to stay home and raise her three children (Ashton arrived three years ago). To her surprise, she was nominated for the 2004 CCMA Independent Female Artist Award for her single "Happiness" released on her own label in 2003, recorded as a hobby rather than a career move. "I laughed when I heard that. I wasn't trying for a huge

comeback and re-mortgaging the house. It was simply doing something I really enjoyed at one point in my life."

Will the nomination alter her plans? Hardly. "That's the first week of September, school starting, and an exciting time for the kids that I don't want to miss out on." ■

Born in Roblin, Manitoba

Won a CKDM Dauphin radio contest – prize: studio time in Winnipeg

ALBUMS: Tara Lyn Mohr (1995); Stuff That Matters (1999)

HIT SINGLES: "Stuff That Matters", "Save Me", "I Will Be Loving You", "What He Used To Be", "Happiness"

Canadian Country Music Association Rising Star award in 2000

Big break came when Chantal Kreviazuk was stuck in traffic and her A&R rep asked Danny Schur who else he had been working with

Winnipeg producer Craig Fotheringham helped develop her songwriting from age eleven

Linda Ronstadt producer Peter Asher co-produced Tara Lyn's album Stuff That Matters

Lived in Nashville for three years

Lives in Port Hope, Ontario, and is focusing on raising her family

# DIANNE HEATHERINGTON

IN 1970, SINGER DIANNE HEATHERINGTON was the undisputed queen of the Winnipeg pub scene. A dynamic performer with few peers, she was a larger-than-life personality equally capable of gut-wrenching emotion or joyous rapture. With her band the Merry-Go-Round, Dianne packed the Plaza, City Centre, Maryland, and St. Vital Hotel pubs night after night, and her future looked bright as she left the city bound for fortune and fame in Toronto. The Guess Who even recorded a song about her in 1973.

Dianne's gift for singing appeared early. "There was always music in the house and Dianne always sang," notes younger brother Ken. "I recall Dianne and my other sister Pat singing a lot at the piano. Dianne was self-taught on piano — everyone in the family seemed to have a pretty good ear. Or they would sing along to records. She loved the Beatles because of their harmonies. And she loved Dusty Springfield: 'Son Of A Preacher Man' and 'You Don't Have To Say You Love Me'. She liked any signature female singers that had a little more R & B." Born and raised in Fort Rouge, Dianne attended St. Ignatius and St. Mary's Academy parochial schools, where she sang in choirs.

Encouraged by her choir master to pursue professional work, Dianne began singing for the CBC, appearing on several local productions including *Let's Go*, with the Guess Who as backing band. "We didn't have a colour TV so we had to go out and rent a hotel room to watch it in colour," smiles Ken. Working day jobs at Rypp's Pharmacy, as a secretary or waitress, Dianne began singing in the pubs by the late 1960s. "She started with some guys from Kelvin High School as the Starlight Combo," recalls Ken. "She went on to some other bands before the Electric Banana, the first band she became prominent with." The Electric Banana was competent enough, but Dianne wanted to work with better musicians. Eventually she formed the Merry-Go-Round with keyboard player Hermann Frühm, drummer Steve Banman from Sugar & Spice, guitarist Chris Anderson, and ex-Fifth bass player Melvin Ksionzek. Together they set out to conquer the pubs.

In September 1970 the pub scene got a lot bigger once the drinking age was lowered to eighteen. Dianne Heatherington and the Merry-Go-Round soon became the talk of Winnipeg and participated in several local rock festivals, the best known being ManPop '70. Initially held outdoors in the football stadium, rain forced a hasty retreat into the Arena, where a makeshift stage was erected. All the name acts performed except Led Zeppelin, safely ensconced in their rooms at the International Inn until accosted by Dianne. "She shamed Led Zeppelin into playing," laughs Hermann. "She told them, 'All these people are here to see you and you're chickening out?' She was in one of her flamboyant rages. She spoke to them like they were her little brothers or something. No fear whatsoever." In the end, Led Zeppelin performed.

In 1971, CBC offered Dianne her own national TV show as a summer programming fill-in, but it became an instant hit across the country. By then, there were several personnel changes: ex-Love Cyrcle guitarist Rob Langdon joined (later replaced by former Mongrels guitarist Duncan Wilson), and Crescendos drummer Vance Masters also signed on. Last onboard was bass player Bill Wallace, from Brother. This new lineup set about developing original material that they debuted in clubs that fall. One person impressed with their tunes was Kenny Rogers, who caught the band's set at a gig in Saskatoon. Kenny booked Dianne and the group to appear on his CTV television series *Rolling On The River*,

then invited them to Los Angeles to record for him, sealing the deal with a credit card for expenses. In January 1972, they set off for LA, spending a week laying down five or six tracks. "We recorded all our own stuff including 'Long Time Coming', 'The Great Garbage Strike of 1912', 'Special Events Day', 'Jesus Came To America" and a couple of others," recalls Hermann. "All this on a handshake."

Returning to Winnipeg, Kenny offered them a contract for an album under the new name Catweazel. "Then, all of a sudden, Guess Who manager Don Hunter started paying attention to the band,"

**IN 1971, CBC OFFERED DIANNE HER OWN NATIONAL TV SHOW AS A SUMMER PROGRAMMING FILL-IN, BUT IT BECAME AN INSTANT HIT ACROSS THE COUNTRY.**

notes Hermann. "I was saying, 'Come on guys, we've been offered a contract here!' but they were seduced by Hunter. Weeks went by and I'm still getting calls from Kenny asking what was happening. In the end he just gave up. Hunter never came through with anything but six months later Bill joined the Guess Who." The band folded soon after and Dianne headed out to Toronto (becoming the subject of "Bye Bye Babe" on the Guess Who's *Artificial Paradise* album).

Working the clubs and local television circuit in Toronto backed by former Winnipeg musicians such as Gary Taylor, Leonard Shaw, Dave Garber, Mark Rutherford, and Sandy Chochinov ("The Panamanians"), Dianne signed

with CBS Records, releasing one album, *Heatherington Rocks*, in 1980, followed by a tour of Germany and Holland. "How do you catch that passion and energy she had onstage in the studio?" says Ken. "That album just didn't capture her." In 1983 she tried cracking the Big Apple. "We did a weekly gig at Joe's Bar on 6th Street in New York," recalls Gary Taylor. "We had a four-piece rock band on Saturday nights and on Friday nights we did country hits. Dianne did the show in a Patsy Cline-style dress, introducing the songs with a Texas accent. People believed she was from Nashville. She didn't tell them any different."

Returning to Toronto in 1985, Dianne pursued an acting career, appearing in *Cocktail* and *The Liberace Story*. "She sang jazz exclusively for two years, then decided she was past her prime and retired from the music scene," says Gary. Dianne then formed her own movie security company. "She employed many of our musician friends and helped them pay their rent." In February 1994, Dianne returned to Winnipeg to reunite with the Merry-Go-Round for a gala fundraiser on behalf of the Manitoba Museum's Get Back exhibit, stunning everyone with her amazing vocal presence. Sadly, however, she died in 1998 of ovarian cancer.

"Dianne's focus was always on the music," says Ken. "That was her passion. She could deliver a ballad with incredible intensity that I have never seen matched. Her heart turned inside out and she left herself open and vulnerable."

Dianne touched the lives of all who knew her. "Many of the singers I know in Toronto consider her the best singer they'd ever heard in the clubs here," concludes Gary. ∎

Born in Winnipeg
BANDS: Electric Banana, Merry-Go-Round
ALBUM: Heatherington Rocks (1980)
SINGLES: "He's A Rebel"; "Rock & Roll Gypsies"

Hosted her own national CBC TV series, *Dianne* in 1971
Moved to Toronto in the mid '70s and played clubs
Appeared in the movies *Cocktail* and *The Liberace Story*
Dianne was the inspiration for the Guess Who song "Bye Bye Babe"

Kenny 'The Gambler' Rogers produced tracks in LA for Dianne and the Merry-Go-Round
Convinced a reluctant Led Zeppelin to perform at Winnipeg's ManPop Festival

# TOM JACKSON

TOM JACKSON

**P**ERHAPS BETTER KNOWN THESE DAYS for his acting than his singing, Tom Jackson still defines himself first and foremost as a singer. "It depends on where you're from in the country," he says, deep baritone voice resonating. "On the Prairies they know me first as a singer who's an actor now. And in places where they didn't know I was a singer, people picked up on my acting career and discovered later that I was a singer through television." Makes no difference. Music remains Tom's passion and gave him his introduction into the world of acting while he was a struggling performer in Winnipeg coffeehouses.

Born to an English father and Cree mother on the northern Saskatchewan One Arrow reserve near Batoche, Tom developed an early affinity for music. "My uncles would always come over and bring their instruments, and my mother would sing. I had a guitar when I was seven or eight years old."

Moving to Winnipeg in 1963, Tom left school at fifteen to perform in local coffeehouses. "I was really caught up with the folk music era. There was a coffeehouse called the Purple Pit at the Indian & Métis Friendship Centre at 376 Donald Street and I played there a lot with Lindsay Cronk, Graham Jones and Doug Elias. Graham showed me how to advance my guitar playing. My first professional gig was warming up for them at Assiniboine School. I can still recall standing up in that school gym playing my songs."

In 1971, Tom recorded an independently-distributed single, "White Man Listen", funded by the Manitoba Indian Brotherhood. A friendship with local folk singer/songwriter Rick Neufeld spurred on Tom's own songwriting. "I fancied myself a connoisseur of poetry, in particular musical poetry. I was a big fan of Kris Kristofferson and Paul Simon. So when I started writing I was very conscientious about making sure that the songs would not be fluff."

Tom supported his budding music career through other means. "I had a

longstanding relationship with a pool table, a backgammon board, dart board, chess board and anything else you could play one on one. I subsidized my passion for music by spending many hours at these pursuits." Adds Rick Neufeld, "Tom was a wicked card player. I lost a few guitars to him in card games."

A trip to the Mariposa Folk Festival proved inspirational for the aspiring singer/songwriter, who witnessed performances by Joni Mitchell, Bob Dylan and Neil Young. "I played some coffeehouses in Montreal where I met Leonard Cohen, who came out to listen to this Native guy singing."

On the periphery of the Winnipeg music scene through the 1970s, Tom worked with a series of local musicians. "I had a band called Tom Jackson and Friends which was Fred Dawes, Bill Merritt, Chris the Shark, Norm Dugas, Dave Wood, the Kozub sisters, Dave Kramer. There were lots of places to play in Winnipeg back then and a real music community, which allowed you to become a better musician. But my greatest influence in music at the time was Rick Neufeld. I still talk about all the good times at Rick's farm out in Ste. Anne in my storytelling show *Stories and Songs and Tomfoolery*."

Tom also found himself in demand to sing on television. "I believe I have probably performed on more musical variety

shows than many other performers, without actually having a recording career or a record out." While not burning up the pop charts, singing nonetheless gave Tom his entrance to an acting career. "My ability to act, I believe, can be credited to my commitment to performing live onstage. I used to get so emotionally wrapped up in what I was singing. If I believed in the song, the audience would believe in it. I would emotionally commit myself to the song. That is a great skill to have as an actor." Approached to do a storytelling segment for the Canadian edition of *Sesame Street*, Tom then received an offer from Winnipeg's Prairie Theatre Exchange in 1979 and took the plunge. "I just figured I'd give it a try. The show was very successful and went on from Winnipeg to New York. So I traded instruments onstage, from guitar and singing to acting."

Over the next twenty years Tom appeared on stage and screen, small and large, including appearances on *Star Trek* and *North of 60*. But music remained central to him, releasing albums beginning with *Tom Jackson*, recorded in Winnipeg, followed by *Love, Lust And Longing*, and a project for the Salvation Army, a country-gospel album entitled *Sally Ann*. He has released ten albums, six under his own name, including his most recent, *I Will Bring You Near*, and been nominated for two Juno awards. As *Scene Magazine* declared, "His lyrics reveal a warmth and insight into his wrong-side-of-the-tracks

Born on the One Arrow reserve in Saskatchewan and moved to Winnipeg as a teenager

Recorded a 1971 single "White Man Listen" for the Manitoba Indian Brotherhood

Has appeared on dozens of televisions shows including *Sesame Street* and *Star Trek*, and starred in *North of 60*

ALBUMS: The Huron Carole (1988, 1994, 1998); Sally Ann (1990); Love, Lust and Longing (1992); No Regrets (1995); That Side of the Window (1997); I Will Bring You Near (2001); On The Holiday Train (2003)

Canadian Aboriginal Music Award for Best Producer (1999); Order of Canada (2000); Lifetime Achievement Award from the Ontario Country Music Association (2000); Queen's

Jubilee medal (2002); named Canada's best activist by *Time* magazine

Early in career a frequent performer at the Purple Pit in the Indian & Métis Friendship Centre, Winnipeg

His annual Huron Carole concerts have raised more than $3 million for food banks

Performs a one-man show entitled Stories and Songs and Tomfoolery

upbringing." In between these projects came Tom's best-known and most enduring legacy, the Huron Carole.

While living on the streets in Toronto in the 1980s, Tom still managed to organize a fundraising concert for a crisis centre, the centerpiece of the concert being "The Huron Carole". He'd first become aware of this song back in 1965 when performing on a Winnipeg Christmas special. Returning to Winnipeg soon after the Toronto fundraiser, a local food bank was threatened with eviction, so Tom staged the Huron Carole concert. "We raised enough money to keep the wolf from the door for the next three months. Now it's a national event." The annual Huron Carole concert series, featuring a star-studded lineup of Canadian performers, has raised more than $3 million for food banks across Canada.

In 1997 Tom organized the Red River Flood Relief Benefit concert in Winnipeg, bringing together ex-Guess Who partners Randy Bachman and Burton Cummings as well as BTO member Fred Turner for a memorable night of music. He also spearheaded the Say Hay concert in support of drought-stricken Canadian farmers, raising $1.8 million.

Tom's philanthropic efforts have not gone unheralded. In 2000 he was appointed an Officer of the Order of Canada and received the Queen's Jubilee medal two years later. *Time* Magazine named him one of Canada's best activists and he has been awarded honourary degrees from Laurentian, Winnipeg, Victoria, Trent, Lakehead and Calgary universities. He recently created Tomali Productions in Calgary as an umbrella organization to oversee his many artistic endeavours, from film production to music.

Despite his many achievements, memories of the Winnipeg music scene remain strong. "I can remember even in the bad moments always having fun," he says. "It was such a blessing for me. The Winnipeg music scene over and above any place else was a life saving and life giving experience for me." ∎

# TERRY JACKS

**T**rust your paperboy. That was the lesson Terry Jacks learned after everyone in the music business cautioned him against recording what would become one of Canada's biggest selling singles ever, "Seasons In The Sun". "They all said it would ruin my career," laughs Terry. "'That sucks, Jacks. Too sappy.' One day I played it for my paperboy and he loved it. So I put it out, went to Hawaii and when I got back, the switchboards had lit up at every radio station that played it."

**RECORDING THE MOVING JACQUES BREL COMPOSITION "SEASONS IN THE SUN" WAS MOTIVATED BY THE DEATH OF A CLOSE FRIEND.**

Born and raised in south Winnipeg as the son of a doctor, Terry lived at 172 Oxford Street and attended River Heights School until age ten. "My best friend was Gerry Schwartz, who's now a powerful businessman. We used to play together on the construction site next door."

His interest in music was kindled while still here. "To me songs are little pictures, and I like to make these little pictures that hit someone the way they hit me when I was growing up in Winnipeg. Records were like little pictures. That's why I didn't do a lot of performing. I would make my little picture and then move on, like an artist doing paintings."

In the late 1950s Terry's family moved to Rochester, Minnesota for four years. "I had a paper route and every bit of my money went into rock 'n' roll records — Everly Brothers, Elvis and Buddy Holly. He was my idol. I would comb my hair like Buddy Holly and stand in front of the mirror and sing his songs."

Moving to Vancouver, Terry acquired a guitar and was soon playing in local bands, including the Chessmen. "I was going to get kicked out of the Chessmen because I wasn't a great guitar player, but I wrote a song called 'The Way You Fell' and it went to #2 in Vancouver. We had been an instrumental group but all of a sudden we were a vocal group and I was the singer." The success prompted Terry to drop out of university to pursue music, hitchhiking to Los Angeles in the mid

'60s, where he learned about record production. An early lesson in the underbelly of the music business revealed the importance of controlling his own product, after a song he sent to a record producer in LA ended up recorded by another artist with no credit to Terry. "I learned that I needed to have my own publishing company." With his next venture, The Poppy Family, Terry controlled everything. "I had my own record company. I wrote my own songs, produced and arranged the records, published the songs and managed myself and I had Susan singing the songs. So I had no obligations to anyone." Meeting Susan Pesklovits following an appearance on *Music Hop*, the two formed the group.

In 1969, The Poppy Family scored a worldwide smash hit with Terry's "Which Way You Going Billy", selling over 3 million copies. "Imagine being twenty years old and a millionaire. Everyone kept saying I had to go on the road but I didn't want to. I just wanted to write. I never went into it to make money or be famous, I just wanted to paint those little pictures that inspired me when I was a kid." "That's Where I Went Wrong" became another hit but Terry was determined to lend his own voice to the Poppy Family. "I got sick of having to write songs for the female gender. Neil Young was coming out then and he couldn't sing so I figured why not me? So I recorded 'Where Evil Grows' and that became a #1 record.

Then I did 'Concrete Sea' and I just figured I didn't care what people thought, I wanted to sing. And then came 'Seasons in the Sun.' I won Male Vocalist of the Year two years in a row so I guess I could sing." He and Susan split after six years of marriage.

Recording the moving Jacques Brel composition "Seasons in the Sun" was motivated by the death of a close friend. Recalling the song about a man suffering a broken heart because his wife left him, Terry rewrote the lyrics. "I used some of Jacques Brel's lyrics but I rewrote almost half of it. Nobody knows that because I didn't get any writing credit." Poet/songwriter Rod McKuen, who translated Brel's original song, was credited alongside Brel. "Jacques told me I should have gotten credit for it."

Initially, Terry intended the song for the Beach Boys. "I was a hot producer in Canada at the time so they invited me down. They cut a version of 'Seasons In The Sun' and it was really beautiful with those Beach Boys harmonies." But the sessions proved problematic after Brian Wilson decided to resume production duties. In the end Terry recorded it himself in Canada, where it became a giant hit. "I came home one day and Bell Records in the US had their representative waiting for me with a cheque for $100,000." The single sold over 12 million copies worldwide.

"'Seasons' is a song critics love to hate. I read where it was named the worst record ever to come out of Canada, yet it was the biggest selling Canadian single. In the last interview Kurt Cobain ever gave, he said one of his idols was Terry Jacks. 'Where Evil Grows' was one of his favourite songs, and he stole the riff from that for a Nirvana song. He loved my guitar sound on 'Seasons In The Sun'."

Further singles followed "Seasons" including Buddy Holly's "I'm Gonna Love You Too" and "Rock 'n' Roll I Gave You The Best Years Of My Life", before Terry retired from the business to focus on his environmental concerns. "I saw all the destruction that the pulp mills were doing to our air and water. I began looking into it and making headlines." He spent ten years on the front lines of Environmental Watch, receiving a United Nations award for his efforts. In 2004 Terry was inducted into the British Columbia Music Hall of Fame alongside another ex-Winnipegger, Randy Bachman.

"I would not be anything without Winnipeg," insists Terry. "Think about it — Neil, Randy and me — three of the biggest Canadians in record sales all from Winnipeg. There's something about Winnipeg. It's the rock 'n' roll heart of Canada." ∎

Born in Winnipeg; moved to Vancouver in his early teens

**Bands:** the Chessmen, Poppy Family, solo artist

ALBUMS: Which Way You Goin' Billy (1969), Poppy Seeds (1971), Seasons In The Sun (1974)

HIT SINGLES: "Which Way You Goin' Billy", "That's Where I Went Wrong", "Where Evil Grows", "Concrete Sea", "Seasons In The Sun"

Sold 13 million copies of "Seasons In The Sun"; Won Juno Male Vocalist and Single of the Year (1974)

"Seasons In The Sun" originally recorded with the Beach Boys; Kurt Cobain a big fan

Left music in late 1970s to become environmental activist; honoured by the United Nations

**B**randon's Angela Kelman became a country pop diva with Canadian sensation Farmer's Daughter on a route that, while not exactly cornfields to Cadillacs, was still a circuitous one. In the late '90s, the trio — Angela, Jake Leiske and Shauna Rae Samograd — was at the top of the heap with gold albums, chart-topping singles and videos, and sold out tours, an odd circumstance for someone who earned her chops in lounges and supper clubs rather than county fairs. "Country pop is not my favourite style of music yet I've had my biggest success with it."

**A THIRD HIT ALBUM, THIS IS THE LIFE, INCLUDED A COVER OF THE BTO ROCKER "LET IT RIDE" WITH RANDY BACHMAN GUESTING ON THE TRACK. AMERICAN SUCCESS BECKONED.**

Born in Brandon, Angela was singing by the time she began school. "I knew by age five that this was what I wanted to do." In high school she became a member of C.P. Express, an extra-curricular pop group assembled by Crocus Plains teacher Gerry Perkin. "I moved on from singing to a hairbrush in front of a mirror to getting up in front of an audience of high school kids, which is pretty scary." Under Perkin's tutelage Angela learned harmony singing, a skill that would serve her well. C.P. Express recorded a one-off single written by Angela and the group as a grad fundraiser. She also recorded "Heaven Tonight", produced by two local disk jockeys.

Angela's professional experience began fronting Cold Duck, a Top 40 band featuring the sixteen year old. "I thought, 'You mean I can get paid to do this?'" Following a brief stint at Brandon University's Faculty of Music, she lit out for Winnipeg to pursue her career, teaming up with veteran pianist and arranger Tom Dahl, who previously worked with pop star Lisa Dal Bello. Tom and Angela performed for seven years in supper clubs and lounges such as Rae & Jerry's Steakhouse, Rumors Comedy Club, and the Oval Room. "Tom taught me a lot about entertaining, how to make an audience comfortable and how to talk to an audience. Those are very important skills for a performer." She recorded commercial jingles, co-hosted CBC TV's *The Crystal*

*Club*, and worked with pop performer Rocki Roletti.

In 1986, Angela joined The Argyles, a Winnipeg-based Manhattan Transfer-style vocal quartet, and spent three weeks performing at Expo '86 in Vancouver before embarking on an Asian tour with engagements in Malaysia, Kowloon, and an American naval base in the Philippines. In 1989 she enrolled in the Vocal Institute of Technology at the Musician's Institute in Hollywood, California. "I felt like I needed to learn more. I refined my voice and learned to project." In Los Angeles, Angela moonlighted with a dance band playing the Marriott Hotel chain. Homesick for Canada, she relocated to Vancouver in 1991 taking a gig in the lounge at the Big Bamboo club.

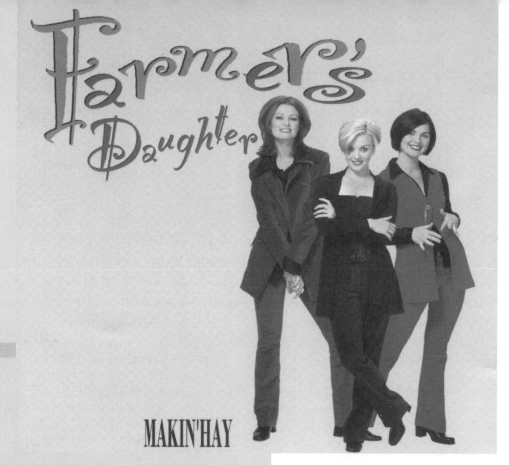

# Farmer's Daughter

**MAKIN' HAY**

"Some friends of mine knew of these girls who were starting a country trio. I wasn't singing country music. Jake Leiske heard a demo I had done in LA — pop and hip-hop stuff — and thought, 'She's good but she's not country.' When they approached me, I listened and thought, 'This is good.'" Jake and Shauna Rae Samograd had already worked with two other singers before drafting Angela to fill in for a weeklong engagement at the PNE in the summer of 1993. "Gerry Lieske, Jake's Dad and Farmer's Daughter's manager, got me in a corner and said to me, 'You are going to join this group and it's going to be sensational!' At that point I had been feeling quite down about approaching thirty. I had set goals for myself that hadn't happened yet. So the timing was right. A year later we all quit our day jobs and went on the road."

*Girls Will Be Girls* catapulted Farmer's Daughter into the spotlight with seven hit singles. Angela's jazz and pop sensibilities along with her harmony training helped to craft a unique vocal blend, leaning as much on pop as country. Country music had entered the video age and the three attractive women were perfect for that format. "My Mom could turn on her TV and see me two or three times a day and think, 'She's doing all right'." *Makin' Hay* became their breakthrough album, going gold and yielding their biggest hits "Cornfields Or Cadillacs" and "Lonely Gypsy Wind". "We were huge by the late '90s but we were away from home so much. In one year we were out on the road for 270 days."

A highlight came in 1997 when the group toured Canadian forces bases in Bosnia. "They were so appreciative of us entertaining them because we were bringing a piece of home to them." They also performed for troops in Egypt and the Golan Heights, as well as war-torn Eritrea in Ethiopia. That same year Farmer's Daughter won Juno and CCMA awards for Country Group or Duo of the Year.

A third hit album, *This Is The Life*, included a cover of the BTO rocker "Let It Ride" with Randy Bachman guesting on the track. American success beckoned. "It felt like we were on the edge of something big, but we were too eclectic for American country music. But what really blew us out of the water was the Dixie Chicks. This concept that we had was being done by someone else." A *Best of* album followed but the momentum was lost. "We loved each other like sisters but there was underlying competition and a lot of difficult personal stuff to deal with so I needed some time off." The hiatus allowed Angela to pursue her own musical goals including the bossa nova-flavoured *Café Brasilia* album and a children's album — "I wanted it to be musically educational as well as fun so I wrote every song with different animal characters." Another of Angela's side projects is the Polyester Philharmonic, a ten-piece retro '70s band.

When Shauna Rae opted for a solo career in Nashville, Angela and Jake regrouped as the Daughters, adding singer Laura Rose. "We'll probably release a single just to see what'll happen." But she has not abandoned her own aspirations. "I really need the freedom to pursue my own music. You have to diversify if you're working full time." Angela cites her prairie roots as keeping her grounded. "There is no pretentiousness in Manitoba. You just do what you do." ■

---

Born in Brandon, Manitoba

GROUPS: CP Express, Cold Duck, Tom & Angela, The Argyles, Farmer's Daughter

Moved to Vancouver and joined Farmer's Daughter in 1993

Farmer's Daughter recorded BTO's "Let It Ride" with Randy Bachman on guitar

Was one of the Rigatoni Sisters in Rocki Roletti's band in the 1990s

ALBUMS: Girls Will Be Girls (1994); Makin' Hay (1996); This Is The Life (1998); Best of Farmer's Daughter (2000); Café Brasilia (2004) Angela May's Magnificent Musical Menagerie (2005)

HIT SINGLES: "Calling All You Cowboys", "Cornfields Or Cadillacs", "Lonely Gypsy Wind", "Now That I'm On My Own", "Freeway"

AWARDS: six BCCMA Awards, Juno Award for Best Country Group (1998), CCMA Country Group of the Year Award (1997)

Performs solo, with the Daughters, and with '70s retro band Polyester Philharmonic

Angela May's Magnificent Musical Menagerie nominated for 2005 Juno for best children's album

# KILOWATT

## KILOWATT

**A**s members of the Guess Who, guitarist Greg Leskiw and bass player Bill Wallace experienced life at the top of the rock 'n' roll pantheon. When they reunited in 1981, both were determined to take a run at that brass ring one more time with Kilowatt, a hard-rockin' quartet that was a serious contender in the Canadian rock sweepstakes.

Following his departure from Crowcuss, Greg released a solo album called *Be My Champion* in 1979 that he credited to LesQ. The album showcased a wide range of musical styles. "I've always been considered eclectic," says Greg, "but it's always something I've tried to avoid." Greg assembled the LesQ band and set out on the road. The lineup remained fluid with players coming and going until 1981, when Greg, guitarist Steve Heygi and drummer Harvey Kostenchuk were joined by Bill Wallace.

LesQ cut a nine-song demo tape at Wayne Finucan's studio with Norm Kinney, who had engineered Gino Vannelli's recent album, as producer. The tracks were complex in structure, akin to Greg and Bill's early Crowcuss material. "We were throwing all kinds of things into the arrangement. They weren't two and a half minute tunes." A cassette tape of the tracks, entitled simply *Q*, became a hot item sold at the group's shows.

During a regular gig at the Osborne Village Inn, Toronto guitarist Domenic Troiano caught a set. A former band mate of Bill's in the Guess Who, Domenic offered to produce the band, who were now calling themselves Kilowatt. Signing with Toronto-based independent label Dallcorte Records, Kilowatt cut their self-titled debut album in Toronto with Domenic. "Basically, Kilowatt's songs were way over arranged and needed to be simplified. Domenic cut to the essential part of the song to make it work." During the sessions, Harvey Kostenchuk was replaced by Bob Brett.

Driven by Steve Heygi's rapid-fire guitar, *Kilowatt*, released in 1982, was an impressive debut album of all original material mostly from Greg, who also handled lead vocals. "Rock 'n' roll was loud and heavy then, and I was trying to work with that. I was trying to be a rock guy." The album was well-received, with "Kids Are Crazy" released as a single as

> **...WITH KILOWATT GREG SUCCEEDED IN CREATING A BODY OF MUSIC THAT TYPIFIES THE BEST IN CANADIAN ROCK OF THE 1980s.**

the group made several television appearances and toured. Fans came to appreciate the group's no-frills rock, something few expected from Greg or Bill.

While the other members embraced the heavier rock approach, Greg found it increasingly difficult to sing in that style. "It was hard work. My voice would be shot after the fourth song. I was singing at the top of my lungs. Everybody was singing that way then, just belting from the top of their range. You had to because of the high-energy music. But it was unnecessarily loud, in retrospect."

By the time sessions rolled around for a follow up album Greg was beginning to resist compromising his concept of the songs. "Kilowatt wasn't what I had envisioned to begin with but it's something that developed out of the musical environ-

ment at that time. I related better to the music on the early demos we did than what it became after we went to Toronto."

Greg began losing interest during sessions for *Currents*, issued in 1984. Bill Wallace was contributing more to the band by this point, posting several tracks on the album including lead vocal on the poignant "I'm Not A Kid Anymore". "Troiano did a fair amount of rearranging, especially on the second album. He also brought in a keyboard player." One of Greg's most enduring songs, "Ma Cherie" made its debut on the album. Out on the road following the release of the album, Kilowatt was stunned by the sudden closure of Dallcorte Records. "The record company actually broke down before we did. We never had a sense that it was on a solid footing." The collapse hastened the end of Kilowatt. "It wasn't a happy ending. The wheels just started falling off the cart. It was recuperation time for me. I took a year off afterwards."

Retreating to his own home studio to record younger local bands, Greg found the experienced rejuvenating. "I recorded tons of bands," he says, "just amazing groups out of Winnipeg." During this period he resurrected Mood Jga Jga for a belated second album before assembling a very personal project, Swing Soniq. Bill Wallace took a complete left turn following the dissolution of Kilowatt, enrolling in the Faculty of Education at the University of Manitoba, emerging four years later with a teaching degree in music. After several years at R.B. Russell vocational school, Bill currently runs the music department

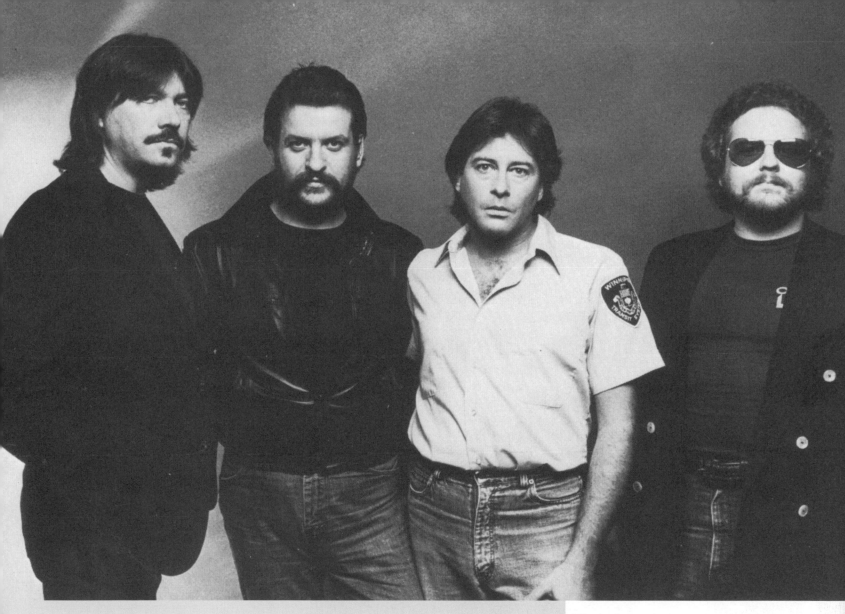

at West Kildonan Collegiate in north Winnipeg, where he will soon be working out of the recently announced Randy Bachman Performing Arts Theatre there. In 2000 he took a sabbatical from teaching to join up with the reunited Guess Who after Jim Kale faltered early on in rehearsals, a role Bill had assumed twenty-eight years earlier. He could not pass up an opportunity to relive past glories. He toured Canada and the United States with the Guess Who for the next three years.

Guitarist Steve Heygi currently lives in the interior of British Columbia where he gigs locally. Bob Brett is in Winnipeg. In 1996 Domenic Troiano was inducted into the Canadian Music Hall of Fame.

Greg is circumspect about his time in Kilowatt and what the group tried to achieve. He now feels that he was trying too hard and in doing so surrendered too much of his own musical integrity in a quest for the big time. "Oh yeah, I wanted success. I wanted hit records. Kilowatt was a good shot. But I fell into that same scene that so many people do of always trying to adapt to something that isn't quite appropriate for them."

Nonetheless, with Kilowatt he succeeded in creating a body of music that typifies the best in Canadian rock of the 1980s. ∎

Formed in Winnipeg in 1981 by ex-Guess Who members Greg Leskiw and Bill Wallace

Began as LesQ before changing personnel and band name

ALBUMS: Kilowatt (1982); Currents (1984); Headquarters (1999); The Jam Factory Sessions (1999)

HIT SINGLES: "Lovers On The Run", "Kids Are Crazy", "I'm Not A Kid Anymore"

Albums produced by ex-James Gang and Guess Who guitarist Domenic Troiano

Wallace and Leskiw first played together in the Logan Avenue Comfort Station (1968)

Bill Wallace later teamed up with ex-Guess Who member Donnie McDougall to form The Best of the Guess Who band

Greg Leskiw later re-recorded two Kilowatt songs, "Step Aside" and "Ma Cherie" in a jazz style on Swing Soniq's 1998 debut album

**F**OR ANY YOUNG ARTIST, recording your debut album can be an unnerving experience. For Winnipeg singer/songwriter Chantal Kreviazuk, the overwhelming expectations caused by hype and a big contract added to an already stressful situation. That she succeeded is testament to her talent, strength of character, and perseverance.

Hardly a household name in 1995, the suburban Charleswood-raised performer was suddenly thrust into the media glare when newspapers across Canada trumpeted a $1.5 million recording contract with Sony Music. The problem was that her career was launched on hype rather than substance. "I had to prove myself in the eyes of the public," Chantal concedes, the story crucial for her to clarify, "because they're thinking, 'Hmm, let's see what she can do for a million and a half dollars!' It shouldn't have been like that. It was something that was pinned on me at the very beginning and I've never been able to get away from that."

But her story has a happy ending. Chantal's debut album *Under These Rocks and Stones* silenced skeptics. Her songwriting was masterful, her delivery and phrasing impeccable. Chantal was, indeed, world-class. Her subsequent albums only reinforce that fact. "I always knew that I was going to be a contributor to the arts. I was playing the piano when I was three and singing, acting and doing musical theatre. I had so much fire and

passion." Songwriting, too, came quite naturally to the precocious youngster. "I never thought, 'I'm going to sit down and write a song.' It was just very stream of consciousness. I remember singing my mom songs to sort of kiss her butt when I was a bad kid. 'You're the best Mommy and I love you'. When I got a little older and started feeling the angst of hormones and puberty my songwriting really became my comfort, my own inner strength and support."

Attending exclusive Balmoral Hall School for Girls offered Chantal further opportunity to develop her talents. "They recognized that I had a particular gift for music." Whether singing, playing piano in assemblies, or tackling the lead in musical productions, Chantal's creativity was encouraged. "I was a multi-tasking kid with a ton of energy and they helped me to handle pressure. It was good for me." Other performance experience came via the annual Manitoba Music Festival and at seniors' institutions arranged by her music teacher.

A motorcycle accident in her late teens forced Chantal to the sidelines but allowed her to focus more attention on her songwriting. Seeking out the Pumps/ Orphan leader Chris Burke-Gaffney, whose hit song "Miracle" inspired her, Chantal nurtured her craft under his tutelage. "When you're a kid and you have a hunger for music and a hunger for songwriting, you want to surround yourself with people who understand you and where you're going musically. Chris gave me that gift."

Sony Records heard Chantal's emotionally charged demo recording of her song "Surrounded" and signed her. "'Surrounded' was about a person in my life who committed suicide, so it's an important song for me. It taught me that when you're an artist to put your soul into your music because when you perform it, it never stops. That song is never going to go away for me in my life."

Sessions in Los Angeles under the direction of veteran producer Peter Asher, whose credits include James Taylor and Linda Ronstadt, were overwhelming. "It doesn't get any bigger than A&M Studios in Los Angeles. I had Tom Petty at the end of the studio working on a record, Adam Sandler in the room next door rehearsing for his world tour, and Keanu Reeves and Dogstar recording across the way. These were my friends, my audience, for six weeks."

The release of *Under These Rocks And Stars* marked the arrival of a stunning new talent. Further solidifying her prominence was landing a track, "Leaving On A Jet Plane," on the *Armageddon* movie soundtrack and scoring an invitation to join Sarah McLachlan's Lilith Fair tour. Chantal also contributed "Feels Like Home" to the *Dawson's Creek* soundtrack and the theme song for the NBC series *Providence*. In 2000 she won the Juno Award for Female Singer of the Year.

Determined to record her follow-up album under less duress, Chantal chose to record closer to home. Recorded in Toronto, *Colour Moving And Still* remains her personal favourite. "It's a pretty consistent album. I could sit down and do a concert of those songs and 'Surrounded' and call it a day." Her marriage to Toronto's Our Lady Peace lead singer Raine Maida contributed to the more

positive experience reflected in the songs. Reviews were glowing. In 2002, Chantal released her third album, *What If It All Means Something*, which, once again, earned critical praise.

Overshadowing her own performing career in recent months has been her songwriting collaboration with fellow Canadian superstar Avril Lavigne. Chantal was able to bring the wisdom of her own experience and a grounding to the partnership. "One of the greatest lessons that I was able to pass along to Avril was that there can't be pretenses attached to songwriting. I just said, 'Let's get back

to your heart and to you.' It was a bit cathartic for me being with her."

Despite homes in Toronto and Los Angeles, Chantal retains her hometown roots. "In Winnipeg, there wasn't this entertainment business quality that is pretty competitive and contrived. Loving music or making music was just so real. It's natural and genuine and that's really rare and beautiful.

"I'm as Manitoban as they get. I always say you can take the girl out of the 'Peg but you can't take the 'Peg out of the girl." ■

Born in Winnipeg

Discovered by Orphan singer/songwriter Chris Burke-Gaffney and Danny Schur

ALBUMS: Under These Rocks and Stones (1997), Colour Moving And Still (1999), What If It All Means Something (2002)

HIT SINGLES: "Surrounded"; "Feels Like Home" (from Dawson's Creek soundtrack); "Leaving On A Jet Plane" (from Armageddon soundtrack); "Before You"

AWARDS: Juno Award for Female Singer of the Year (2000)

Chantal collaborated with teen singing sensation Avril Lavigne on the pop star's sophomore album

She is married to Our Lady Peace vocalist Raine Maida

Her most personal song, "Surrounded", is about the suicide of a close friend

# JOEL KROEKER

**A** FOOTLOOSE CHILDHOOD LEFT AN INDELIBLE IMPRINT on singer/ songwriter Joel Kroeker. *Melodrama*, his first major label release on True North/Universal, has garnered the young artist critical praise for its insightful lyrics and soulful presentation. "Just looking at the themes lyrically on *Melodrama*, there's talk about endings and coming to terms with transitional periods in people's lives, and a deep longing and nostalgia," says the Winnipeg-born musician. "As a child it was kind of hard to have a consistent sense of who you are when you're making friends, then losing them, then making other friends and moving away."

**"IF THERE'S A STORY SO FAR THIS YEAR IN THE CANADIAN MUSIC INDUSTRY, IT'S JOEL KROEKER."**

In a very short span of time, Joel has established his credentials as one of Canada's finest new songwriters. "For every great musician who walks this earth, there are, relatively speaking, very few truly great songs. Joel Kroeker has a few of them," wrote the *Regina Leader Post* while *The Calgary Sun* concluded, "If there's a story so far this year in the Canadian music industry, it's Joel Kroeker."

Joel's nomadic existence began after his journalist father moved the family to Fresno, California when Joel was an infant, uprooting a year later for Chicago first, then Hillsboro, Kansas, and back to Fresno for a three-year stint. Joel returned to Winnipeg at the start of grade seven, settling in East Kildonan and enrolling in Mennonite Brethren Collegiate Institute. There he took up the guitar, forming his first band, the Crunge, in high school.

"It was an all-original band but the war in the band was between Zeppelin lovers and Van Halen lovers. I was a Van Halen lover. 'Eruption' was the very first song I ever learned."

Enrolled at the University of Winnipeg, Joel later transferred to the University of Manitoba's Faculty of Music, studying composition and guitar performance. He also formed the Kin, "an avant-garde experiment for me." He soon shifted his focus away from bands towards a solo career. "I started writing songs that I could perform by myself and that's when I started singing. I just figured I needed to do this by myself."

Moving on to the University of Alberta for post-graduate study in ethnomusicology and popular music, Joel's thesis was on western Canadian singer/songwriters. He ended up fulfilling his academic requirements by writing a master's thesis

Born in Winnipeg

Lived in Fresno, California, Chicago and Hillsboro, Kansas before returning to Winnipeg

ALBUMS: Naïve Bohemian (1999); Melodrama (2004)

AWARDS: Best New Recording Artist by Alberta Recording Industry

Association (1999), Film Score of the Year for the documentary Tokyo Gardens

Played in Winnipeg bands The Crunge and The Kin

Graduate of Mennonite Brethren Collegiate Institute, Winnipeg

Has a Masters degree in ethnomusicology and popular music from the University of Alberta

Guested on Randy Bachman's JazzThing album and Bravo TV special

Co-wrote songs with Lee Aaron on her Beautiful Things album

on his own experience promoting his independently produced album, *Naïve Bohemian*, to the music industry. "I was basically trying to get into the industry. I sent that out and in a circuitous way that's how I got True North and Universal involved." *Naïve Bohemian* reached #7 on the Canadian National Campus Radio Specialty chart and was picked up by Edmonton-based Spirit River Distribution. On the strength of the album, Joel was named Best New Recording Artist by the Alberta Recording Industry Association in 1999. Other projects kept him busy: a collaboration with heavy metal queen-turned jazz stylist Lee Aaron, and scoring soundtracks for three Canadian films, winning Film Score of the Year for the documentary *Tokyo Gardens*. He also guested on fellow Winnipegger Randy Bachman's daring jazz album, *JazzThing*. "That was a huge thrill because he's an icon. I grew up playing BTO covers. And then I toured with him and we did a Bravo TV special and it's been great."

Signing a unique 50/50 partnership between independent label True North and the mighty Universal Records for distribution, Joel recorded *Melodrama* in Toronto with producer Danny Greenspoon, who recruited some top session players including Randy Bachman.

Unexpectedly, given Joel's versatility and talent on guitar, the songs on *Melodrama* are more lyric-driven than guitar-focused. "That was very intentional. I have a fascination with the guitar and I always have but I'm at a stage right now where I find the song is much more important to me than the guitar. That's why the album is diverse in style. I like to think of it as twelve demos that I'd like to pitch to see if anyone else wants to do these songs, because that's more important to me than the guitar aspect."

Joel's songs resonate with emotions that draw the listener in. "I try to deal with archetypal images or images that are universal in some way and try to take my own personal story and make it into a metaphorical image that will be a larger energy source. Common themes like love and loss come up and I personalize them with my own stories. Sometimes that's scary."

Now residing in Vancouver, his hometown remains a source of inspiration. "I feel very connected to Winnipeg, partly because my family is still there. It's like the anchor of Canada for me. I also think that sense of nostalgia or melancholy on the album is a Winnipeg thing for me. Somehow that's the Winnipeg mentality or psyche and I hear it in a lot of different kinds of music."

Joel's master plan is to build a career for the long haul rather than flash quickly on the scene. "I have no interest in having one of these short, tumultuous, exciting careers that's over right away. I want to put out twenty albums and keep doing this until I'm eighty-five. The people I respect are artists like Bruce Cockburn who are in it for the long haul. He is the template for what I'm trying to do, have commercial success and still have a social conscience addressing issues."

Signing with Cockburn's label True North was a positive step. "When I grow up I want to be like Bruce Cockburn," he laughs. ■

# D A N I E L  L A V O I E

**I**T'S QUITE A DISTANCE FROM TINY DUNREA in southwestern Manitoba to the elegant concert halls of Paris, France. But singer/songwriter Daniel Lavoie made that leap. He is regarded as one of the greatest recording artists in Quebec and France, has sold millions of albums, starred in theatrical productions in Europe and the UK, and written songs for Céline Dion. With all this enormous success, Daniel still values his connection to Manitoba.

"I'm a prairie boy and I always have been," says Daniel from his home in Quebec, on the eve of another high-profile European tour. "I like flatland and open skies and I think that's always shown in my music. I'm a small town boy, and that doesn't leave you. Being from a small town in Manitoba, and from a minority Francophone community as well, has affected my outlook on life."

Born in Dunrea, southeast of Brandon, the son of a local grocer, Daniel's roots are firmly planted in Manitoba soil. His grandfather farmed near the town and other relatives lived nearby. "It was a perfectly Canadian community, half English, half French, and they lived separate cultures for almost eighty years. We had a French parish with a priest and nuns. It was a very peaceful cohabitation, although the separation was nonetheless clear."

Despite a strong French presence, Daniel grew up unaware of Francophone music. "My mother played opera and classical music all the time, so music has always been an important part of my life. No popular music or French music, though. We didn't have that much contact with French culture outside the community. French folk songs weren't part of our tradition. I had an uncle who loved country music and turned me on to Hank Williams."

Learning piano from the nuns, Daniel harboured no ambitions for a music career. At fourteen he entered boarding school at St. Boniface College where he discovered rock 'n' roll. "We had

a band called the Nomads, and later the Spectres, and we played Surfaris songs and the Ventures at community clubs in St. Boniface. I played saxophone."

By the mid 1960s a vibrant Francophone music scene thrived exclusively in St. Boniface and Daniel got caught up in it. "There were two teachers trying to get us in touch with our culture. French music was just starting to open up. It was a very interesting period. It didn't touch anyone in the English part of Winnipeg because French music is very lyric-oriented, and if you didn't speak the language you would have thought it was silly music, but for us there was some good stuff happening. We even had our own club in St. Boniface, Les Cent Nons, and it still exists."

In 1967, Daniel's ensemble entered the Jeunesse Oblige Francophone music competition sponsored by CBC Radio Canada and traveled to Ottawa for the semi-finals. "To participate, you had to have a singer/songwriter in the group. So I wrote a song and sang it, and we won."

Following graduation he headed to Quebec, performing in the burgeoning club scene. "That was the golden age of Quebec nationalism and the arts, music, poetry, literature, were all so incredible. I had never seen anything like it. I couldn't imagine going back to Manitoba at that point." Signed to London Records, his debut album was released in 1974, featuring "J'ai Quitté Mon Ile", which became a popular song in Brazil and Portugal where other artists recorded it.

**BY THE MID 1960S A VIBRANT FRANCOPHONE MUSIC SCENE THRIVED EXCLUSIVELY IN ST. BONIFACE AND DANIEL GOT CAUGHT UP IN IT.**

*Nirvana Bleu*, released in Quebec and France in 1979, yielded three hit singles: "Angéline", "La Danse du Smatte" and "Boule qui Roule". His biggest success came four years later with *Tension Attention* selling over 2 million copies and including the hit single "Ils S'aiment". Daniel was now spending as much time in France as he was in Quebec. "Quebec is not a very big place, so you go to Europe. There was a really solid market there rather than in English Canada." Attempts at launching an English-language career in the US ran aground despite initial promise after the daytime drama *General Hospital* used one of his songs. LA-based Curb Records released *Woman To Man*, but management problems kept his English-language career from taking off. "I didn't much want to run three careers so I let the English side go."

Instead, Daniel made the transition to movies in the early 1990s, appearing in several Quebec productions. "I'm not an actor but I was offered different roles over the years. Some of them I accepted just to see what it was like." He recently starred as Félix LeClerc in a television biopic of the revered Quebecois performer.

In 1998, Daniel starred in songwriter Luc Plamondon's rock opera *Sand et les Romantiques*. "I had been recording and touring for many years and was bored with it. So when Luc asked if I wanted to do it I said, 'Sure, why not?'" The success of the production led to a two-year starring role in another of Luc's productions, *Notre-Dame de Paris* in France. "That was the closest thing to the Beatles I've ever known," he marvels. "Pandemonium! A thousand people waiting after the show wanting to rip our clothes off. I've never seen anything like it." He also appeared in the London production in a translation by Tim Rice.

In 2002 Daniel starred in the musical comedy *Le Petit Prince* in France for eight months.

Daniel's own recording career remained in limbo until 2004 when he released *Comédies Humaines*. "Universal Music in Paris wanted me to do an album. I told them I wasn't writing stuff that was being recorded very much these days. It's a very personal record, very special for me. It got the best reviews of any record I've done." His songwriting career continues to flourish with recent hits for Bruno Pelletier, Natasha St. Pier, and Céline Dion. "I have the best of both worlds. I'm doing the artistic, non-compromising part with my own recordings, and still writing the songs that get radio play for others." In 1999 he appeared with Céline Dion as part of a gala Millennium concert at the Montreal Forum. He has also recorded three albums of children's music.

In the early 1990s the Francophone community in St. Boniface named the patio at the Franco-Manitoban Cultural Centre "Terrasse Daniel Lavoie". No commemorative marker exists in Dunrea. "There's no one there who remembers me."

As for his future, "I can't predict what can happen. I've been working a lot with young singers and musicians and I've really found that stimulating. So I still enjoy doing this." ∎

Born in Dunrea, Manitoba

Graduate of College St. Boniface

ALBUMS: Nirvana Bleu (1979); Tension Attention (1983); Woman To Man (1994); Comédies Humaines (2003)

HIT SINGLES: "J'ai Quitté Mon Ile", "Angéline", "La Danse du Smatte", "Boule qui Roule", "Ils S'aiment"

AWARDS: Numerous Felix music awards in Quebec including Male Artist of the Year (1980, 82, and 84); Artist of the Year (1985); Song and Album of the Year (1985); Francophone Album of the Year (1987); Pop Rock album of the Year (1990); and Children's Album of the Year (1997); la medaille Jacques-Blanchet (1986)

Starred in Luc Plamondon's rock operas Sand et les Romantiques and Notre-Dame de Paris in Paris and London, as well as in Le Petit Prince

The patio at the Franco-Manitoban Cultural Centre named "Terrasse Daniel Lavoie"

Appeared in 1988 alongside Sting, Peter Gabriel and Bruce Springsteen at Amnesty International concert at Montreal's Olympic Stadium

# ALANA LEVANDOSKI

**S**HE HAS BEEN CALLED "THE 'IT' GIRL of Canadian Roots Music" by CBC Radio host Bill Stunt. Stunt launched his series *Roots Underground* with Alana's "Jezebel's Ringing", off her debut album *Unsettled Down*. Profiles have appeared in every major magazine across Canada and her name is dropped in the most exclusive music circles as the next major singer/songwriter to emerge from Manitoba. Yet, despite the notoriety, Alana remains firmly grounded in her rural roots.

"My mom showed me the local paper," says the Kelwood, Manitoba native. "Under the Kelwood news section is a paragraph about me going to Nashville and the second is about my grandma cutting her geraniums back to prepare for spring. There is definitely still a small town mentality here and it is refreshing. I think it's hilarious, but I wouldn't have it any other way."

Born in McCreary, Alana was raised in nearby Kelwood, population 300, and attended school in Riding Mountain before home schooling with her parents. She comes from a long line of farmers in the vicinity. "Family was immensely important and my mother, being a die-hard genealogist, was determined that we would know our heritage. My Polish roots had escaped wars and come to North America under adverse circumstances. My Scottish ancestors came seeking a better life and my English great-grandfather came seeking adventure. On both sides of my family there was a sense of pride for Canada as many of my forefathers had cleared forest, ploughed land, hunted, raised families and died on the same land they were born."

Literature, poetry, theatre and music became Alana's passion and her enlightened parents encouraged her artistic interests by erecting a stage with curtains in her room where she and her friends performed. "I was not held back from my natural abilities or from my inclination to be expressive, my natural desire to be a child."

At nine she joined her parents' gospel band, adding guitar at age twelve. "My musical influence as a young child consisted mostly of gospel music. But the music that was being sung in my little country church was the good stuff. I didn't know it, but this was music that was being recorded at that very time by artists like Emmylou Harris and Dolly Parton." In her later teens she broadened her musical vistas with CSNY, John Denver, Corey Hart, even Canadian country music legend Wilf Carter. "I was into a wide range of music including Simon & Garfunkel, Garth Brooks, Beethoven, Bruce Springsteen, Joni Mitchell, Nirvana, Neil Young, Pink Floyd, and my very favourite of all, U2. Music and writing were such an essential part of my life that I began to do little else. I listened to the wonderful words, to the meaning and the simple melodies. It is interesting that most of my heroes wrote songs in a very raw fashion. I also loved the poetry of Dylan Thomas, Carl Sandburg, Sylvia Plath, Paul Simon, Joni Mitchell and Bob Dylan."

Completing her high school education at home, Alana embarked on her own odyssey, spending time in Boston and Europe before settling in Winnipeg and pursuing her music career as a writer. Here she absorbed musical influences and made connections, including Manitoba Association of Recording Artists' (MARIA) Sam Baardman and singers the Wyrd Sisters. "I joined a band called Jamoeba, a six-piece jam band that played organic dance music. I was the lead vocalist. This band was great for getting me back on stage." Alana also began performing on her own, often backed by members of the group. Taking her savings for a trip to India, Alana instead invested it in recording time with local producer Norm Dugas, yielding a three-song demo with her songs "Red Headed Girl", "Prairie Sun", and "Misty Sea". Showcase performances including a spot at the Winnipeg Folk Festival in 2003 as well as the Ontario Council of Folk Festivals brought further attention, and she signed a publishing deal with Brycemoor Music and booking agency Paquin Entertainment. Warner Music Canada offered a development deal allowing Alana to record her debut album, *Unsettled Down*, in 2003, with Norm Dugas supported by the New Meanies' Damon Mitchell and Sky Onosson, Doc Walker guitarist Murray Pulver, drummer Christian Dugas, and Ken 'Spider' Sinneave of Streetheart and Loverboy. When Warner Music trimmed its roster, Alana took the tracks to Boston-based roots/Americana label Rounder Records, signing a deal with them.

Alana's songs draw on her gospel and traditional country roots melded with a contemporary outlook and context. As one writer noted, "Her lyrics are often hailed by music fans for her ability to avoid being literal and still have the realness and familiarity that is essential to good song-writing." Her experience in Nashville proved valuable for her. "I love old country music and old gospel music. What I enjoyed in Nashville was jamming with David Peterson, who played old country music, and going to the African Methodist Church on Sunday to hear some of the most incredible gospel music ever."

While finding the recording experiences intense, Alana also found them satisfying. "The vision I had for this record was that I wanted it to sound bigger than people expected it to sound. I wanted the record to be thought-provoking, to relate to everyday people, and I wanted it to make people's toes tap. Many sides of me were revealed that I had locked up or forgotten about, even parts that I had never known. I realized really, for the first time that not everybody can write. Not everybody can hear what I hear and that the tapestry we were weaving would have been different if I had chosen a different guitar player or drummer or if I had gone with a different producer."

While the future certainly looks bright for Canada's newest "It" girl, Alana will never lose her small town sensibilities. "I love performing at small venues where people are drinking and dancing. There's a community feel to that. I love the feeling that you get when something you give is received. It's a high, a total high." ∎

Born in McCreary, Manitoba; raised in Kelwood, Manitoba

Debuted at Winnipeg Folk Festival in 2003

Signed development deal with Warner Music Canada in 2003

ALBUM: Unsettled Down (2005)

Song "Jezebel's Ringing" used to launch CBC radio series *Roots Underground*

Once played in a six-piece Winnipeg-based dance band called Jamoeba

# MACLEAN & MACLEAN

MACLEAN & MACLEAN

BETWEEN 1974 AND 1998 MacLean AND MacLean RELEASED SEVEN ALBUMS, INCLUDING A BEST OF ENTITLED *DIRTY THIRTY*, TOURED CANADA RELENTLESSLY TO PACKED HOUSES, AND TOOK THEIR BRAND OF TOILET ROCK TO EUROPE AND THE UK.

**W**HILE SOME ARTISTS HAVE MADE MUSIC HISTORY, few can claim to having made legal history. MacLean & MacLean, brothers Blair and Gary, did just that in the late 1970s, forcing Ontario to rewrite its antiquated liquor laws after they won a landmark legal case. In doing so, the popular duo struck a blow for free speech and the freedom of club owners to hire whom they choose.

"By that time, community standards were catching up to us," acknowledges Blair MacLean, "Everybody said it, only we were doing it onstage." "It" was the dreaded F word. "You hear it now on television, and even worse."

Born in the mining town of Glace Bay on Nova Scotia's Cape Breton Island, Blair and Gary grew up around music. "There was a lot of singing in the house. On Saturday nights the folks would all go to the Armoury for a dance, then come home, drink moonshine and sing songs. We used to listen at the top of the stairs. Gary and I would listen to all these cheesy records, like Mario Lanza, and imitate them."

Joining the Air Force in 1960, Blair was posted in Gimli, Manitoba where he formed a folk music duo with fellow recruit Wayne Hooper. "I got my first guitar for three dollars at boot camp," he recalls. "It was handed down from each training course group before they moved on. The strings were a half inch off the neck, but that was my introduction to playing music seriously. Folk music was big and we learned all the folk songs back in the barracks, rehearsing for hours every night." Moving to Winnipeg, the two, christened the Glee Men, won CJAY's Talent Show and proceeded to perform in city beverage rooms.

Meantime, Gary was a member of popular folk group The Sherwoods back in Cape Breton. "They dressed in green with all this Robin Hood shit," laughs Blair, who convinced his younger brother to come out to Winnipeg. "There was money to be made here in Manitoba." Gary and another Sherwood came out by train and joined up with the Glee Men before returning to Nova Scotia. With Wayne also departing, Blair recruited Victor Pasta and Cathy Hunter. On a

return home for a family wedding, he convinced Gary to come back with him, and with the addition of bass player Mike McMahon, the Vicious Circle was born. "We had a following. People would show up hours before the pubs opened, knitting and crocheting until the show started. We would have the place packed." Mixing comedy and song, the quartet was one of the most popular attractions in the pubs by 1969. "We heard a Don Rickles album called *Hello Dummy*, where he insulted the audience, and borrowed stuff from him. But we had good harmonies and people loved our songs, too."

Donnie McDougall, former Mother Tucker's Yellow Duck guitarist, and drummer Gord Osland joined up in the early '70s and the group found itself recording at Chicago's RCA Studios, under the aegis of Guess Who frontman Burton Cummings, who lived with Gary. "Whenever Burton was around he would sit in with us." Nothing was ever released. In 1972, McDougall joined the Guess Who (his song "Glace Bay Blues", written with the MacLeans, appeared in the band's *Live At The Paramount* album) and Blair and Gary decided to perform as MacLean & MacLean. "It was the same idea as in the Vicious Circle, with descriptions of songs and then the tune, only the descriptions got longer and the introductions became stories and bits."

A concert appearance at Toronto's Massey Hall resulted in a recording contract with GRT records and *Toilet Rock*, produced by Lighthouse founder Skip Prokop, was recorded live at the Chimney club. "We were supposed to do a hundred dates with Lighthouse but got as far as Swift Current when some reverend's son heard us say 'fuck' onstage

and went ballistic. The minister got everybody involved — the morality squad, the newspapers. That was our first national story." Further controversy ensued.

At a performance in London, Ontario, liquor inspectors heard the duo's set, which included crowd favourites like "I've Seen Pubic Hair" and "Fuck Ya" and issued a threat to all pub owners that they risked their liquor license if they hired MacLean & MacLean. Blair and Gary countered with an injunction challenging the liquor board's preventing them from working. In the end they won, and the liquor laws in Ontario were revised to limit the power of the board. In Sault Ste. Marie, the local Crown Attorney went after the duo. "He sent out cops with tape recorders in their purses and then had a linguistics expert translate the tape as evidence in court. We heard it and it had no resemblance to what we were saying. It was hilarious. So we had to get linguistics experts to define what we were doing. We had Clayton Ruby defending us. We had to go out and keep committing the crime in order to pay the lawyers." Eventually a not guilty verdict was upheld by the Supreme Court. "We were pretty infamous."

Between 1974 and 1998 MacLean and MacLean released seven albums, including a best of entitled *Dirty Thirty*, toured Canada relentlessly to packed houses, and took their brand of toilet rock to Europe and the UK. They appeared at the Edinburgh Fringe Festival and the first Just For Laughs Comedy Festival in Montreal. In the early '80s they were joined by Burton Cummings for a seven-week Canadian tour. "Burton loved our harmonies. We used to sit around, get ripped and sing songs together. Burton had a real comedy side to him doing

impersonations, so it gave him a chance to do that."

In 1998, the two called it quits after twenty-six years on the road. Gary moved into radio, becoming a popular DJ at CKY until his death in December 2001. Blair returned to Cape Breton and turned his love of art into a business creating ornate candles and grain art (his works hang in Paris, Beijing and Moscow), before moving back to Winnipeg to look after Gary's teenage sons. A posthumous MacLean & MacLean live album has been released by Blair.

In recent months Blair has performed with Gary's sons, doing the old repertoire. "They're great musicians so we get together and bang off the tunes. It's MacLean & MacLean & MacLean & MacLean. Funny thing was, when they were growing up, Gary wouldn't allow any MacLean & MacLean records in the house. Now they know the material better than I do." ∎

Both born in Glace Bay, Nova Scotia; moved to Winnipeg in the early 1960s

GROUPS: the Glee Men, the Vicious Circle

ALBUMS: Toilet Rock (1974); Locked Up For Laughs (1981); Suck Their Way To The Top (1982); Cruel Cuts (1985); Dirty Thirty (1998); MacLean & MacLean Live (2004)

Hit singles: "Dolly Parton's Tits" was a UK chart hit and theme song for British TV show *Over the Top*

AWARDS: An unofficial honourary Juno presented to them in 1980 by host Burton Cummings, for Best Post-show Party (Blair uses it as a doorstop)

Their debut album, Toilet Rock, was produced by Lighthouse drummer Skip Prokop

Hosted the first Nasty Nights at the Montreal Comedy Festival (1986) and returned for the Nasty Nights 10th Anniversary (1996)

Were the reason Burton Cummings had to cancel the Guess Who's only Carnegie Hall appearance (1972) and live recording (too much partying the previous night)

**F**OR SOME ARTISTS, MUSIC IS A CALLING. For pianist/composer Robbie McDougall, music was a means to a higher calling. In 1985 the talented Winnipeg musician, who had enjoyed a #1 record across Canada and appeared on just about every national television show, became Reverend Father Robbie McDougall. But while he serves God and the Catholic Church, he continues to be actively involved in music.

**WITH HIS ALMOST WAIST-LENGTH POKER-STRAIGHT HAIR AND FLOWING CAPE, ROBBIE PRESENTED A DASHING IMAGE, SEATED AT A GRAND PIANO PERFORMING HIS OWN ELABORATE INSTRUMENTAL COMPOSITIONS.**

"Through the years I've always kept music as a priority," he says. "Even in my pastoral care work I use music with people. That's what a lot of these cassettes I've done were recorded for. I worked with schizophrenic patients and other mental health-related problems and I was also a chaplain. So I used music. I just thought that God can speak so easily through music, so why not use it. I started composing tunes and helping people relax. That was a wonderful experience."

To say that music was a part of the McDougall family growing up in St. Vital is gross understatement. Brothers Billy, Donnie and Alan all played professionally. Billy drummed for a number of artists including Chad Allan and Ray St. Germain; Donnie founded 1960s hippie sensations Mother Tucker's Yellow Duck before joining the Guess Who in 1972 (he still plays in the reunion lineup); and Alan played keyboards in Crawford. Following years of formal piano training, Robbie played in a series of local rock groups including the Gentry and Power Company. As a solo pianist he performed before the Queen, the Prime Minister, and all ten premiers in 1967. "That was really exciting stuff for a kid." He also guested on recording sessions in Chicago for Winnipeg group the Vicious Circle, featuring friends Blair and Gary MacLean.

Signed to Guess Who manager Don Hunter's Quasimodo agency, Robbie set out to pursue a solo career as what one journalist termed "a long-haired Liberace".

With his almost waist-length poker-straight hair and flowing cape, Robbie presented a dashing image, seated at a grand piano performing his own elaborate instrumental compositions. One such composition was "The Theme", reminiscent of epic Hollywood movie theme songs with magnificent flourishes and lush orchestration. Recorded in 1972 at Toronto's Manta Sound and produced by Guess Who arranger Ben McPeek (who scored the orchestration on "These Eyes") the recording also boasted members of the Toronto Symphony and Boss Brass. The single was instantly hummable. Robbie signed with RCA Records in New York, who released the single in the US in 1972, while in Canada it was released by Nimbus 9, the label and production company owned by McPeek and Guess Who producer Jack Richardson.

"It was a #1 record in Canada in 1972 and '73 and won a BMI award for airplay in 1972. I also won an award from Yamaha Music Canada for my contribution to Canadian music." The success led to appearances in concert with Sonny & Cher, Jose Feliciano, Dionne Warwick, and rock group Lighthouse. One particular performance remains memorable. "I played the Winnipeg Arena on the ice for Schmockey Night. They had me seated at a grand piano and they pulled me around the ice as I played 'McArthur Park' and we kept hitting bumps. It was so bizarre."

Robbie followed up with the theme song from the Gordon Pinsent movie *The Rowdyman* again arranged and produced by Ben McPeek. A self-titled album came out that same year.

In 1974 Robbie wrote and performed *A Pilgrimage To Jerusalem*, a television special for Winnipeg's CKY TV and later created *Music, Magic & the Eclipse of the Sun* for CKND TV, as well as recording *A Celebration of Hope & Joy* that was granted apostolic benediction by Pope Paul VI and aired on CBC radio in 1975. His musical themes clearly revealed a leaning towards sacred music and it was no surprise to those who knew him when he abandoned his thriving pop career to enter the priesthood. Robbie studied for seven years at seminaries at Laval University in Quebec and St. Joseph's College in Indiana. He was ordained Reverend Father in 1985 and entered parish work first, then did counseling at hospitals.

Since then he has recorded twenty-four cassette tapes and a CD of instrumental relaxation music that are used for music therapy, notably in his work with schizophrenic patients as a chaplain in local hospitals. Today he teaches theology, runs workshops and does retreat work for the Catholic Church, bringing his music to all three activities. "I use my piano and songs in all my teaching. I just love music." He also spent a year as composer in residence at St. Paul's College in Winnipeg.

"I founded Adoramus Music in 1975 and that is still going strong today. That's a Latin word for adore. I founded it first as a publishing house, then as a place for me to channel my own music. All the retreats I do now operate out of Adoramus Ministries, which is associated with the Archdiocese of St. Boniface."

Robbie was the subject of a 1987 CBC TV special *The Music of Father*

*Robert McDougall*, filmed at Rainbow Stage. He continues to travel and has played for Mother Teresa in Calcutta. "My authorities have asked that I be available for retreats anywhere in Canada. That's my main job. When I'm back in Winnipeg between trips, I do replacement work in any parish where there is a need if the priest is away. And I still do work in hospitals." Since 1988, Robbie has performed a non-denominational devotion service five times a year for Alderwood Group Funeral Homes at Green Acres on the eastern edge of Winnipeg. "It's kind of a 'we remember' service in music and words, both for those who have passed on and those we want to honour and thank."

In 1990 Robbie and the entire McDougall family founded a non-profit memorial foundation in the name of

Robbie's younger brother Gerald, who was tragically killed in a bicycle accident at age twenty-four. They hold benefit concerts and annually award a bursary to a university-bound student studying the religious sciences. "We named it after Gerald because he was so young when he died. It keeps his name alive. Gerald is still helping people. It was my way of dealing with his loss." Recently Robbie officiated at the memorial service for another close friend, Gary MacLean of the Vicious Circle and MacLean & MacLean.

Robbie has no regrets about leaving the world of pop music to serve God. By integrating his music into his ministry he has been able to bring joy to many more people and greater satisfaction to himself. ∎

Born in Winnipeg

Bands: Terry & the Gentry; recorded with the Vicious Circle, solo artist

ALBUMS: Robbie McDougall (1972); Celebration of Hope and Joy (1975); A La Glorie de Marie (1976)

HIT SINGLES: "The Theme", "The Rowdyman" (theme to the Gordon Pinsent movie)

BMI award for airplay in 1972; apostolic benediction by Pope Paul VI for A Celebration of Hope & Joy

Wrote and performed A Pilgrimage To Jerusalem for CKY TV; Music, Magic & the Eclipse of the Sun for CKND TV; A Celebration of Hope & Joy for CBC radio; and The Music of Father Robert McDougall for CBC TV

Robbie is the brother of Guess Who guitarist Donnie McDougall

Recorded twenty-four cassettes and a CD of instrumental music for music therapy

Ordained as a Roman Catholic priest in 1985

# LOREENA MCKENNITT

LOREENA MCKENNITT

**M**ORDEN-BORN LOREENA MCKENNITT is an artist who defies categorization. Her music is a melting pot of Celtic, folk, pop, medieval madrigals, Middle Eastern mysticism, and world beat so distinctively her own that trying to label it is futile. While she sometimes uses the phrase "eclectic Celtic", it is simply Loreena McKennitt's music, instantly recognizable from Manitoba to Marrakesh. She is an artist of the past and present, near and far away, the familiar and the mysterious. Whether busking in Toronto's St. Lawrence market or performing before Her Majesty, Queen Elizabeth II, Loreena has the power to captivate and transport her audiences.

**"I BECAME ASSOCIATED WITH PEOPLE WHO WERE INTERESTED IN THE BROADER SCOPE OF FOLK MUSIC," SHE RECALLS. "THERE WAS AN INFORMAL FOLK CLUB THAT WOULD GET TOGETHER ON SUNDAY EVENINGS. A NUMBER OF THOSE MEMBERS CAME FROM THE BRITISH ISLES AND SO PEOPLE WOULD BE SINGING THOSE SONGS."**

Raised on a farm outside Morden, Manitoba, the daughter of a livestock dealer and a nurse, Loreena's introduction to the arts came via highland dancing, before a car accident left her with two broken legs. Her mother then enrolled her in piano with instructor Olga Friesen, an early mentor. "Olga was very creative musically but also visually and conceptually," says Loreena, "which you don't find every day, especially in small communities."

When Olga moved to Winnipeg, ten-year old Loreena continued to study with her. "That first year my mother drove me to Winnipeg on Saturdays, but within the year I was putting myself on the Grey Goose bus in Morden in the morning, and it would drop me off on Pembina Highway. I would walk to Olga's house, have my lessons, then have the rest of the day to kill in Winnipeg. That was my Saturday for many years. Would I let children do that today? I don't think so," she laughs.

Completing her final high school year at Winnipeg's exclusive Balmoral Hall School for girls, Loreena's musical education continued amid the rich cultural life of the city. "I became associated with people who were interested in the broader scope of folk music," she recalls. "There was an informal folk club that would get together on Sunday evenings. A number of those members came from the British Isles and so people would be singing those songs.

You would also hear about the recordings they were listening to. From this came the next generation of my musical influences and the more overtly Celtic influences which would be Steeleye Span, Planxty, Bothy Band, Alan Stivell, Mary Black. When I heard that music I was smitten by it. There was something incredibly infectious about that musical sound."

Working by day at her father's office at a Winnipeg stockyard for the next three years, Loreena nurtured her music career by night in coffeehouses, lounges and theatrical productions. The city offered her an opportunity to pursue her music and to experience an awakening. "The awakening was in terms of that folk club that I was a part of and the chance for me to develop my own performing capacity and style," she says. "There were small venues where people would have me and it wasn't the end of the world if it didn't work. I also got involved in musical theatre — Rainbow Stage and the Hollow Mug. I played in the Drummer Boy Lounge at the Hotel Fort Garry and the Ramada. I sang at the Winnipeg Folk Festival and at small coffeehouses like the Ting on Broadway. When I look back, clearly I was trying to find my place.

"I actually aspired to be a veterinarian but there were opportunities that kept presenting themselves to me," she admits. "There would be the odd little

CBC radio event or a variety show for CBC television in Winnipeg." Enrolling in Agriculture at the University of Manitoba, she quit three months in. "I decided that I would always wonder how far I could have gone in music. So I thought I would park my agricultural studies and head off into the music realm, and whenever it reached a plateau I would re-evaluate."

In 1978 she travelled to Toronto as a finalist in CBC's *DuMaurier Search For Talent* show. Two years later she journeyed to Prince Edward Island to appear at the Charlottetown Festival. In 1981, Loreena landed a role in the chorus in *HMS Pinafore* at the prestigious Stratford Festival and moved to the Ontario community, where she resides today. Pursuing a theatrical career, music again overtook her. "There was a woman in the wardrobe department who happened to have a harp,"

Born in Morden, Manitoba

Performed at Rainbow Stage and the Hollow Mug

ALBUMS: Elemental (1985); The Visit (1991); Mask And Mirror (1994); A Winter Garden: Five Songs For The Season (1995); The Book Of Secrets (1997); Live In Paris And Toronto (1999)

HIT SINGLES: "The Mummers' Dance"

AWARDS: Juno Awards for Best Roots/Traditional Album (1992) and Best Roots/Traditional Album (1994); Billboard International Achievement Award (1997); The Order of Canada (2004)

Besides Canada and the United States, Loreena has had gold and platinum records in Australia, New Zealand, Brazil, France, Spain, Italy, Greece, Turkey

Sold over 13 million records worldwide

Started her own record company, Quinlan Road, to market her albums

Performed for Queen Elizabeth at the Golden Jubilee Celebrations (2002)

Recording new album for release in 2005

"I'VE ALWAYS BEEN EXCITED OR
DRAWN BY THE NEXT WAVE OF NEW
MATERIAL OR NEW HISTORY THAT
LIES BEFORE ME," SHE SAYS.
"THERE HASN'T BEEN A LOT OF
TIME FOR REFLECTION ON
THE SUCCESS AND THAT'S PROBABLY
GOOD, BECAUSE IT'S KEPT
MY FEET ON THE GROUND."

she recalls. "I used to borrow it and sit in the stairwell at the Festival Theatre and putter around. Then I was in London, England in '83 and came by a harp in Hampstead and brought it back to Canada. And that was that." The instrument would become universally associated with her.

"I think the most pivotal recording I heard that inspired my harp development was Alan Stivell's *Live In Dublin*. I was really taken with that sound. It wasn't just traditional. I really liked the way he fused rock and other elements with some of the traditional music and instruments."

Loreena had already begun composing and adapting music for theatrical productions, so the next step was to record her own album in 1985. "The sound engineer at Stratford had just bought some recording equipment. We set his equipment up in a church and started recording. That was the basis of *Elemental*." The album of traditional and Celtic lyrics set to original music composed by Loreena was completed at a studio in Elora. Without a record label, Loreena took the bold step of forming her own, Quinlan Road Productions, named after her rural residence in Stratford. "It was

really established as a matter of default. I had no idea who all the record companies were at the time or even how to get a hold of them so I just figured I would create this on my own."

Busking at Toronto's St. Lawrence Market or the Harbourfront for the next three years and selling her CDs directly provided a modest income. Two more independent albums followed, *To Drive*

*The Cold Winter Away* and *Parallel Dreams*. Her breakthrough release was *The Visit*, in 1991, which was distributed worldwide by Warner Music Group. *The Visit* sold well over one million copies, and Loreena suddenly found herself in great demand.

"The success really grew in an organic way," she says. "There were definite progressions through each recording so it didn't happen overnight."

The success of *The Visit* was eclipsed by 1994's *The Mask And Mirror* and in 1997 by *The Book of Secrets*, each selling in the millions. "Obviously there are a lot of perks that come with this kind of success," she says. "It was an unbelievable luxury building *The Book of Secrets*. We

camped out at Peter Gabriel's studio in the UK over five three-week blocks and there were about twenty-six players who came in and out. It was absolutely fantastic."

By retaining her independent record label and licensing her recordings, Loreena has managed not only to retain artistic control but also to reap a greater financial return. Her worldwide sales total a staggering 13 million albums and garnered two Juno Awards. However, she has also demonstrated a strong philanthropic commitment not only to her local community, but to society at large, whether funding the creation of a community centre in Stratford by rescuing an abandoned school or, more personally,

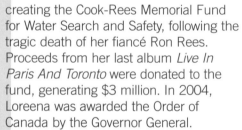

creating the Cook-Rees Memorial Fund for Water Search and Safety, following the tragic death of her fiancé Ron Rees. Proceeds from her last album *Live In Paris And Toronto* were donated to the fund, generating $3 million. In 2004, Loreena was awarded the Order of Canada by the Governor General.

Loreena continues to view her musical journey as one of learning and exploring. "I've always been excited or drawn by the next wave of new material or new history that lies before me," she says. "There hasn't been a lot of time for reflection on the success and that's probably good, because it's kept my feet on the ground."

Despite the magnitude of her success, Loreena retains a fond affection for her Manitoba roots. In 2002 she returned to perform for the Queen, and then donning her gum boots the following year to help her brother Warren for several months on his Morden farm. "I'm grateful I was allowed to experience the beginnings I did in Morden," she says, "and then the wonderful feast of opportunities in Winnipeg. I feel blessed that I was in the Manitoba kitchen while all this was cooking." ■

# BIG DAVE MCLEAN

"DAVE MCLEAN HAS BEEN STAL-
WARTLY KEEPING UP THE BLUES
TRADITION FOR YEARS," OBSERVES
BLUES GUITARIST AND ACOLYTE
COLIN JAMES. "HE'S ONE OF THE
GREAT UNDISCOVERED BLUESMEN."

**Y**OU DON'T PICK THE BLUES, the blues pick you. It's a calling, not a career move, and those who choose that road do so out of sincere dedication to the music. Winnipeg blues man Big Dave McLean has been treading that path for more than thirty-three years and has earned respect and admiration from many of the genre's finest practitioners.

"The blues is something you just can't fake," Dave says, an inimitable, larger-than-life personality. "You can tell the shit from the Shine-ola." Few know the blues better than Dave. "Dave McLean has been stalwartly keeping up the blues tradition for years," observes blues guitarist and acolyte Colin James. "He's one of the great undiscovered bluesmen." With his trademark tweed slouch cap and shiny National dobro guitar, Dave is a fixture on the Canadian blues scene and a staunch advocate for the genre.

Born in Yorkton, Saskatchewan, the son of a Presbyterian preacher, and raised in Winnipeg, Dave's blues journey began in his teens via the folk circuit playing guitar, harmonica and washboard in various ensembles, performing jug band and old-time songs, until a chance encounter with his own personal mentor and inspiration.

"I saw John Hammond Jr. at the Mariposa Folk Festival in Toronto in 1969 and he absolutely blew my mind. I'd never heard this kind of music before coming out of one guy. So I kind of thank him and blame him for getting me started in the blues." Accompanying himself on National dobro guitar and harmonica, Hammond captivated Dave and set his life's course.

Dave began performing solo acoustic Delta blues in coffeehouses like the Wing'd Ox, The Ting, and Latin Quarter, often joined by harmonica player Gord Kidder. The nickname Big Dave predates his music career but stuck with him. "I'm six foot three. When I got into the blues there was Little Walter and Big Walter so I just figured it had a nice ring to it."

Throughout his career, Dave has performed alone or fronted Chicago-style blues bands. "We were one of the first to play electric instruments at the Winnipeg Folk Festival and the folkies almost killed

• Big Dave with mentor John Hammond Jr.

us." When the music didn't pay the bills, he took on occasional jobs. "I was a car jockey, a land surveyor, construction worker, I did dishwashing jobs in just about every hotel in Winnipeg. But music was always the constant."

Dave was instrumental in launching a thriving blues scene in Winnipeg. "I used to play the Occidental Hotel, the Bell, the Sutherland. They were the only places that would hire the blues. It was like the Wild West or the south side of Chicago. I just figured if you want to get something happening you have to start somewhere. I got the Bella Vista going, I was a part of the Royal Albert days, Times Change club, I hosted a blues room in the basement of the Marlborough, and I ran jams for nine years at the Viscount Gort."

In 1977 Dave met another major influence on his music, the legendary Muddy Waters, father of electric Chicago blues. "I opened for him at the Centennial Concert Hall and we really hit it off." What cemented the friendship between the prairie upstart and the Chicago master was an original composition dedicated to him. "I wrote 'Muddy Waters For President' when I opened for him in Saskatoon in 1980. I played it that night. After the show Muddy said to me, 'I really like that song.' He invited me to his hotel in Winnipeg three days later to play him the whole song. Man, the pressure was on. I've got to play this song I wrote about Muddy Waters *with him sitting right there!'*"

Dave won Muddy's stamp of approval. "I had to pinch my arm to make sure I wasn't dreaming. He gave me his home phone number in Chicago and told me to give him a shout." Muddy died in 1983 before getting the opportunity to record Dave's song, but the two developed a close bond.

In 1989 Dave recorded *Muddy Waters For President* at Bud's On Broadway club in Saskatoon, releasing the cassette independently. The album was later remastered for release as a CD. Nine years later he cut his first official studio album, *For The Blues… Always*, for Stony Plain Records, produced by Colin James at his studio in Vancouver. "I knew Colin when I used to play the Regina folk circuit. He really hooked onto my heels and we became friends. He had some of the best players on the West Coast playing on my album." Critics raved about Big Dave's authentic blues delivery and selection of songs including classics like "Dust My Broom", and "Rollin' and Tumblin'". "Recording was never why I got into this business," he concedes. "It took me twenty-eight years to do it the first time."

A second Stony Plain album, *Blues From The Middle*, followed in 2003,

recorded at Winnipeg's Private Ear studios and featuring an eleven-minute studio recording of Dave's signature song "Muddy Waters For President". Dave hopes to do an acoustic blues album next.

Big Dave McLean has appeared across Canada, including the Harbourfront Blues Festival in Toronto, Montreal and Ottawa Blues Festivals, Windsor and London Blues, Stratford, the Thunder Bay Blues Festival, and has even toured Australia and Tasmania.

"I just like playing in front of people," says the amiable musician. "When I get tired of that well, I guess I'm done. I've had people say to me, 'Someday you'll be a success,' but, hey, I've been doing this for over thirty years, raised a family of three kids, a wife, house, car. I've got friends all over this country. If that ain't success, doing what I love to do, then I don't know what is." ∎

Born in Yorkton, Saskatchewan; moved to Winnipeg as a child

BANDS: Chicken Flat String Band, Black Betty, Crosscut, solo artist

ALBUMS: Muddy Waters For President (1989), For The Blues… Always (1998, produced by Colin James), Blues From The Middle (2003)

TURNING POINT: meeting bluesman John Hammond at Mariposa Folk Festival (1969)

Befriended blues legend Muddy Waters after playing him "Muddy Waters For President"

Hosted blues jams at the Bella Vista, the Royal Albert, Times Change, Viscount Gort, and the basement of the Marlborough

Has toured Australia and Tasmania

# MCMASTER & JAMES

IN 2000, SOUL-BASED DUO McMaster & James were the darlings of the pop music world. Young, talented and photogenic, they were perfect for the video age and their faces were everywhere. But beyond being pop sensations, the two were skillful songwriters, able to craft funk-fuelled soul hits like "Love Wins Everytime" and "Thank You", that ruled Canadian radio airwaves.

"It was really exciting during that time, a real adventure," recalls Luke McMaster, who, with partner Rob James, were still in their early twenties. "It was a weird feeling being famous." But the experience was not without its lessons. "It gives you an appreciation for the whole business and what it takes. There are a lot of enjoyable things about it, but it's really hard work. You're constantly promoting yourself, even if you're at the grocery store. You can't brush people off. All that can be draining."

The duo formed after Luke moved to Winnipeg from Brandon in the mid

1990s to attend the Professional Musician's College. A late bloomer in music, he began by writing lyrics in his mid teens, picking up the guitar shortly before graduating. After two weeks at Brandon University he lit out for Winnipeg. In the capital he performed solo in coffeehouses doing a mix of Cat Stevens, Beatles and original songs before forming the band Double Vision, playing schools and clubs.

Working with local producer Chris Burke-Gaffney, of Orphan and Chantal Kreviazuk fame, Luke met Winnipegger Rob James. "Chris and I were writing

Luke McMaster born in Brandon, Manitoba; Rob James born in Winnipeg

BANDS: Two Face and house band at 8 Trax on Main Street

ALBUM: McMaster & James (2000)

HIT SINGLES: "Love Wins Everytime", "Thank You", "Bad Thing"

Secured their BMG recording contract at a showcase at Bruce Junior School in the Winnipeg suburb of St. James

Performed a showcase at LA's legendary Whisky A Go-Go in 2003

Contributed songs to Canadian Idol winners Ryan Malcolm and Kalan Porter

Currently writing and recording separate projects

Rob recently signed on to appear in rainbow Stage's production of Miss Saigon

together but he was going out of town for several weeks, so he recommended I hook up with Harlequin guitarist Glen Willows, who had a studio in his house. Rob was working with Glen, too. We happened to be there at the same time. I played him some of my songs, he played me some of his, and we decided to get together to write. Not to start a band or anything. We wrote a song real fast and that doesn't always happen. And our voices blended really well. Everyone told us we should start a band or a duo like Hall & Oates, who I always loved. So it went from there."

The two formed the band Two Face, working as house band at the 8-Trax club while writing and demoing songs with Chris, Glen and Danny Schur. "As time went on Chris became the driving force. He had the studio downtown and we just ended up there doing more writing with him." On the strength of demo tapes he produced, Chris managed to convince a rep from BMG to audition the band in an unlikely venue.

"One of the schools that I had a really good relationship with was Bruce Middle School in St. James, and one of the teachers, Bob McKinnon, arranged for us to perform a showcase in their theatre. We had an A&R rep from BMG come out to hear us. It was packed with kids who went crazy for us and it really gave the label a vision of what this thing could do."

Released in February 2000, McMaster & James, produced in New York and Vancouver and featuring songs by Luke, Rob and Chris, earned positive reviews as the single "Love Wins Everytime" went into heavy rotation as a video. "BMG put a lot behind us and put a lot into the videos. We had a lot of fun

with it." "Thank You" became a Top 20 hit nationally, earning the duo a SOCAN award for airplay that year and appearing on the double platinum compilation PlanetPop. The two toured Canada opening for 'N Sync, Christina Aguilera, Joey McIntyre and Prozzak. They played at the Pan Am Games opening ceremony to some 40,000 people in 1999, and headlined at Vancouver's PNE. "That was crazy

**...DESPITE PERFORMING A SHOWCASE AT LA'S LEGENDARY WHISKY A GO-GO CLUB ON SUNSET BOULEVARD, MCMASTER & JAMES FAILED TO CONNECT IN THE US.**

with 20,000 people singing along to our songs. I couldn't even see to the end of all the people." The album went gold.

But despite performing a showcase at LA's legendary Whisky a Go-Go club on Sunset Boulevard, McMaster & James failed to connect in the US. "Unfortunately it's a tough market to crack because they'll have ten McMaster & James artists and you're on the bottom of the list even if you're better. They're just so much bigger."

Sessions for a follow up album in Philadelphia, capturing that city's sophisticated funk, failed to impress BMG. "We recorded tons of material but it was one of those things where we just agreed to disagree with our label. They wanted us to go in a different direction than where we wanted to go. We had a real Philly sound to this stuff, really vibey, but we used more real instruments this time, real drums. We wanted a more organic sound and brought in our band. The label didn't

want us to do that. They wanted it to stay mainstream. We wanted different things so we got to the point where we parted company with BMG. We wanted to be ourselves."

Moving to Toronto, both singers began writing and working with other artists. "McMaster & James is currently on hold right now. Rob and I are both doing some solo things. But I wouldn't say it's out of the question that we might get together again." The two continue to write together and in 2003 released the independent single "Bad Thing".

While Rob is currently pursuing a solo album, Luke has been collaborating with a number of artists including Winnipeg legend Randy Bachman, co-writing a song with the BTO founder for Canadian Idol winner Ryan Malcolm's album (Rob also co-wrote a track on the album). "It was such a thrill for me to write a song with Randy Bachman. I couldn't believe I was sitting there with him." Luke is currently producing and writing for recent Canadian Idol sensation Kalan Porter's debut release. Having been the pop flavour of the month, Luke can empathize with the young singer. "Kalan is very young but he's handling it well. He understands what it's all about, all the demands on you." In addition, Luke has written and produced tracks for the band Driver. He and co-producer Tranny Wu operate Big Beat Conspiracy, a writing and production company.

And of the influence of the Winnipeg music scene, Luke reflects, "There's so much great music in Winnipeg, so when you're around all that you think, 'Well, I'm supposed to be successful in music because I'm from Winnipeg.' It's inspiring." ■

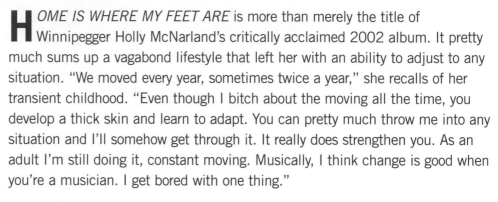

# HOLLY MCNARLAND

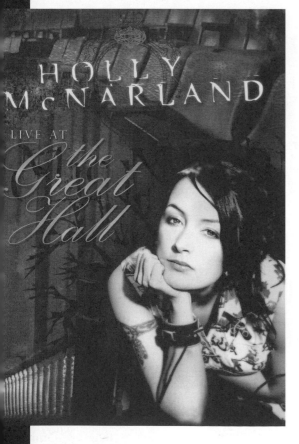

**H**OME IS WHERE MY FEET ARE is more than merely the title of Winnipegger Holly McNarland's critically acclaimed 2002 album. It pretty much sums up a vagabond lifestyle that left her with an ability to adjust to any situation. "We moved every year, sometimes twice a year," she recalls of her transient childhood. "Even though I bitch about the moving all the time, you develop a thick skin and learn to adapt. You can pretty much throw me into any situation and I'll somehow get through it. It really does strengthen you. As an adult I'm still doing it, constant moving. Musically, I think change is good when you're a musician. I get bored with one thing."

By the time she settled in Winnipeg at age eleven, Holly had lived in The Pas, Brandon and Portage la Prairie. "I was sort of made all over Manitoba," she laughs. Even in Winnipeg she continued to uproot, attending a half dozen schools in as many different neighbourhoods before dropping out of Vincent Massey Collegiate in Fort Garry to pursue music. "At that point I was obsessed with singing and playing." Taking a job pumping gas at a Mohawk gas station in Fort Rouge, she practised guitar and began writing her own songs. "Basically that's all I did, play guitar. I took my guitar to work and played in the garage while the guys pumped the gas."

Best known as a rocker, Holly grew up singing country music. "My mom sang country music pretty much all my life. Before I was born she and my dad were in a band. She played guitar and sang. So that's where I got it." An appearance at a Brandon talent show almost ended Holly's career before it even started. "When I was about twelve my girlfriend Naomi and I scrounged enough money and took the bus to Brandon. I went up onstage at the Keystone Centre and sang 'Blue Bayou' and sucked big time. It was terrible. They played it in the wrong key for me. I was so humiliated."

In her later teens a job as door girl at Osborne's Tom Tom Club gave Holly the opportunity to perform before a more appreciative audience. "They would let me play after all the other bands were done. I'd play as people were leaving. People started staying and that's how it began." Friend Luke Doucet invited her to open for his band Acoustically Inclined at the Spectrum. "Oh my God, I was so excited. That was the room in Winnipeg. I was so nervous." She also frequented open mike nights at the Blue Note Café. "I was writing like crazy and pretty much doing all my own stuff." A friend then turned her on to Ani deFranco's music. "She was so brutally honest and that opened things up for me to express myself more."

In 1993 Holly headed west to Vancouver. "I just felt like I needed to go. I didn't have a job, I couldn't get a band together in Winnipeg, so I figured it would be easier in Vancouver. I was nineteen and really terrified but I was determined to do it." She unsuccessfully auditioned as a backup singer for Sarah McLachlan, recorded a five-song demo for Sarah's label Nettwerk, and eventually released Sour Pie, an independently distributed six-song EP produced by ex-Winnipegger Dale Penner. The EP became a hit on the indie charts and on college radio. "I just kept plugging away at it and it all just unfolded."

Universal Music took notice and signed Holly, releasing *Stuff* in 1997, recorded in Los Angeles and San Francisco. Comparisons to Alanis Morissette, P.J. Harvey and Sarah McLachlan were frequent, one critic dubbing the album "full of female angst and emotions". A single, "Coward", became a chart hit. Signed to Universal in the US, Holly and her band toured there frequently. *Live Stuff*, released two years later, was recorded in Las Vegas and at Toronto's Phoenix Club. "I always thought that my live show was better than anything I'd ever recorded." The album boasted a surprising cover of MOR popster Phil Collins' "In The Air Tonight". "He's kind of on the fromage side, but what a talented guy. That song is so good."

Married to MuchMusic videographer and *Much West* host Jay Mirus, an ex-Winnipegger whom she met in Vancouver, and pregnant with their first child, sessions for *Home Is Where My Feet Are* stretched out over three years. "I wasn't in a hurry. I wanted to be a mom for a while. When Nege was about nine months old we moved down to Malibu for a couple of months, recording with Mark Howard. But nothing was right, the record company wasn't happy, so it ended up taking three years on and off with other producers to finish. It took way too long, but that was good for the family because there was so much time between sessions. I was pretty much with Nege for his first three years." She finds the title an apt description of her life. "It's so me. I just sort of land somewhere and make do."

Following the album's release, Holly briefly moved back home to Winnipeg. "I missed it. I was homesick. I felt like I needed family around me and around Nege. But I couldn't handle the cold so we moved back to Vancouver. I still get homesick. Ideally, I'd love to have a place here and a place in Winnipeg. I miss it, I miss my friends and family, but I can't take the winters."

Does she still have that vagabond spirit? "No, because Nege is now in school so I've got to try and stay here for awhile. I don't want him to go through what I did."

Currently without a recording contract, Holly continues to write, but she feels herself drawn to her country music roots. "I think I always had those roots, although in my teens I was fighting it saying 'I hate country music!' I'm thinking more acoustically right now. In the last few years I've been listening to a lot of stuff that my mom used to listen to. It's in my voice and vocal technique. I'd love to do an acoustic album, maybe recorded at home."

If so, there is one song she would like to tackle. "I was watching a movie the other night and 'Blue Bayou' came on and I said to Jay, 'I've got to record that song! It's payback. I've got to prove to everyone I can do it right.'" ∎

Born in The Pas, Manitoba

Lived in Brandon and Portage la Prairie before moving to Winnipeg at age eleven

ALBUMS: Sour Pie (1995); Stuff (1997); Live Stuff (1999); Home Is Where My Feet Are (2002)

HIT SINGLES: "Coward", Elmo", "Numb", "Water"

Once worked as the door girl at the Tom Tom Club on Osborne Street

Auditioned unsuccessfully to be Sarah McLachlan's backup singer

Currently writing in preparation to record her next album

Married to MuchMusic videographer and ex Winnipegger Jay Mirus

# MOOD JGA JGA

**H**OW MANY BANDS WAIT TWENTY-FOUR YEARS BETWEEN ALBUM RELEASES? For Mood Jga Jga, the quarter century interval only made them stronger and more creative. Despite forming in 1972, and with several bands to individual members' credit since, Mood Jga Jga remains a living entity that has never broken up, only taken long periods of hiatus.

**TAKING SIX MONTHS TO DEVELOP THEIR SOUND, THE QUARTET DREW ON TRADITIONAL AS WELL AS PROGRESSIVE JAZZ TO CONCOCT A HEADY BREW OF MELLOW POP JAZZ.**

In 1972 during a US tour, Greg Leskiw abruptly left the Guess Who following a concert in Corpus Christi, Texas. Elevated to the ranks of Canada's greatest hit makers two years earlier, he no longer felt part of the group. "It wasn't my thing," Greg concedes. "I had my own dream and I guess I was stubborn about it." Having stepped aboard a train that was already rolling on a full head of steam, he now wanted to be his own engine.

Returning to Winnipeg he set about assembling his dream group. After a false start with Larry Pink, Bill Wallace and Craig Hamblin, Greg and longtime friends drummer Gordie Osland and bass player Bill Merritt formed a trio but there was still something lacking. "Hermann Frühm completed the band. If that hadn't happened there wouldn't have been a Mood Jga Jga." With the breakup of Dianne Heatherington's Merry-Go-Round, the keyboard wizard was freed up and Mood Jga Jga (pronounced "jah jah" for the uninitiated) was born.

Greg explains the origin of the unusual moniker. "It came from Gordie's son, Sam. He was just a little guy. Around the dinner table one day he was banging on the plates with his knife and fork and he kept saying 'Mood jga jga, mood jga jga' over and over. And it stuck in my mind. It was tough to say, tough to spell, but there was something about it, the look of it. There's probably better ways to spell it because everybody mispronounced it. We were at Warner Brothers records being introduced to everyone in the building as 'Mood Jeegah Jeegah' and we didn't

pick up on the hint: 'Change your freakin' name!'"

Taking six months to develop their sound, the quartet drew on traditional as well as progressive jazz to concoct a heady brew of mellow pop jazz. "We were always pushing the envelope. It was our own concept of our sound. My roots weren't rock 'n' roll. We wanted to be different and it worked with the way I was singing and still works today."

Surprisingly, their distinctive sound was derived not from Greg's virtuoso guitar talents. "When you listen to the first album it's built around Hermann's keyboard. It wasn't a guitar-based band. I played more rhythm guitar but it's really the piano that takes it someplace special." A highly regarded guitarist, Greg has been willing to step back throughout his career to let others shine. "That was always my dream; to have it sound like a group."

With former Guess Who road manager Jim Millican as manager, Mood Jga Jga signed with Warner Brothers records. In the summer of 1973 they went to New York to record with producer Phil Ramone, renowned for his work with Paul Simon, Phoebe Snow, and Billy Joel. "We were looking for someone who had done some work in the jazz field and who was ready to step into pop to do some producing. Phil was the guy." Working with Phil remains a highlight. "He was walking musical history, won all those Grammys and awards, had just finished *There Goes Rhymin' Simon* and working with Burt Bacharach, and here we were recording with the guy!"

Cut at A&R Studios in Manhattan, *Mood Jga Jga* is a rare gem, a wholly fresh sound dominated by Greg's clever writing. "I had written 'I Am What I Am What I Am' just before leaving the Guess Who. I also had 'Gimme My Money'." He regards "Daybreak" as capturing the essence of what Mood Jga Jga represents. The hard-rocking "Queen Jealousy" was the debut single, inspired by an unlikely source. "I met this five-string banjo player who showed me how to get that picking style for the opening riff muting of the strings. That was always my contribution guitar-wise, intros and riffs that were quirky and off the beaten track." Besides stellar musicianship, the album also reveals the group's vocal strength. "Mood Jga Jga is an unbelievable vocal band. All of us sing."

Reluctant to promote such an eccentric-sounding album, Warner pulled back, leaving the group to suffer its own fate. "The signs were there. First of all a delayed release. Then it was, 'Let's just release it in Canada.' The record didn't happen like it should, and then they decided to cut back their roster and we were dropped."

A spellbinding live group, Mood Jga Jga continued to gig in western Canada, opening for the likes of the **Mahavishnu** Orchestra and appearing in concert at the Manitoba Theatre Centre, as well as a memorable performance on the roof of the Winnipeg Art Gallery. Gordie Osland recalls another unforgettable gig. "We played a set in the nude at the Sandstone Club in LA. They called it a 'sensual awareness club.' It's interesting playing drums naked. You gotta be kind of careful."

Attempts at recording a second album financed by Greg fell apart (several tracks appeared on Greg's solo album *Be My Champion*). Bill Merritt left, replaced by Ian Gardner. "We were committed to improvisation. Bill, however, thought it wasn't commercial. I could see his point. What we wanted to be was a pop band so what were we doing with eight-minute jam sessions?"

Mood Jga Jga never officially broke up, reconvening for sporadic gigs over the next two decades, even after Hermann relocated to British Columbia. In 1991 they recorded a six-song tape for CBC before returning to the studio in 1997 to write and record *Boys Will Be Boys,* released independently. "We just decided to get together and do it. What it shows is the amazing chemistry between us."

None of the four rules out another Mood Jga Jga album someday. "The band is such a strong, creative entity that it should be recorded again," insists Greg. "Everyone in the band is still such a strong player. Here we are still talking about the band 30 years later, so who knows?"

While critics at the time considered Greg's defection from the Guess Who ill-advised, he has no regrets. "If I had the choice between staying in the Guess Who or making music with Mood Jga Jga, there's no question. It would be Mood Jga Jga." ∎

Formed in Winnipeg in 1972 by ex-Guess Who guitarist Greg Leskiw

Former members of the Guess Who, Wild Rice, Vicious Circle, and the Shags

ALBUMS: Mood Jga Jga (1974); Boys Will Be Boys (1997)

HIT SINGLE: "Queen Jealousy"

Debut album recorded in New York with legendary producer Phil Ramone

Managed by ex-Guess Who road manager Jim Millican

Drummer Gord Osland founded the Winnipeg International Children's Festival

Once played nude club in a Los Angeles club

# MAE MOORE

M M A E O M O R E

**W**HO SAYS YOU CAN NEVER GO home again? After a forty-year absence, in the summer of 2004 singer/songwriter Mae Moore returned to her hometown of Brandon, Manitoba to appear at their annual folk festival. "I've been wanting to go back for years and was wondering why they never hired me before," she says, from her home in British Columbia's Gulf Islands.

Mae, who titled her second album *Bohemia*, has also led a bohemian life. Born in Brandon, she lived with her parents and older sister on Princess Avenue, and took piano lessons at Brandon College. She was introduced to jazz by her father, a trumpet player. "It was an influence," she suggests, "but I never really liked jazz until I moved to Vancouver and studied it at Capilano College for a few years." Rock 'n' roll came via her sister's record collection and the boys down the street. "The very first time I heard a live rock band was in Brandon walking home from Fleming School through the alley."

The family moved to BC only to head east to Toronto two years later. Then they relocated to St. Thomas, Ontario two years after that, where Mae completed high school. An early interest in art pointed toward a possible career, but her post-secondary art studies were interrupted when she found herself pregnant. "I moved to Halifax/Dartmouth to live with my sister until my daughter was born. I gave her up for adoption, then moved back to Ontario to finish my art studies." Already playing guitar, Mae's musical aspirations and songwriting skills were nurtured at a popular coffeehouse, Smales, in London, Ontario. "I felt I would never be able to make my living from visual art, so I went into music by default. But I never thought of pursuing music as a recording career."

It wasn't until she moved to Vancouver in 1979 that Mae's professional career began, playing electric guitar in New Wave band Foreign Legion before becoming a solo acoustic performer. Her first break came in 1985 when a song she co-wrote, "Heaven in Your Eyes", was recorded by Loverboy for the *Top Gun* soundtrack. "That's probably the thing

Born in Brandon, Manitoba

Performed with New Wave band Foreign Legion in Vancouver before going solo

ALBUMS: Oceanview Motel (1990); Bohemia (1992); Dragonfly (1995); Mae Moore (1999); Mae Moore: Collected Works 1989-1999 (2000); It's A Funny World (2003); Oh My! (with Lester Quitzau, 2004)

HIT SINGLES: "Red Clay Hills", "I'll Watch Over You", "Bohemia", "Genuine", "Watermark"

AWARDS: SOCAN Award for Most Played Song (1996)

Co-wrote "Heaven in Your Eyes" for Loverboy on the *Top Gun* soundtrack

Singer Jann Arden signed Mae to her Big Hip Records label and produced "Mae Moore"

A serious car accident in Prince Edward Island almost ended her career in 1997

people might know me for more than anything else. I'm very grateful for it because it opened some doors for me, but I really have no attachment to it."

Securing a recording contract with Sony Music with help from Barney Bentall, Legendary Hearts' guitarist Colin Nairne, and Spirit of the West's Geoff Kelly, Mae recorded *Oceanview Motel*, a debut boasting the hits "I'll Watch Over You" and "Red Clay Hills". "I remember in high school asking myself if I could have one thing in the world what would I want, and that was to hear one of my songs on the radio."

"Red Clay Hills" remains one of her best-known songs. "It was influenced by an article I read in *The Globe and Mail* about the building of a fixed link between PEI and the mainland, and I thought what a terrible thing for this beautiful place in the ocean. For some reason being from Manitoba, smack dab in the middle of the country, I had this strange affinity for islands."

Mae toured Canada through the next year, followed by a trip to Australia to record her follow-up, *Bohemia*. The title track, a breathy Rickie Lee Jones-style beat poem, became a Top 10 hit in 1992. The album was also released in the US and later in Japan and Germany. "I always thought of myself as a songwriter first, setting a landscape for each song, seeing things the way a painter does."

*Dragonfly* followed in 1995, earning Mae another hit with "Genuine" going on to receive the SOCAN Award for Most Played Song in 1996. "Sony had just dropped me so when I got the call that I'd won the award it was sweet vindication."

Without a recording contract, Mae took time off for a personal mission: to locate and reunite with her daughter. "It's a fairytale ending. She's beautiful and I couldn't be happier." While residing in PEI, Mae was involved in a serious car accident that laid her up for more than six months. It took the intervention of a fan and friend to bring Mae back into a recording studio. "During my recuperation I got a call from Jann Arden asking me if I wanted to do a record with her on this little label she'd started, Big Hip Records. So I did and that was my self-titled album. It was very generous of her to do that for me." Around the same time, Sony released *Mae Moore: Collected Works 1989-1999*, gathering together many of her best songs from her previous three albums.

Mae recorded her next album, *It's A Funny World*, in the comfort of her Gulf Islands home, with the result being simpler arrangements, sparser instrumentation, and a jazzier feel. She also re-recorded four of her best-known earlier songs, "Red Clay Hills", "Superstitious", "Bohemia", and "All I Can't Explain". "They're still songs that I perform live and I wanted to give them an updated treatment. They still mean a lot to me."

US-based Paras Records issued *It's A Funny World* in 2003, but because it was a small label, distribution was spotty. "It was very heartbreaking for me because I still feel it's my best work."

Recently married to noted blues guitarist and Juno award winner Lester Quitzau, Mae and Lester have released *Oh My!*, an acoustic album that has received enthusiastic reviews and a Western Canada Music nomination. "It's just two guitars and two voices, very bare

bones. We recorded it in our living room, engineered it ourselves, and we got a five-star review in an audio magazine in Germany that is very sticky about their sound quality."

In the future Mae plans to record another album with Lester, as well as a personal project, a jazz album of her own compositions. "Not your traditional jazz but more along the lines of *Funny World*, keeping that vibe."

Despite the lengthy absence from Brandon, Mae continues to feel a spiritual bond with the prairies. "People ask me where I'm from and I struggle with that question because in my heart I still feel like I'm from Manitoba. I think the landscape and the openness influenced my writing. I think I was influenced very early on by the sense of freedom that being born on the prairies gives you." ■

# RICK NEUFELD

RECENTLY, CBC RADIO IN WINNIPEG discovered that Manitoba was one of only two provinces lacking an official song. So host Roger Currie went in search of a suitable musical anthem. The overwhelming choice of listeners? "Moody Manitoba Morning". Singer/songwriter Rick Neufeld isn't surprised, some thirty-five years after penning the tribute to his home province's pastoral pace. "Try to come up with a song that has Manitoba in it," he chuckles. "There just aren't any."

Born in Deloraine and raised in Boissevain, Rick spent his youth on farms, and rural life has remained with him. "I was always a rebel and a restless soul." Moving to Winnipeg in the mid 1960s to attend the University of Manitoba he discovered that his rural education had not sufficiently prepared him for studies in architecture and he dropped out, taking a job in a drafting office. Bitten by wanderlust, he and a friend took off to Europe, where he discovered a love for music. "I had an uncle who played guitar as a kid and I had dabbled in music when I was younger." In Munich he met Rick Hahn. "Rick's dad was Bob Hahn who was a legendary jingles writer back in Canada. When I came back from Europe I stopped off in Montreal for awhile, met Bob, and played him a couple of my songs. It was kind of an epiphany because he liked them. When I got home he sent me a letter saying he was going to be producing a band and wanted to use one of my songs."

The band was the Five Bells (later the Bells) and the song was "Moody Manitoba Morning", among Rick's first compositions written on his return to Canada and not yet recorded by him. He explains his inspiration. "When you've never been anywhere and you go to Europe and come back home, you're just so amazed at how magnificent it is here, so I was moved to write that song." The Five Bells went on to score a Canadian hit with their soft pop rendition in 1969. American folk/country singer George Hamilton IV also enjoyed a hit with the song in the US. "It's been covered by so many artists I'd have to do a Google search just to find all of them." George recorded more of Rick's songs and suddenly he found himself in demand as a singer/songwriter.

The Manitoba Mennonite community, the largest outside Russia, embraced Rick as a local Mennonite hero. "*The Mennonite Mirror* did a great article on

> **"AS SOON AS I STARTED DRIVING FOR BRUCE I IMMEDIATELY KNEW THAT WAS WHAT I WANTED TO DO. I DIDN'T WANT TO SLUG IT OUT AS A MUSICIAN ANY MORE."**

me. I still get newsletters from the Mennonite Collegiate Institute in Gretna where I went for a year in the 1960s."

For Manitoba's 1970 centennial year Warner Brothers Records invited Rick to cut his own version of "Moody Manitoba Morning", backed by "Boissevain Fair", a nostalgic remembrance of the annual county fair. Soon after, Bob Hahn started his own record label, Astra, and signed Rick to record his debut album under the aegis of Canadian country music legend Gary Buck. *Hiway Child* wasn't quite what Rick had in mind. "I had absolutely no input in that whatsoever. It wasn't so much a conscious effort to be country except that there was a market for it."

Rick took his newfound country sound to Nashville in 1971, performing at the Grand Ole Opry. "Tom T. Hall invited some of us Canadians to showcase at the old Ryman Auditorium. I remember Gordie Tapp was there as well as Stompin' Tom Connors, who had an extra amp on stage that turned out to be a fridge for Canadian beer. I hung out a lot with Kris Kristofferson and Randy Scruggs down there."

Moving over to RCA, Rick released three singles between 1974 and 1975, one, "A Love Worth Living", raising a few eyebrows after Rick insisted the word "whore" remain in the lyrics. "That was the most hip song I had written but, obviously, a lot of radio stations wouldn't play it." Residing on a farm in St. Anne, Manitoba, Rick and Don 'Fiddler' Zueff worked as a duo prior to recording *Prairie Dog*, which featured an all-star cast of Winnipeg players including Burton Cummings, Garry Peterson, and Bill Wallace of the Guess Who and folksinger Tom Jackson. "Burton had a big hand in the production of that album and he loved doing it."

*Manitobasongs* was credited to Rick Neufeld & Prairie Dog and was recorded live onstage at the Centennial Auditorium in Brandon and released on his own

Prairie Dog Records. Rick went on to host two CBC television shows in 1976, *On The Road* and *Songsingers*. The Prairie Dog lineup, including Gord Osland, Bill Merritt, Chris Anderson and Don Zeuff, scattered following a tour of northern Manitoba.

While Rick grew weary of touring, he had not tired of travel. Purchasing and renovating an old excursion bus, he began driving other acts out on tour. One of his first clients was Graham Shaw and the Sincere Serenaders, The experience brought him in touch with another friend, Toronto folksinger/songwriter Bruce Cockburn, who tapped Rick and his bus for a western Canadian tour. "As soon as I started driving for Bruce I immediately knew that was what I wanted to do. I didn't want to slug it out as a musician any more."

Eventually Rick moved to Salt Spring Island and continues to drive for Sarah MacLachlan, the reunited Guess Who, and American jazz-pop sensation Norah Jones. The 2003 Iraq War put a damper on some of his driving after American customs officials denied him a visa to work across the border.

On Salt Spring Island, an artistic enclave of painters, poets, writers, songwriters and performers, Rick remains somewhat anonymous, better known as a driver than the composer of an enduring Canadian cultural signpost. "I've never performed here. They don't know me as a musician." Photography has become a recent passion for Rick who now operates "Noofoto" and has become the unofficial photographer around the community. A photo he took of Norah Jones recently appeared in *Rolling Stone* magazine.

Looking back, Rick feels very gratified that "Moody Manitoba Morning" remains in the public consciousness as a Canadian classic. "There were some people who insisted it doesn't exactly flatter the province because it says 'Nothing happens, it never does.' But that was the whole point of it. What we really like about Manitoba is that the pace of life is manageable. Bob Hahn tried to get me to change it to Mississippi or Montana but I stuck with Manitoba and I'm glad I did." ■

Born in Deloraine, raised in Boissevain, Manitoba

Studied architecture at the University of Manitoba

ALBUMS: Hiway Child (1971); Prairie Dog (1975); Manitobasongs (1978)

HIT SINGLES: "Moody Manitoba Morning", "Long Way Home", "Hiway Child", "A Love Worth Living"

Hosted his own CBC television series The Songsingers and later co-hosted *On The Road* with Colleen Peterson

Played at the Grand Ole Opry in Nashville (1971)

Burton Cummings played on and helped produce Rick's Prairie Dog album

Became an entertainer tour bus driver for the likes of Sarah MacLachlan, the Guess Who, and Norah Jones

Now a well-known photographer

**T**HE BIRTH OF A CHILD CAN BE AN AWE-INSPIRING moment. For Winnipeg songwriter Chris Burke-Gaffney, the event served as inspiration for a hit song. In 1983, his band Orphan scored a cross-Canada Top 10 hit with "Miracle", penned following the birth of Chris's son, Nick. "Miracle" would also serve as the launching pad for a high profile music business career for Chris that continues unabated today.

"Miracle" and Orphan's history both date back to the popular late 1970s band the Pumps, formed in south Winnipeg by school friends Chris and drummer Terry Norman Taylor. The two met at St. Ignatius school as neophyte rock 'n' rollers. "Terry played a Jimi Hendrix record for me when I was thirteen, and as soon as I heard that record I knew that's what I wanted to do," says Chris. "It was my epiphany." Over the next five years the two jammed with other neighbourhood rockers, but it wasn't until they met lead guitarist Lou Petrovich that the Pumps was born. The three were later joined by keyboard player Brent Diamond, formerly of Hurricane Hannah, as the group began gigging regularly. Their music — blending punk, New Wave, rock and original material composed mainly by Chris and delivered with great energy — garnered a loyal following and enthusiastic reviews.

Managed by Frank Weipert and future Winnipeg mayor Sam Katz, the Pumps signed a recording contract with Polygram Records in 1979. Then they travelled to Le Studio in Morin Heights just outside Montreal (frequented by the likes of Elton John), to record their debut album. British pop producers Jon Astley and Phil Chapman were recruited for the sessions. Final mixing was done at London's Olympic Studios where the Who, Led Zeppelin and the Rolling Stones all worked.

Released the following year, *Gotta Move* captured the group's dynamic power pop repertoire with favourites like "Coffee With The Queen", "Success" and "Bust The TV". Reviews, including a feature in *Maclean's* magazine, were encouraging as the Pumps toured North America, opening for AC/DC, Triumph, and Prism. The future looked bright for the Winnipeg quartet.

A dispute with Polygram, however, left them unable to release a follow-up. "We ended up having to wait out our three-year contract before we could sign with someone else. That was discouraging, because we had gone from a semi-successful Canadian album to playing in clubs again." In the interim, Lou Petrovich was replaced by Steve McGovern.

Following their recording hiatus, the Pumps signed with CBS Records and began recording a long-awaited sophomore album. The delay, however, had not been good for the band's reputation, so they agreed to change their name to Orphan. CBS brought the group to New York to record at the Power Station, where pop stars Duran Duran had recently recorded. Their producer was Tony Bongiovi, whose nephew Jon also worked at the studio. "Although he now goes under Bon Jovi, Jon used to come in and sweep the floor in his uncle's studio. He loved our band and would make all these suggestions to us. We just used to think, 'Get lost kid.' Two years later he releases a record and sells 10 million copies." Jon Bon Jovi remembered the guys in Orphan. "He came to see us play when he was on tour to say hello."

During the recording of *Lonely At Night* Chris introduced a song composed in the Pumps era. "The guys thought

'Miracle' was a little too light for what we were doing, but we decided to record it. The arrangement was inspired by Tom Petty's 'Here Comes My Girl.'" With its throbbing bass line and synthesizer swells, "Miracle" was dripping with hit potential. Released in 1983 it went Top 10 across Canada, redeeming the expectations created by the Pumps. Orphan toured across Canada and released a second CBS album, *Salute* in 1985, however the group failed to come up with a strong follow-up single to "Miracle", and dissolved later that year.

Chris and Terry bounced back with Deadbeat Honeymooners alongside bassist Blair DePape (Chris switching over to guitar) and lead guitarist Barry Player, recording one self-titled album for Anthem/Sony. The timing just wasn't right. "That was the year the Nirvana record came out and the whole sound of straight rock changed to grunge. We had a joke that we had the fastest moving record on the charts, moving straight down."

Weary of the road grind and with young families to support, Chris and Terry took a gig as house band at two downtown Winnipeg clubs operated by Sam Katz. "We played a rock 'n' roll set at the Rolling Stone cabaret, then changed into sparkly jackets, went over to the Bank cabaret, a dance club, and played disco. It was great; only three nights a week and I didn't have to leave town."

During his free time, Chris embarked on a new career. "I wanted to ease out of playing and get more into production and writing." One of the first clients to come knocking was a teenager from suburban Charleswood named Chantal Kreviazuk. "Chantal was a huge fan of 'Miracle' and wanted some help with songwriting. She had a phenomenal voice and was a good pianist, but she also had that X factor of being a star. I thought I could get her a

deal because I still had a lot of contacts in the business." Chantal then invited Chris to manage her.

"I never thought I was the manager type but there was nobody else that could do it, so I did that for a few years, started my company and started managing a couple of other artists. And that's where I am now." In 1996 he formed CBG Artist Management with a roster boasting Winnipeg pop duo McMaster & James and more recently Saskatoon singer/songwriter Kyle Riabko. Chris is producing Kyle's debut CBS album in Los Angeles. The Prairie Music Association named Chris Manager of the Year three years running (2000, 2001 and 2002). He continues to write and record and has

posted songs in several movies and television shows, including *Chicago Hope*, *Real World* and *Providence*. Despite the pull from larger music centres, he continues to live and work in Winnipeg. "It's been a struggle for the last ten years, but I am a Winnipeg champion and I believe it can be done from here." He is currently the driving force behind a multi-media consortium seeking to build a large music facility in Winnipeg that will house management, song publishing, recording, video and booking, all under one roof.

Chris remains proud of "Miracle". "I've written hundreds of songs but that one still stands up. You're lucky to write five or ten really great songs. I think 'Miracle' was one of them." ■

Formed in Winnipeg in 1978

Began as the Pumps before becoming Orphan

ALBUMS: Gotta Move (1980); Lonely At Night (1983); Salute (1985)

HIT SINGLE: "Miracle"

Recorded at New York's Record Plant where Jon Bon Jovi was the gofer

Once managed by future Winnipeg mayor Sam Katz

Two members formed the Deadbeat Honeymooners

Recently reunited for gigs around Winnipeg

Chris Burke-Gaffney currently producing Saskatchewan sensation Kyle Riabko

**F**EW CANADIAN RECORDING ARTISTS are as likely to cause a mob scene in a grocery store as children's entertainer Fred Penner. While adults may spot a musical hero at the mall, they are unlikely to give him a hug. But children have no such inhibitions, nor do teenagers and young adults who grew up on Fred's songs and TV shows.

**FRED PENNER'S CAREER TRAJECTORY, FROM AMATEUR FOLK SINGER TO INTERNATIONALLY-ACCLAIMED CHILDREN'S ENTERTAINER, HAS BEEN SERENDIPITOUS.**

"There is this domino affect," states Fred. "Somebody will approach and ask, 'Are you Fred Penner?' Then more people come over and before long there's this wave of people seeking autographs or wanting to meet me. Somebody will say, 'Oh yeah, I remember him. Didn't he crawl out of a log?'"

Fred Penner's career trajectory, from amateur folk singer to internationally-acclaimed children's entertainer, has been serendipitous. "A lot of the direction was beyond my control," he admits. Born in Winnipeg in 1946, the son of a career Canadian Forces officer, Fred attended half a dozen elementary schools.

"I would often check in after the school year began and I remember walking into a class, the kids all silent, and the teacher saying, 'Class, this is Freddy Penner. Please make him welcome.' And there I would be in front of an audience. That made an imprint on me."

At Kelvin High School Fred rubbed shoulders with another budding musician. "I remember seeing Neil Young's old hearse parked outside the school. He had such an aura about him. I remember him in his black jacket surrounded by people. He was a star already." But Fred was listening to folk music and toting a rifle. "When everyone else went to Crescentwood Community Club to hear the Guess Who, I was in Air Cadets." Taking up the guitar at age twelve, he formed the Folk Four at Kelvin.

After getting a BA in economics and psychology from the University of Winnipeg, Fred had little desire for nine-to-five routine. "I knew that I didn't want to be an economist. I just thought, 'What have I done that has given me some feeling of gratification?' — and it was always music. I just never knew you could make a living as a musician. That was not an option, certainly not from my parents' Mennonite background."

Two other events helped push Fred toward music: the deaths of his sister Susie and then his father's a year later. "These two intense mortality checks were a turning point for me. I had fulfilled a son's responsibility in completing university, I was the first in the family to do so, and my sister had been a musical inspiration for me." Taking a job as a childcare worker at Children's Home of Winnipeg and Knowles Home for Boys, Fred performed in local coffeehouses. A mutual friend suggested he team up with a former Air Cadet buddy, Al Simmons, whose band Out To Lunch had recently folded. With Bob King and later Mike Klym on drums, they formed Kornstock, a zany mid 1970s pub band.

"I was this folk guy and Al was doing bar band stuff but with Al's level of insanity," Fred recalls. "I was in shock that this could actually work." The group toured for four years. "Working with Al I learned a lot about spontaneity. In the middle of a song Al would suddenly stop and say, 'Number 4' and that was our cue to grab our Snap, Crackle, Pop hats and go into the Rice Krispies commercial. People would be stunned. The key was always to make contact with the audience, and make them participate. That was good preparation."

But Fred wanted something more musically satisfying. "Kornstock was Al's trip," he says. "I wanted to find a balance, not just be crazy all the time." At a gig in Toronto, he met future wife Odette, a dancer moving to Winnipeg to work with the Contemporary Dancers. Quitting Kornstock, he took on roles at Rainbow Stage. Then he formed a children's dance theatre company with Odette, called Sundance, performing in schools and with the Manitoba Theatre for Young

People. Odette choreographed while Fred provided musical accompaniment. A Sundance performance started Fred's recording career.

"After a show a local doctor offered to finance a recording. He liked my voice and what I stood for. I went into Finucan Studios in fall 1979 and recorded my first album with kids from Montrose School. I delved back into my folk music brain and found this great old song called 'The Cat Came Back' and we recorded it." The album was released on children's entertainer Raffi's Troubadour label and Fred toured with Raffi for the next five years. In 1985, Fred and manager Gilles Paquin formed Oak Street Records to release his subsequent albums. At the same time, CBC approached Fred to host a national TV series, *Fred Penner's Place*. The popular weekday show ran for twelve seasons, nearly 900 episodes, and Nickelodeon picked it up in the US, where Fred enjoyed a following of some fifty-five million American viewers.

Eleven more albums followed over fifteen years including *Happy Feet, Ebeneezer Sneezer, Company's Coming*, and most recently *Sing With Fred*. Fred has received countless accolades including two Juno Awards, the Best Children's Album of the Year in *Entertainment Weekly*, and the Order of Canada in 1994. He was honoured by the Canadian Institute of Child Health, and received the Parents' Choice Award as the "Canadian Minister of Positivity". In 2002 he received $25,000 through the CIBC Children's World Market Fund to redirect to the charity of his choice. Fred chose the Down's Syndrome Association. "For me, that was a total validation of my life's work because my sister Susie had Down's Syndrome," he acknowledges.

Fred resists being called a children's entertainer. "I consider myself a family entertainer," he says. "There are some children's entertainers who have less substance to what they do. About half the songs I write are totally palatable for an adult audience. Maybe I'll do something more for grown-ups. But not because I feel a lack of fulfillment.

"What I do touches lives. I've had parents come up to me and tell me that their child passed away but my music meant so much to the family. In the autograph lines I'll have the little ones wide-eyed with their parents, and teenagers too. I've even had Goth kids with the black hair and clothes, and they're just kids at heart. It's such a trip to see that whatever I did is still inside them." ∎

Born in Winnipeg

BANDS: the Folk Four, Kornstock, solo artist

ALBUMS: The Cat Came Back (1979), A House For Me (1986), Fred Penner's Place (1988), Ebeneezer Sneezer (1991), Happy Feet (1992), Fred's Favourites (1998), Sing With Fred (2002)

AWARDS: Juno for Best Children's Album (1988, 2002); Prairie Music Award for Outstanding Children's Recording (1999); the Order of Canada (1994); Best Children's Album of the Year in the US *Entertainment Weekly*; the US Parents' Choice Award

Fred played Captain Hook in the MTYP production of *Peter Pan*

Hosted CBC TV's *Fred Penner's Place* for twelve years (seen by 55 million viewers on Nickelodeon in the US)

He attended Kelvin High School in Winnipeg at the same time as Neil Young

Fred writes all the music for YTV's *Tipi Tales*

**MOVING TO TORONTO, SCRUBBALOE CAINE TORE UP EVERY CLUB AND CONCERT HALL, SCORING AN OPENING SLOT FOR THE GUESS WHO AT TORONTO'S CANADIAN NATIONAL EXHIBITION, WHERE THEY CAUGHT MANAGER DON HUNTER'S ATTENTION.**

**B**ACK IN 1973, WITHOUT ANY DOUBT *the* band to catch live in Winnipeg was Scrubbaloe Caine. Driven by bluesy twin lead guitars and fronted by mini dynamo Henry Small on vocals and electric violin, the oddly-named sextet was the talk of the Canadian music industry. Composed of members from across western Canada but based in Winnipeg, Scrubbaloe was emerging as the next big thing. Managed by Guess Who svengali Don Hunter and boasting a Guess Who alumnus within their ranks, what could possibly go wrong?

The group's origins went back to the late 1960s with Vancouver soul outfit the Trials of Jayson Hoover, a popular club act that included guitarist Jim Harmata, keyboard/harmonica player Al Foreman, and bass player/singer Donny Gerrard. In the summer of 1971, the band came through Winnipeg for an extended gig at the Fireplace on Pembina Highway. When they returned the following spring they had transformed into Cannonball, with Donny Gerrard gone to join Skylark (who enjoyed a huge hit single with "Wildflower"). In his place was diminutive vocal powerhouse Henry Small. Hailing from Beacon, New York, a child prodigy on the violin, Henry moved to Alberta in the latter '60s, joining Edmonton-based group Gainsborough Gallery before hooking up with Cannonball. Rounding out the group was Bob Kidd on bass, Calgarian Bill McBeth on drums, and guitarist Paul Dean from Invermere, BC.

With a blues-based hard rock sound, Cannonball rolled eastward for an extended residency at a Quebec City nightclub. There Cannonball became Scrubbaloe Caine. Henry explains the strange moniker. "We were sitting around in our room listening to Buffalo Springfield when somebody said, 'That's kind of a cool name, why don't we call ourselves Scrubbaloe Dingfield.' So we kept the Scrubbaloe and somehow got Caine. Nobody even knew what it was. Screwballou? Scooby doo? What the hell were we thinking?"

Moving to Toronto, Scrubbaloe Caine tore up every club and concert hall, scoring an opening slot for the Guess Who at Toronto's Canadian National Exhibition, where they caught manager Don Hunter's attention. Hunter signed the group. Looking for a suitable vehicle for former Guess Who bass player Jim Kale, Hunter parachuted Jim in to replace Bob Kidd, and moved them to Winnipeg. "We thought that since Kale had been in the Guess Who, that would be a good career move for us." But the presence of a

Formed in Calgary as Cannonball; based in Winnipeg from 1973

Members of Scrubbaloe Caine were also in the Trials of Jayson Hoover, Cannonball, Gainsborough Gallery, and the Guess Who

ALBUM: Round One (1973)

HIT SINGLES: "Feelin' Good On Sunday", "Travelin'"

Managed by Guess Who manager Don Hunter

Derived their name from Buffalo Springfield

Ex-Guess Who bass player Jim Kale joined (1973-74)

Guitarist Paul Dean went to form first Streetheart then Loverboy

Singer Henry Small later toured with the Who's John Entwistle

bona fide rock legend within their ranks unsettled the group. "We had never seen anything like Jim Kale before.

"In those days everyone wanted to be what the Guess Who was so we came to Winnipeg." Hunter negotiated a recording contract with Guess Who label RCA Records and arranged sessions at RCA's Music Center Of The World studios in Hollywood. But while the Guess Who enjoyed the luxury of several weeks in the studio, Scrubbaloe Caine was allowed just six days for their debut album. It was a recipe for disappointment. Complicating the hasty sessions was the destabilizing presence of drugs.

"We were never happy with the album. We never had the opportunity to go into the studio for a month and play around. Some of the guys had very little recording experience. Obviously I think it could have been better. Like a lot of bands that play great live, we just never had the opportunity to record properly. Once they get into the studio it's a whole other thing."

*Round One* failed to capture Scrubbaloe Caine's natural energy. Despite strong writing and skillful playing, the sound was flat. RCA pulled back on promoting the album in the US, leaving the band to flounder. Two singles, the hoedown-flavoured "Feelin' Good On Sunday", featuring Henry's spirited electric violin, and a ballad, "Travelin'", charted across Canada. "We were getting airplay in parts of the US but Don Hunter was just too involved with the Guess Who."

The group gigged sporadically before grinding to halt. "We just never had the same energy." Jim Kale bailed out and was replaced by local bass player Gary Stefaniuk. "Jim was just overwhelmed by the rock star lifestyle in the Guess Who and never really recovered."

Al Foreman was next to go, followed soon after by Henry. "After Al left that was pretty much it. Dean and McBeth carried it on for a while as a four-piece but that didn't last very long." The four-man lineup, with newcomer Pat Riley on bass, cut a single, "Feelin' Down", for the tiny Amherst record label, before folding in 1976.

Returning to Calgary, Paul Dean joined the Great Canadian River Race

before moving on to found Streetheart and later Loverboy. Henry declined an offer to join Loverboy, instead forming Small Wonder, a popular Toronto club act that recorded two woefully neglected albums for Columbia Records in the latter '70s. He bounced back in Burton Cummings' backing band before joining Vancouver's Prism and John Entwistle's solo band (Entwistle was the Who's bass player). With Entwistle's outfit Henry wrote, arranged and produced the album *The Rock* and toured extensively. Today, Henry can be heard as the morning man at 98.3 CIFM in Kamloops, BC, and operates Small World Recording Studios. In 2002, he released a solo album, *Time*, and recently gigged with ex-Winnipeggers Gord Osland and Steve Heygi.

Al Foreman continues to play clubs in Vancouver, while Bill McBeth does the same in Calgary. Gary Stefaniuk went on to Graham Shaw and the Sincere Serenaders. Guitarist Jim Harmata lives in Vancouver. Bob Kidd died in a car accident several years ago.

Henry maintains that nothing could match the onstage energy Scrubbaloe Caine generated. "I don't think I've known that kind of excitement onstage since. I've played with some of these better known people but I still would go back to Scrubbaloe as the pinnacle for me." He believes that individual members created a rare chemistry together that could ignite audiences. "We didn't know it at the time, of course. It was a great combination because Jimmy could lay down a groove and Paul could work off that. That really prepared Paul for Loverboy, to be honest. Bill McBeth was never a great drummer in a technical sense but as far as putting out energy and being a real character to watch onstage, he was one of the best."

And what of his own contributions to Scrubbaloe Caine? "Being a young guy then I was just very physical onstage. And I had a really strong, high voice, which has long since gone to the wind, but those guys gave me a platform for me to shine." ∎

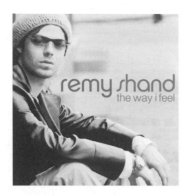

**R**ECEIVING PRAISE FROM YOUR FANS is always gratifying for a recording artist. But when one of your fans turns out to be Sir Elton John, and he heralds your work on *The Rosie O'Donnell Show* before millions of viewers, that is high praise indeed. When Rosie asked whom he was listening to, Elton said "Remy Shand," and praised Remy's debut album *The Way I Feel*. "There's a boy called Remy Shand from Winnipeg," he said. "It's great to hear that kind of music, with real talent."

"That was wicked, man," recalls the Winnipeg singer/songwriter/producer. "After that happened we got a call from his management company saying if I got a call from a guy in the middle of the night saying he was Elton John, I shouldn't hang up."

Remy spent four years conceiving and recording his album in his parents' house in suburban Garden City, playing most of the instruments himself. He is a self-confessed studio junkie who prefers being cloistered in a recording facility to performing live. The staggering success of *The Way I Feel*, debuting at #1 in Canada and selling 750,000 copies worldwide, forced the reclusive star into the public limelight. He seems to be adjusting to his newfound fame just fine. "It is totally amazing. Sometimes I still can't believe it myself."

Born and raised in North Winnipeg, Remy's early musical aspirations were encouraged by his father, who showed him the basics of guitar. A keen interest in rhythm 'n' blues, soul, Stax and Motown music was kindled after his father brought home a box of abandoned albums. "After that I pretty much taught myself by just listening to records and figuring out what the instruments were doing. I really got into it." Home-schooled until grade ten, Remy attended St. John's High School largely for the band program, absorbing all he could hear and experience, including recording techniques. "I researched for years about recording and engineering. I would read everything I could about different producers and engineers. I started out with a lot of trial and error but I never got tired of it. I wanted to know everything that was happening."

Playing with local bands proved less satisfying than calling his own shots so Remy decided to follow his own muse. "I was playing in experimental rock bands, but no one else in Winnipeg wanted to sing my kind of music." While Remy was thinking more in terms of a songwriting career than as a singer, Remy's manager, ex-Winnipegger Steve Warden, secured a recording contract with Universal Music, Canada. The contract gave Remy the financial freedom to return to his home studio and craft *The Way I Feel* at his own pace. "I promised my parents I'd accomplish something in music and they saw me put my head down and really accelerate. So they supported me through it. My music bills were as much as the mortgage on our house." His demos were so impressive that a bidding war ensued. Motown, the premier soul label in the US, won.

All the songs on the album are drawn from the young performer's own life experiences, suggesting an old soul inside the youthful man. "This record is purely about relationships. I've pretty much covered my ups and downs of the past four or five years, but *The Way I Feel* really represents where I'm at now, which is in a great place. There's no fiction; it's all true stuff. One breakup drove a lot of the lyric writing. For this album, the topic is love." Remy recently married Winnipeg singer Maiko Watson, formerly of pop sensation Sugar Jones, who sings backup in his band.

Released in 2002, the album had several hit singles including the title track, "Take A Message" boasting his remarkable falsetto, and the Al Green groove "Rocksteady". "I want to make people feel the magical feeling they do listening to Marvin Gaye and Stevie Wonder, and soul music in general," he remarked at the

time of the album's release. "That's the reaction I had listening to them, and that's the reaction I wanted to project. It's still just one percent of what I can do." The album sold multi platinum in Canada as well as a quarter of a million in the US.

Promotional tours in the UK and Europe boosted record sales further. Remy assembled a backing band and hit the road the following year playing across North America. "I've got a wicked band out there," he said to a reporter from the *Ottawa Sun*, "they've got range and we can take it anywhere." Remy found a comfort level onstage playing an array of instruments. His touring brought him back home where, in November, he played his second-ever hometown concert at the Burton Cummings Theatre. Earlier that year he personally handed over a cheque for $10,000 in support of the St. John's High School music program, encouraging students in his brief speech to keep the school band program thriving.

Remy was overwhelmed to learn that he had been nominated for four Grammy awards including best male R&B vocal performance and best R&B song for "Take a Message", best traditional R&B vocal performance for "Rocksteady", and best R&B album for *The Way I Feel*. "It's unbelievable," he told *Winnipeg Sun* reporter Rob Williams. "The big one for me was being nominated in the traditional R&B category because I'm not a neo-soul person. I don't believe in that term. It's like, 'Coke is It.' Everyone who's fusing that old soul back into songwriting —

D'Angelo, Erykah Badu, Maxwell, Shelby Lynne, Macy Gray — that's who I relate to."

After living in Toronto while his album climbed the charts, in 2004 Remy returned to Winnipeg to hole up — this time in his own home — recording a much-anticipated follow up album expected sometime in 2005. Once again the sessions will proceed at his own pace with few pressures or distractions, only Remy's own perfectionism.

Asked recently if the lure of America would draw him to leave Canada, Remy insisted, "I live here, I work here, I'm never going to move. It's a hard thing because you want your music to be heard around the world, but I'm the type of person to let Canada know that I love my identity as a Canadian. I love it so much and it's just important that people know that."

"He's a great ambassador for Winnipeg," says Steve Warden. "He always talks about Winnipeg and he's very proud of his Winnipeg roots." ∎

Born in Winnipeg

BANDS: Leaderhouse, Further, Chelsea Drugstore, solo artist

ALBUM: The Way I Feel (2002)

HIT SINGLES: "Take A Message", "Rocksteady"

Nominated for 4 Grammies (2003) for Best Male R&B Vocal Performance, Best Traditional R&B Vocal Performance, Best R&B Song, and Best R&B album; 2 Prairie Music Awards for Best Pop Recording and Best Producer (2003), Juno Award for Best R&B Recording (2002)

Recorded his debut album at his parents' Garden City condominium in Winnipeg

Appeared on *The Tonight Show* and *Live! With Regis and Kelly*

Married to Winnipegger and ex-Sugar Jones singer Maiko Watson

Donated $10,000 to the St. John's High School band program

# GRAHAM SHAW & THE SINCERE SERENADERS

**F**OR SOME GROUPS, THE BONDS that unite individual members can be deeply rooted in shared experiences and aspirations, and can override the commercial dictates of the cold-hearted music industry. When his record label suggested that he ditch his band, Winnipeg's Graham Shaw chose to stick with his band-mates — and it may have cost him his career as a recording artist. He has no regrets.

"Bobby Colomby from Blood, Sweat & Tears was my A&R guy," says Graham. "He got me in a room with some Capitol Records executives and begged me to fire the band. They said they could get me the A-list of session players, including the guys who played with Steely Dan. I was in tears after I left the meeting, but I couldn't do it. Then I probably became a pariah for them because I wouldn't do what they wanted. That may have affected my career vector in the long run."

Born in Calgary, Graham came to Winnipeg in 1965 at age thirteen. His father had played in a Depression-era family band, so music was in Graham's veins. "My piano teacher told me back when I was eight or nine that I changed tunes to suit myself," he says. "I still can't read music." Living in St. Vital, he formed his first group, the Mushroom Band, in the mid 1960s with Graham on guitar, piano and vocals. They recorded a single, Graham's "Don't Come Down", for local Syntax Records. Enrolling at the University of Manitoba, he left after three years, one credit shy of an Arts degree. "I flunked Shakespeare," he laughs. Working by day for the CPR and the Winnipeg Art Gallery, Graham continued to pursue a music career as a journeyman player in various local bands including the Deverons, Terry & the Gentry, Electric Banana, and the Musical Odyssey, all the while writing songs.

By the mid '70s Graham had established a solid reputation as a songwriter and musician, and formed Graham Shaw & the Sincere Serenaders. After some flux the stable lineup became drummer Gord Osland, Gary Stefaniuk on bass, guitarist Danny Casavant, and two back-

Born in Calgary; moved to Winnipeg at age thirteen

BANDS: Mushroom Band, Deverons, Electric Banana, Sincere Serenaders

ALBUMS: Graham Shaw & the Sincere Serenaders (1980); Good Manners In the 80s (1981)

HIT SINGLES: "Can I Come Near"

AWARDS: Juno for Most Promising Male Vocalist (1980)

Went on to write and record commercials for The Bay, Esso ("You're On Your Way With Esso"), Home Hardware, Canadian Tire, Budweiser, 7-Up, Labatt's, Bacardi Breezer

Composed music for CBC's *Venture, Marketplace, The Health Show, 24 Hours*, and *Land And Sea* as well as the *Theodore Tugboat* series (which ran in sixty-eight countries)

up singers, Susan Lethbridge and Ilana Zaramba. "At first we did covers, then we would throw in a couple of original tunes, and finally we did all originals." Working the pub circuit, Graham attracted the attention of influential Toronto managers Bernie Fiedler and Bernie Finklestein, who guided the careers of Bruce Cockburn, Dan Hill and Murray McLaughlan. On the strength of a demo recording at Winnipeg's Roade Studios, the two Bernies signed Graham and negotiated a recording contract with Capitol Records in the US. The band was flown to LA in 1979 to record their debut album, with Kenny Edwards from Linda Ronstadt's band as producer. "The record company really just wanted Graham, but he fought for the band," recounts Susan.

As Graham ruefully notes, "I produced a six-song demo for $8,000 at Roade Studios that got me the deal in LA. Then we burned up $140,000 in LA making a crappier record than we did at Roade." Graham rejected the idea of firing his band, and the self-titled album was released with little fanfare in 1980. "I remember all the big label nabobs saying it wasn't going to fly." A single, "Can I Come Near", charted across Canada but not without a little subterfuge. "It was 4:45 long, which was too long for radio formats at that time, so Finklestein put 4:00 on the label so it would get airplay. It was #1 to #5 depending on the region. At that point it was the most radio-friendly tune we had."

"Can I Come Near" earned Graham the 1981 Most Promising Male Vocalist Juno Award. "It felt very satisfying but I'm now a trivia question because I beat out Bryan Adams," he laughs. The

Serenaders toured Canada with Dr. Hook and appeared on several television shows. *Good Manners In The '80s* failed to produce another hit single and the Serenaders parted company with Capitol Records. A couple of singles credited to Graham Shaw alone appeared on Fiedler and Finklestein's True North Records

> "My piano teacher told me back when I was eight or nine that I changed tunes to suit myself," he says. "I still can't read music."

before the Serenaders folded in the mid '80s. At that point Graham was fed up and left Winnipeg. "I woke up one day and said, 'I'm moving to Toronto,' gassed up my '69 Firebird and left."

This precipitous decision brought the singer/songwriter a whole new career. "I lived off my royalties for a bit before realizing I still needed money," he says. "So I put together a vocal demo and sent it off to a jingle company, and all of a sudden I was singing every jingle on the planet. Then I started writing jingles. At the same time I was composing television theme music and making a good living from that."

Graham's jingle credentials are impressive. "I did 'You're On Your Way With Esso', and all the Bay commercials, including producing Céline Dion and Anne Murray. I sang on a McDonald's commercial. The list is anywhere from Home Hardware to Canadian Tire. I spent about ten years doing a lot of jingles and

making a lot of money." In addition, Graham composed incidental music and theme songs for CBC TV's Newsworld channel as well as the television series *Venture, Marketplace, The Health Show, 24 Hours*, and *Land And Sea*. But his biggest payday came when he was tapped to compose the music for the long running children's series *Theodore Tugboat*, which ran in sixty-eight countries round the world.

Graham continued to keep his hand in rock, writing songs with Alice Cooper, Triumph's Rik Emmett, Zappacosta, songwriter Eddie Schwartz, and Valdy, and working with famed producer Bob Ezrin on a Jeff Beck project. He also recorded a Christmas album with the Nylons. *Raw Shaw* is a collection of his best-known recorded work.

Recently Graham returned to Winnipeg to produce an album for ex-Generator singer Jennifer Hanson, younger sister of Serenaders' member Susan Lethbridge. The project involves recording all Shaw originals including "Can I Come Near".

What does Graham regard as his greatest Winnipeg accomplishment? "I suggested a cover charge in the pubs because bands were filling the houses and selling a lot of booze. That was the first cover charge I remember in Winnipeg. There used to be a lot of fights in the pubs but once the cover charge came in folks came to see the music. So that's my legacy, that and a couple of decent tunes." ■

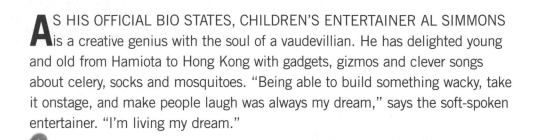

**A**S HIS OFFICIAL BIO STATES, CHILDREN'S ENTERTAINER AL SIMMONS is a creative genius with the soul of a vaudevillian. He has delighted young and old from Hamiota to Hong Kong with gadgets, gizmos and clever songs about celery, socks and mosquitoes. "Being able to build something wacky, take it onstage, and make people laugh was always my dream," says the soft-spoken entertainer. "I'm living my dream."

That dream began when Al was a young kid growing up in south Winnipeg where he would entertain family and friends, dressing up in costumes and performing comedy routines. "I knew I wanted to be an entertainer, I just didn't know what route to take." At age twenty, opportunity knocked at an Air Cadet dance. "The singer didn't show up, so the band played all their songs as instrumentals. I sang all of them from the audience so they ended up inviting me onstage to sing. If I didn't know the words I just made them up. After that I thought, 'Man, this is what I want to do.'"

Encouraged by Gary MacLean of the Vicious Circle, Al quit his job with Manitoba Hydro and placed an ad in the newspaper: 'Singer with gigs looking for band'. "A number of rock bands call me up and I went to auditions. That was horrific. I had a repertoire of Dean Martin songs." Undaunted, he eventually joined Just Us Three, making his debut at the notoriously tough Plaza Hotel pub in 1970. "That was trial by fire. I still have some of the requests from that show and they're unbelievably nasty. 'Get a f$#@ing band!' We had only nine songs. I'm amazed we got through the evening without being killed. They absolutely hated us. To put a guy singing Dean Martin and Frankie Laine songs in the Plaza was just cruel. I bombed as a rock singer. The next week we were in Portage la Prairie and I figured that if I put on a silly hat and acted out the lyrics to an inane rock song, it was hilarious. So I became the funny guy."

Just Us Three became Out To Lunch with Al developing elaborate routines and song parodies, accompanied by his banjo and a growing array of gadgets, including the exploding toilet seat. "Bob Peters, our keyboard player, came up with that name because he thought I was out to lunch." The quintet became a popular fixture on the pub circuit in the early '70s with Al moonlighting as Uncle Al the clown at parties and hosting comedy events.

In 1973, Al formed Kornstock. While rehearsing the new band he became

• Kornstock

re-acquainted with an old Air Cadet buddy. "Fred Penner came over with his guitar and sat in the kitchen playing along to every song we were doing. Finally our guitar player got fed up and walked out. So Fred joined the group." It was a strange mix from the get-go. "Fred knew all these folk songs and I had all these comedy songs but neither of us knew each other's songs. It was becoming Fred's band because he was singing folk songs. My only comeback was my comedy. It ended up being like the Smothers Brothers at first. There was a competition between Fred and me but that's partly what made it work. It had an edge." Eventually joining the group was Bob King on bass, who later became a noted children's entertainer in his own right, and drummer Mike Klym.

"We would sing 'Rudolph the Red-nosed Reindeer' in July in a bar. Or *Sesame Street* songs. The more outrageous we could be, the better. And the best route to go was almost more kids' stuff."

During a week-long bar stand in The Pas, Manitoba, Kornstock was invited to perform at an elementary school. "The kids loved it. The fact that we could take our bar show and perform it for kindergarten kids was astounding. We didn't have to cut out much." Sensing that their strongest audience wasn't yet of drinking age, Kornstock split up, with Fred going on to become Canada's premier children's recording artist.

Al took a more circuitous path, entertaining children as The Human Jukebox. "Captain Bart Bourne built it for me. It looked like a port-a-potty at first. I stuffed in bells, sirens and whistles and did that for a few years. The only thing was that I'd end up with $1.75 in quarters at the end of the day." Still enamored with

gadgets, Al concocted the upright baritone Simbonium, a B♭, four-bell, nine-valve baritone horn, eventually playing the *1812 Overture* with the Winnipeg Symphony Orchestra. Along with his wife Barbara, he starred in the CTV series *All For Fun* from 1981 to 1983, guesting as well on *Sesame Street*. Al appeared at Vancouver's Expo '86 as "A One Man Cast of Thousands", performing two shows a day for seven months. He even found time to run for the Rhino Party.

In 1987, Fred Penner suggested Al record an album for his and manager Gilles Paquin's Oak Street Records. "I always loved music from the '20s and '30s so I wanted to do an album that felt like it was back in that era. I recorded it but no one knew what to do with it. It wasn't kids' music. It was vaudeville, novelty songs. So Oak Street records sat on it. Fred told me to go write more songs, so I wrote about what my kids did over the summer, and everybody said, 'Let's record these!' They put it out and it became a hit." *Something's Fishy at Camp Wiganishie* received a Juno nomination.

"They needed a follow up so they decided to release the first sessions and lo and behold it won a Juno for best children's album. And here it was tunes that nobody knew what to do with." *Celery Stalks at Night* became a runaway success, winning the U.S. Parents' Choice Award. Al was in demand from coast to coast. His third album, *The Truck I Bought From Moe* also received a Juno nomination.

Most recently Al starred in *A Year With Frog and Toad* at the Manitoba Theatre For Young People. He continues to toil away in his workshop in Anola inventing gizmos like Distant Early Warning Jogging Shoes and Ol' Spoke — half horse, half bicycle.

Al credits his family for his career. "I learned more about comic timing playing Go Fish with my Aunt Georgie than from any comedians on TV. My entire family was so supportive of my early comedy and my career. That's why I'm still living here. I have so many ties to the community." ■

Born in Winnipeg

BANDS: Just Us Three, Out To Lunch, Kornstock (with Fred Penner), solo artist

ALBUMS: Something's Fishy at Camp Wiganishie (1992), Celery Stalks At Midnight (1995), The Truck I Bought From Moe (1997)

Hosted CTV series *All For Fun* from 1981 to 1983

AWARDS: Juno Award for Best Children's Album (1995); U.S. Parents' Choice Award (1996 and 1997)

Inventor of the Upright Simbonium, a B♭, four-bell, nine-valve baritone horn, Distant Early Warning Jogging Shoes, Skeeter Vac

Once ran for the Rhino Party; worked as The Human Jukebox; starred in Manitoba Theatre for Young People's *A Year With Frog and Toad* (2004)

# RAY ST. GERMAIN

RAY ST. GERMAIN

> "ROCK 'N' ROLL WAS CHANGING SO FAST BACK THEN. THE BEATLES CHANGED EVERYTHING AND THE ELVIS PRESLEY STUFF WAS QUICKLY LOST ON THE YOUTH. I FELT I WAS BEING LEFT BEHIND."

**H**E IS THE GODFATHER OF WINNIPEG rock 'n' roll, though far too modest to accept such a title. Ray St. Germain, better known for his country recordings and television shows, probably recorded Winnipeg's first rock 'n' roll single back in 1958. "She's A Square", released on Toronto's Chateau label in 1959, was a finger-snappin' slice of Elvis-style rockabilly.

"When CKY radio was signing off the air recently, they stated that 'She's A Square' was the first local rock 'n' roll 45 they ever played, the first Winnipeg rock 'n' roll record," says Ray with justifiable pride.

Born in St. Vital, Ray began his music career in his mid-teens, singing and playing guitar at community club dances as part of the Country Cats and a Kitten with Wayne Finucan, Roy Delarond, Albert Shorting and 'Kitten' Pat McMullin. Then he joined the Hal Lone Pine and Betty Cody Show. "I was hired because I sang Elvis Presley and they wanted it in their show." Ray was a featured performer for three years. The guitar player in the ensemble was Hal and Betty's teenage son Lenny Breau. Between travelling the province with the CKY Caravan and opening for Grand Ole Opry touring shows Ray and Lenny became fast friends.

While Lenny was obsessed with playing the guitar, Ray was more interested in singing. "People say to me, 'You must have learned *something* from him! I remember him saying to me, 'Let me teach you this Chet Atkins stuff.' I tried,

but didn't have the patience to sit with a guitar 24/7 like Lenny. I wanted to sing."

In the latter 1950s there was not much distinction between country music and rock 'n' roll, and Ray found himself riding both horses. "I would do the Elvis stuff one weekend, then next weekend I'd be out with a country band doing Ray Price songs. Most people thought rock 'n' roll wouldn't last more than a couple years back then."

"We had rock 'n' roll travelling shows back in the '50s," recalls Ray. "I remember going out with PJ the DJ, Pat Riordan who was in the Balladeers, and Wayne Walker, the Swingtones and the Angels. Victor Davies, who's now a big symphony arranger, was on piano, he played all the Jerry Lee Lewis stuff with his feet. Dave Young, now a renowned jazz player, was on upright bass."

Leaving Lone Pine, Ray and Lenny teamed up as the Mississippi Gamblers, working drive-ins and teen spots together. "We wore red jackets and black cowboy hats," he laughs. "I looked like Elvis and Lenny looked like Sal Mineo." Around this time, Ray entered CKY radio's tiny record-

Born in Winnipeg

Began career with Hal Lone Pine & Betty Cody Show with Lenny Breau

ALBUMS: *There's No Love Like Our Love* (1997); *My Many Moods* (2003)

HIT SINGLES: "She's A Square", "Raise A Ruckus", "The Métis" "I'm Mighty Proud I'm Métis"

Aboriginal Order of Canada (1985); Aboriginal Wall of Honour (1998); MCMA Entertainer of the Year, Song of the Year, Male Vocalist of the Year, Recording Artist of the Year, Lifetime Achievement Golden Award (1978–1985), member of the Canadian Country Music Hall of Fame

Recorded what is considered Winnipeg's first rock 'n' roll record "She's A Square"

Hosted Winnipeg's edition of CBC TV's *Music Hop* from 1964–1966

Wrote, produced and starred in Global TV's *Big Sky Country* for thirteen seasons

Hosts *The Road Show* on NCI radio 105.5 FM in Winnipeg

Is the voice of the Bear on YTV's *Tipi Tales*

ing studio on Main Street to cut two of his own songs, one of which was "She's A Square". The single was credited to Ray St. Germain and the Satins. "The Satins were actually the Swingtones, who sang backup on the record. Lenny Breau played guitar, Shadow Saunders bass, and Reg Kelln drums." The single climbed to #7 on the CKY Hit Parade chart and was Top 20 in other Canadian markets.

After winning the local edition of CBC's *Talent Caravan*, Ray moved to Toronto but found little work. Returning home he enjoyed a three-year stint hosting CBC Winnipeg's weekly edition of the cross-Canada cavalcade *Music Hop*, from 1964 through 1966. The backing band included Lenny Breau. The Winnipeg slot was dubbed *Hootenanny* in keeping with the folk music boom, with Ray recording its theme song "Raise A Ruckus" as a single in 1964. "We were stars back then because there were only a couple of channels to choose from, and CBC was *the* channel to be on. I did guest appearances on shows like *Juliette*. That's how I met Anne Murray and we later did some TV specials together."

He also enjoyed a long residency at Chan's Moon Room on Main Street. "I was able to work six nights a week in the clubs plus the weekly TV show, which ran for thirty-nine weeks, as well as doing the country fairs and rodeos in the summer. I was able to make a living, buy a house and raise a family." In 1966 *Music Hop* was replaced by the hipper *Let's Go*, featuring the Guess Who.

"Rock 'n' roll was changing so fast back then. The Beatles changed everything and the Elvis Presley stuff was quickly lost on the youth. I felt I was being left behind." Ray made a smooth transition to country music, appearing for years at the Ramada in south Winnipeg.

In 1970 Ray hosted *My Kind Of Country* for CBC TV, a popular showcase that featured many of the biggest names in country music. The show ran nationally for twenty-seven weeks. "It was supposed to be a summer replacement but it was so popular they ran it longer." He later hosted *Ray St. Germain Country* on CKND beginning in 1978, which was picked up nationally after the first year and ran for

thirteen more as *Big Sky Country*. "We did it on a shoestring budget, so we shot it all outside." Ray's two daughters, Chrystal and Cathy, joined him as regular performers on the show.

In his mid-twenties, Ray learned of his Métis heritage and began exploring his roots. "I found a book on Louis Riel and was fascinated by the story." That interest led to "The Métis", the song most associated with Ray's career today. Recorded in 1979, the song recounts the 1885 battle of Batoche. "The record got a lot of airplay and I was surprised because with the words 'Not red enough, not white enough' I wasn't sure everybody would get that. Later I got the Aboriginal Order of Canada for that song because they said it brought a greater awareness of the Métis people."

Ray continues to enjoy the support of the Aboriginal community, and currently

works as program manager and drive-home DJ for NCI (Native Communications Incorporated) 105.5 FM in Winnipeg. He recently released an album, *My Many Moods*, on Arbor Records, which includes "The Métis" and "She's A Square". "I told them, 'if it sells a million copies, just send me the cheque.' I'm sixty-four. I've done the road enough years in my life."

Ray St. Germain still performs around the province. He laughs about a recent encounter with a fan. "I did a show at an armed forces base recently and when I went to check in, the lady said, 'You're Ray St. Germain!' And I said, 'Yes, I am.' I was feeling pretty good that she knew me. Then she added, 'I would recognize you anywhere. Not too many guys wear that Wayne Newton hair cut anymore.'" ■

# LUCILLE STARR

"**Q**UAND LE SOLEIL DIT BONJOURS aux montagnes". Whether you speak French or not, the opening line to Lucille Starr's million-selling 1964 hit "The French Song" is instantly recognizable. Her recording of the Harry Pease and Larry Vincent composition, produced by Herb Alpert (of Tijuana Brass fame) became A&M Records' first gold record. It reached #54 on the Billboard charts and #2 on Toronto's influential CHUM chart for three consecutive weeks during a remarkable fourteen-week run. The record topped pop and country music charts around the world and Lucille found herself a star. Her name remains forever associated with that sentimental bilingual ballad.

Lucille Marie Savoie was born in St. Boniface, Manitoba, and lived on Langevin Street for her first seven years. "My father played the fiddle and my mother sang," Lucille recalls. At the age of seven she moved with her family first to Windsor and then settled in Maillardsville, near Port Coquitlam, BC, where she began her singing career with the Keray Regan Band. Marrying band-leader Bob Regan (Frederickson) the two recorded as the Canadian Sweethearts, releasing a number of singles in the early 1960s including "The Hootenanny Express", and "Blue Canadian Rockies". There were fewer distinctions between country and rock 'n' roll then, so the duo toured Canada with Hank Snow and Wilf Carter. Their debut album, *Introducing The Canadian Sweethearts*, had covers of country, folk and pop songs from "I'm Leaving It All Up To You" to "Blowin' In The Wind".

Relocating to Los Angeles, Lucille met Dorsey Burnette of rockabilly duo Johnny & Dorsey Burnette, who had penned songs for pop star Ricky Nelson. Impressed with Lucille's vocal range and vibrato, Dorsey recommended her to trumpeter Herb Alpert who, along with partner Jerry Moss, was looking for an artist to kick-start their label, A&M records. They matched Lucille with "The French Song".

"Actually, it was re-named that," Lucille told *Country Music News* editor Larry Delaney in a 1988 interview, "because Herb couldn't pronounce the original title. Herb would say, 'I don't care if I can't understand the words… I know this is a hit'." "For six weeks it didn't hit," says Lucille, "and then it took off. It went gold and platinum."

Released in the spring of 1964 at the peak of the British Invasion, "The French Song" captured hearts all over the world. Her debut solo album featured the hit single plus further hits like "Colinda", "Jolie Jacqueline", and a bilingual cover of Ray Price's "Crazy Arms" (later covered using Lucille's arrangement by Ian and Sylvia Tyson). Lucille's yodeling abilities were put to good use on the popular television show *The Beverly Hillbillies* where she provided the singing voice for Cousin Pearl.

Her international acclaim was unprecedented for a Canadian-born artist. In the Netherlands "The French Song" was #1 for nineteen weeks. "I was the first Canadian or American to do a television special in the Netherlands." Lucille's popularity extended to Belgium, Switzerland, Mexico, Guam, the Philippines, Japan, and Korea. She performed in many of these countries, and in South Africa the Prime Minister held a special luncheon in Lucille's honour at their parliament after she occupied five of the Top 10 chart positions in that country at one time. She headlined a five-week tour in South Africa in 1967 where she received several gold records.

In 1965 Lucille was fêted with an invitation to be Grande Vedette (top star) of Amsterdam's Grand Gala du Disques, an international music cavalcade whose lineup included Vera Lynn, the Everly Brothers and the Supremes. She was in illustrious company following on the heels of previous honourees like Frank Sinatra, Barbra Streisand and Charles Aznavour. "I still draw huge crowds there," she says.

Dozens of cover versions of "The French Song" have been recorded by artists ranging from instrumentalist Billy Vaughan and the Sandpipers to country performers like George Hamilton IV and Roy Drusky. The tune became a standard for many French Canadian singers.

> **LUCILLE'S YODELING ABILITIES WERE PUT TO GOOD USE ON THE POPULAR TELEVISION SHOW THE BEVERLY HILLBILLIES WHERE SHE PROVIDED THE SINGING VOICE FOR COUSIN PEARL.**

Choosing a more mainstream country music path, in 1968 Lucille recorded in Nashville with noted producer Billy Sherrill, the man behind hits by Tammy Wynette, Charlie Rich, and George Jones. The partnership yielded two albums and the hits "Too Far Gone", "(Bonjour Tristesse) Hello Sadness" and "Send Me No Roses". During this time her marriage to Bob Frederickson ended; Lucille later married Bryan Cunningham from Sarnia, Ontario.

Returning to the recording studio in 1981 after more than a decade, Lucille released *The Sun Shines Again* on her own Starr Concerts Records. "One thing that I really enjoyed about that comeback album," she told *Country Music News'* Larry Delaney, "was having my son Robert Frederickson play guitar on the session."

At the time, Bob Frederickson was a member of the group Buffalo Springfield Revisited.

Over the next two decades, Lucille continued to tour worldwide releasing *Lucille Starr's Greatest Hits* in Europe in 1982, and picking up another gold record. In 1996 she was added to the Nashville Walk of Stars in the Country Music Hall of Fame.

The Canadian Country Music Hall of Fame inducted Lucille in 1989, spurring a comeback tour for her in Canada as part of the Grand Ole Opry tour. The two-CD compilation *Bound For Movin' On*, a collection of the finest Canadian country music contributions released in 2001, featured Lucille's "The French Song". Never known as a songwriter, Lucille collaborated with longtime admirer Sylvia Tyson on the songs "Pepere's Mill" and "Le Moulin À Pépere" on Sylvia's 1989 album *You Were On My Mind*, singing duets with Sylvia on both tracks. Collector's Choice Records in the US has recently re-released Lucille's catalogue on CD, as has Disque in Europe.

Recently, the citizens of Maillardsville, British Columbia proclaimed 'Lucille Starr Day' on her birthday, May 14, and named Lucille Starr Boulevard in her honour. Lucille was delighted as she attended the Welcome Home event. "Isn't that a riot?" she laughs. "They said I'd never amount to anything. Now I have my own street and I can say, 'Don't ever park on my street!'"

Reflecting on her career, Lucille says, "When I was just a kid all I ever thought about was to get up on a stage and sing. I never thought about stardom or gold records or having a street named after me. It's like the happy ending you read about in story books." ∎

Born Lucille Marie Savoie in St. Boniface, Manitoba; moved to Maillardsville, BC at age seven

Formed the Canadian Sweethearts with husband Bob Regan

ALBUMS: Introducing The Canadian Sweethearts (1963); The French Song (1964); Lucille Starr's Greatest Hits (1982), Sweet Memories (1990)

HIT SINGLES: "The French Song", "Colinda", "Jolie Jacqueline", "Too Far Gone", "(Bonjour Tristesse) Hello Sadness", "Send Me No Roses", "It's The First Time I've Been In Love"

AWARDS: Grande Vedette (top star) of Amsterdam's Grand Gala du Disques (1965); Canadian Country Music Association Hall of Honours (1987); Phonogram's Gold Record Club (1990); The Golden Tulip Award in Holland (1990); Nashville Walk of Stars (1996)

"The French Song" sold over a million copies, earning A&M Records its first gold record

In the Netherlands "The French Song" was #1 for nineteen weeks straight

The South African Parliament hosted a special luncheon in Lucille's honour

Lucille was the singing voice of Cousin Pearl on The Beverly Hillbillies

# AMANDA STOTT

**B**RANDON'S AMANDA STOTT has been in the music business almost half her life. And she's only twenty-two. Signed to her first recording contract at age thirteen, she released her self-titled debut album nationally one month shy of her eighteenth birthday and two months short of her high school graduation. Her peers were surprised to learn their classmate was a country music star. "I didn't really want anything to change so I didn't really mention it," she laughs. "Everyone just knew me for me." And it's that desire to remain true to herself that continues to propel Amanda forward professionally.

Born and raised on a farm northwest of Brandon, Amanda has been singing almost as long as she's been talking. "I was about three years old the first time I actually sang on stage. I sang 'I May Be Small But I've Got A Great Big God' at church." Dad Cyril and brother Conrad backed the budding singer at local fairs and festivals before she was ten, where she belted out country tunes to standing ovations.

"One of my earliest memories was seeing **Reba McEntire** and thinking, 'Wow, she's cool!' That's when I started listening to country music."

Amanda's first break came in 1996 with an invitation to sing at the prestigious Governor General's Performing Arts Awards ceremony in Ottawa. That same year she performed at the Brandon Winter Fair alongside folksinger Valdy, who was so impressed with the thirteen-year-old dynamo that he produced a three-song demo tape in a Brandon recording studio. That tape would ultimately lead to a recording contract.

"We sent that tape to the CCMAs (Canadian Country Music Association) and got accepted to do a showcase, which was really wild because we knew nothing about the process. From that weekend I had management, an agent, and a record company. I went with nothing and came out with everything."

WEA Records offered Amanda a development deal on the spot. "Because I was so young, they wanted to give me time to grow up and get used to this idea of singing because I had never really been in a studio before." The process took the next four years. Meantime, Amanda performed before thousands at Winnipeg's Pan American Games as well as for the prime minister and the premiers.

Rather than encouraging her own songwriting talents, WEA brought in

ready-made songs for Amanda to record. "I made a pact that I would not sing something that I hadn't experienced or that someone my age couldn't have experienced. People know that I believe in what I'm singing."

Issued in the spring of 2000, *Amanda Stott* vaulted the recent high school graduate into the spotlight with promotional videos as her single "Black Is Black" reached the Top 10 on CMT's Top 20 Countdown. Amanda handled it all like a pro. For her first major tour she was teamed up with fellow Canadian teen acts Adam Gregory and the Wilkinsons. "Here I was done high school and this was all I ever wanted to do. So I had a blast."

Further tours followed including two stints with Tom Jackson's annual Huron Carole, an experience that left an indelible impression. "When you go on the tour with Tom you know you're not just going out to play music," says Amanda. "You're really making a difference and helping people." She also performed for Queen Elizabeth II during her Golden Jubilee Tour and travelled to Bosnia to entertain Canadian troops.

Despite several more hits including "Somebody To Love" and "Reachin' For A Star", the album did not meet WEA's sales expectations and Amanda was ultimately dropped by the label. "At the time I was disappointed but I feel it was the best thing for me. I don't think they were really behind me." Without a label, Amanda signed on for the musical production of Winnipeg composer Olaf Pyttlik's powerful rock musical *The Wave*, based on the real life experience of a teacher's attempts to educate students on the dangers of Nazi tyranny. "What attracted me to it was that there were no speaking lines, it was all

singing. I've always said if I could be onstage and not have to talk, that would be the best, because I just love to sing."

Determined to develop her own songwriting, she recently began collaborating with the country's finest writers including Marc Jordan, Christopher Ward, and Stephen Moccio, who has written for Celine Dion. "I felt so out of my league but it's really great to learn from the best." Signed to EMI Canada, Amanda is now focusing her attention on her own songs, with an album project in the immediate future that will consist mainly of her own collaborations. "EMI really want to develop that part of my career, which is great," she points out.

"Since my first album I've changed a lot as a person, musically, stylistically and with my writing," muses Amanda. "I'm

really proud of my first album but I've grown a lot since then."

Now residing in Winnipeg, Amanda is in no hurry to rush the project, entitled *Chasing The Sky*. "We really want to make the right choices but still represent me in how I've changed." Her vision and musical direction, too, have shifted. "I'm playing piano and the music is more piano-based. I don't like to call it pop music, but it's a really organic kind of sound. I'm hoping the country fans and country radio will play it." There is little doubt of that.

Amanda continues to remain true to herself. Half a lifetime of experience has given her that confidence. "You just have to go with what you're feeling and where you're going when you're making the music. I love what I do and I'm very lucky to get to do what I love." ■

Born in Brandon, Manitoba

Began her career singing in church at age three and a half

Signed with WEA Records in 1996 at thirteen

ALBUM: Amanda Stott (2000), Chasing the Star (2005)

HIT SINGLES: "Black is Black", "Somebody To Love", "You're Not Alone"

Appeared in Winnipeg composer Olaf Pyttlik's rock musical *The Wave* (2002)

Toured with Tom Jackson's Huron Carole (2002, 2003); performed for Canadian Forces in Bosnia in 2004

Signed to EMI Records in 2004; currently recording new album

Opened the Canadian Family Farm Tribute in Toronto in 1999 singing "O Canada"

# STREETHEART
## STREETHEART

"I WAS AMAZED WHEN THEY PRESENTED us with the Prairie Music Hall of Fame Award," marvels Streetheart keyboard player Daryl Gutheil on the occasion of the induction of the Saskatchewan-born, Winnipeg-based outfit into the Hall of Fame in 2003. "There we were alongside Neil Young, the Guess Who, Joni Mitchell, and Ian Tyson. I kept thinking 'What the hell are we doing here?' But I guess it says something about the legacy of the band." Indeed it does. Back in the late 1970s there was no band more beloved by fans in western Canada than Streetheart. They were the kingpins of prairie rock.

**"I ALMOST THINK WE HIT OUR PERFORMANCE PEAK WITH THE ORIGINAL BAND EVEN BEFORE WE HAD AN ALBUM OUT."**

Streetheart's roots go back to popular Saskatoon band Witness Inc. who released five singles between 1967 and 1969, including two Canadian hits, "Jezebel" and "Harlem Lady". The band toured across Canada until a serious highway accident left singer Kenny Shields with multiple injuries that needed years of recuperation. Regina band Wascana, featuring Daryl Gutheil on keyboards and bass player Ken 'Spider' Sinnaeve, had become one of the most popular bands in the province, but by the mid 1970s were looking for a new direction. Hooking up with Kenny Shields, they set up camp in Winnipeg as Witness before relocating to Edmonton, picking up drummer Matt Frenette and ex-Scrubbaloe Caine guitarist Paul Dean from the Great Canadian River Race, and Streetheart was born. Teaming up with manager Gary Stratychuk, the band signed with WEA (Warner Elektra Atlantic) Records in 1977.

Released in early 1978, *Meanwhile Back In Paris* became a gold album propelled by a thundering rhythm section, edgy guitar and Kenny's powerhouse vocals. "I almost think we hit our performance peak with the original band even before we had an album out," maintains Daryl. "We were working hard and people were starting to respond." A disagreement with Paul led to his hasty exit replaced by Winnipegger John Hannah, formerly of

Chopping Block, Holy Hannah, and Harlequin. Based in Winnipeg, the group cut the platinum-selling *Under Heaven Over Hell*, produced by Nazareth guitarist Manny Charlton. The album featured a driving cover version of the Rolling Stones' "Under My Thumb" as well as Hannah and Shield's "Hollywood", both chart-climbing singles. Matt Frenette left to join Paul Dean in Loverboy and Streetheart recruited ex-Painter and Hammersmith drummer Herb Ego.

*Quicksand Shoes* failed to top the sales success of its predecessor. "Manny had this idea that we should try to lighten up and write a bunch of singles. But it wasn't guitar-heavy and turned out to be the wrong choice for us. We were known as a hard-rockin' band." Stung by criticism that their original material never quite matched their live strength, the group recorded a powerful cover of the Small Faces hit "Tin Soldier" for the next album *Drugstore Dancer*. "We cut that album at Century 21 studios in Winnipeg with the great engineer Ralph Watts who got a terrific sound for us on a shoestring budget. That album kind of re-established us in many ways."

WEA failed to promote the group south of the border so they signed a distribution deal with Capitol Records and recorded *Drugstore Dancer* for their own Pressure Records. WEA responded by issuing *Action…The Best of*

*Streetheart* culled from tracks off the first two albums.

John Hannah was relieved of duty for health reasons in 1981, replaced by Vancouver-based guitarist Jeff Neill for the recording of *Streetheart*, yielding their biggest hit single with the power ballad "What Kind Of Love Is This". "That was actually done in about an hour as a demo at Century 21 studios before we went to Toronto to record the album. We tried re-recording it in Toronto but in the end used the demo we recorded here in Winnipeg. We spent a month doing nine songs and an hour on one song and that one became the biggest song on the album." The single proved that Streetheart was still capable of writing hit songs.

*Dancing With Danger* maintained the band's reputation, but sales were declining in the early '80s. "We had been doing it for seven or eights years which, by today's standards, is a pretty long career. By then we were running out of steam." Known for its energetic live shows, *Live After Dark*, recorded at concerts in the band's three strongest markets, Winnipeg, Edmonton and Regina, captured Streetheart in full flight.

Inability to crack the more lucrative American market continued to frustrate the group. A falling out with manager Gary Stratychuk resulted in the seizing of the band's equipment and bankruptcy. "It was a mess. It was us against management. I wouldn't wish that on my worst enemy the way that all went down. We still had a recording contract but Kenny, Spider and I, the nucleus from the beginning, didn't want to go on." A compilation *Over Sixty Minutes With Streetheart* remains a steady seller.

"There are a lot of people who think we got a raw deal and should have been bigger but I don't dwell on it," notes Daryl. In recent years, he, Kenny and Jeff Neill revived Streetheart with bass player Blair DePape and Dylan Hermiston on drums. "We're getting a bit of the payoff now. Some nights I can't believe it, everyone out there singing along to those songs."

Health problems plagued Kenny Shields in the early eighties. A star-studded fundraising benefit organized by Winnipeg musicians helped defray recuperation costs. Spider Sinnaeve became one of the most in-demand bass players in the country, gracing records by Kim Mitchell and Tom Cochrane among others and touring with Red Rider, Tom Cochrane and a latter day version of the Guess Who. He is currently a member of Loverboy alongside former Streetheart mates Paul Dean and Matt Frenette, replacing Winnipegger Scott Smith who died in a boating accident in December 2000. John Hannah now lives in Scotland.

At the group's induction into the Prairie Music Hall of Fame in Regina, Daryl, Kenny and Jeff were joined onstage by Spider and Herb. Videotaped messages from Paul and Matt were included in the tribute. "It felt like we did something worthwhile after all," says Daryl with pride. ■

Formed in Winnipeg in 1976; members from Saskatchewan, Alberta and Manitoba

Members of Streetheart were also in Witness Inc., Wascana, Scrubbaloe Caine, Great Canadian River Race, Holy Hannah

ALBUMS: Meanwhile Back In Paris (1978); Under Heaven Over Hell (1979); Quicksand Shoes (1980); Drugstore Dancer (1981); Streetheart (1982); Dancing With Danger (1983); Live After Dark (1983)

HIT SINGLES: "Action", "Pressure", "Under My Thumb", "Here Comes The Night", "Tin Soldier", "Hollywood", "Teenage Rage", "What Kind Of Love Is This", "Look In Your Eyes"

Under Heaven Over Hell produced by Nazareth guitarist Manny Charlton

Inducted into the Prairie Music (Western Canada) Hall of Fame in 2003

Guitarist Paul Dean and drummer Matt Frenette left to form Loverboy

Kenny Shields, Daryl Gutheil and Jeff Neill continue to tour as Streetheart

Spider Sinneave is one of the most in-demand bass players in Canada and currently tours with Loverboy

**A**T THE HEIGHT OF THE VIETNAM WAR in 1969, eight local musicians collectively known as Sugar & Spice recorded one of the classic anti-war anthems of the era. Their exquisitely orchestrated rendition of Peter Yarrow's "The Cruel War" topped the charts across Canada as the group stood poised for American success. Pegged by influential American radio programmer Bill Gavin to be a hit, the single was abruptly pulled from the charts by their US record label, White Whale, and with it went the group's chance for international success.

Sugar & Spice was a merger of two mid 1960s groups from south Winnipeg's Fort Rouge area: rock band the Griffins and the Murphy sisters folk trio — Kathleen (seventeen), Maureen (sixteen), and Aileen (fourteen). The union was the brainchild of ex-Mongrels guitarist John MacInnes, who had a wider vision of the music scene and approached the two factions with a proposition in fall 1967. The three sisters had been performing for years singing their sweet folk songs in coffeehouses and get-togethers. The thought of being backed by electric instruments was appealing, though not to everyone. "Our mother was a bit worried when she saw guys carrying all these amplifiers down our basement stairs," laughs Maureen. Even some members of the band, which consisted of lead guitarist Phil O'Connell, MacInnes on rhythm guitar — Larry Mahler on bass, drummer Ken Richard, and vocalist Geoff Marrin — had doubts. But from the first rehearsals they knew they had something fresh and exciting for the local music scene.

Booking agent Frank Weiner threw the weight of his Hungry I booking agency behind Sugar & Spice, insisting they not appear in public before releasing a single. Guess Who guitarist Randy Bachman

Formed in Winnipeg in 1967

Members of Sugar & Spice were in the Griffins, Mongrels and Murphy Sisters

HIT SINGLES: "Not To Return", "The Cruel War", "Strawberry Wine", "Angeline"

Made their public debut only after releasing a debut single

Played the opening of the National Arts Centre in Ottawa

"The Cruel War" was pulled from US charts after a mistake in the credits

The three Murphy sisters reunited in the Greaseball Boogie Band and sang backup on Bill Amesbury's single "I Remember The Road"

provided the group with "Not To Return". Cut in one quick session at the band's rehearsal room in the downtown Hart Building, the single was released as the group debuted before a sellout crowd at the University of Manitoba. It was a perfectly timed plan. "As far as we knew that's the way it happened with all bands," says Aileen.

In the ensuing months, Sugar & Spice appeared on concert packages throughout western Canada, supporting the likes of Dusty Springfield, B.J. Thomas and the Who. Mrs. Murphy accompanied the band on their first road trip. "She wouldn't let us stay in the same hotel as the guys," chuckles Maureen. Aileen recalls members of the Who trying to pick up the three teenage sisters. The band soon acquired a battered old Greyhound bus and fitted it out with bunks for the grueling miles they faced over the next three years, crisscrossing Canada and the northern US. "We had a lot of really horrible highway accidents with the bus," says Phil. "I began to think that the odds were coming up for us after so many hours on the road." Personnel changes followed as first Mike Elliot, then Steve Banman came onboard on drums, singer Geoff Marrin exited, John McInnes assumed the bass duties, and organist Chuck Gorling joined.

In Ottawa the group opened the National Arts Centre by invitation of Prime Minister Trudeau but as they began performing, the hydraulics operating the rising stage jammed and the group found themselves descending in mid song. For their first major television appearance Weiner brought in a choreographer for the girls. "All three of us ended up moving," notes Aileen, "but in different directions."

As the single "Day By Day" was climbing the charts, the group booked a hasty return to Kay Bank studios in Minneapolis to record a new single. Having performed the Peter, Paul and Mary folk song "The Cruel War" in their folk repertoire as the Murphy Sisters, local arranger Bob McMullin orchestrated a full-blown version for the band. "The thing I remember most," states Maureen, "is when Bob McMullin put the strings on the track. We had been doing that song for years and then I heard all the strings and an incredible cello solo. That was a highlight." Rush-released, "The Cruel War" became a hit right across Canada. The group even recorded a French language version for the Quebec market. "We were #1 in St. Boniface," notes Aileen.

A licensing deal with White Whale Records saw the single released in the US in early 1969. "With the Vietnam War on it was a prime time to release it," says Maureen. All looked rosy until composer Peter Yarrow stepped in, threatening legal action over the omission of his name in the writing credit. Rather than re-press a corrected single, White Whale withdrew it. "Things just stopped going up," says Aileen. The group never fully recovered.

Further singles, including two songs from singer/songwriter Russell Thornberry, failed to stem the decline. Randy Bachman returned with "Judith And The Windswept" and "Whisper Girl Shining" but it was all too late for oldest sister Kathleen, who left in late 1969 with John MacInnes to form the Tweadle Band. Maureen departed the following year to form Fresh Air. "The band was playing too loud," she says. "I ended up with blisters on my vocal cords. I used to have

to scream a lot." Recruiting two Toronto musicians — bass player/singer Brian Miessner and drummer Laurie Currie — Aileen, Phil and Chuck Gorling carried on, shortening the group name to Spice and releasing two further singles, "Strawberry Wine" and "Angeline", and concentrating their efforts on the southern Ontario market, playing clubs and colleges. Aileen was next to leave and Brian Miessner stepped forward as lead singer, adding Winnipegger Glenn Stewart on bass. Phil O'Connell was the lone original. In 1972, he too exited, replaced briefly by Bob White before the group finally quit.

"There never was one person who took charge of the musical direction," laments Aileen, on the slow fall of the group. "It was too much of a democracy." In the mid '90s, Sugar & Spice reunited for a benefit concert in support of the Manitoba Museum's *Get Back* Winnipeg music history exhibit.

Maureen later moved to Toronto and worked with Bentwood Rocker, the Greaseball Boogie Band, and Shooter. Aileen fronted a Winnipeg version of Bentwood Rock and now lives in Kamloops. Kathleen and John MacInnes both earned law degrees while Maureen became a popular broadcaster in Winnipeg. Phil O'Connell works in a local music store. Brian Miessner and Laurie Currie formed the Beatles tribute band Liverpool.

None of the three sisters harbours any regrets about their lost opportunity to make the big time. "They still play 'The Cruel War' on the radio," observes Maureen proudly. "We never got any money from it. I wonder where the money is going?" ∎

<... >

**GREG STILL SEES A BRIGHT FUTURE FOR SWING SONIQ. THE TRIO RECENTLY WON THE COOL JAZZ FM COMPETITION IN WINNIPEG, WITH A PRIZE OF $15,000 TO GO TOWARD SESSIONS FOR A LONG-OVERDUE SECOND ALBUM.**

" **W**HEN I WAS A KID, all I wanted was to be the rhythm guitar player in Django Reinhardt's band," guitarist Greg Leskiw once revealed in an interview. With Swing Soniq, Winnipeg's elder statesman of the guitar is living his original dream. Combining the syncopated rhythms of pre-World War II hot jazz, swing standards, original songs, and free-flight soloing, Swing Soniq is a rare treat to the ears. Their infectious sound has won them many fans along with the 2004 COOL FM Jazz contest.

Formed by Greg in 1997, the original trio — Greg, guitarist Greg Lowe, and bassist Danny Koulack — epitomized the one-time Guess Who guitarist's longtime musical vision of presenting authentic swing-era jazz to younger audiences. While there have been hints of his leanings throughout his career, including his two-year stint in the Guess Who with songs like "Grey Day" and "One Divided", Swing Soniq is the realization of those earlier experiments.

"My roots weren't in rock 'n' roll," he says. "My dad played '40s stuff and that's what I first learned." Joe Leskiw lived in Brandon and played in several dance bands, including the Syncopaters. While his contemporaries cut their musical teeth on Elvis and Chuck Berry, Greg played an entirely different repertoire. "I learned a lot of jazz standards, some of the songs that appeared on the first Swing Soniq album, like "Moonglow". My dad taught me jazz chords, so I had learned augmented, diminished, sevenths, minors and how to play all over the fretboard. He taught me how to play in B♭ and E♭, which were the horn keys, and a lot of those old songs were written in those keys. He was a good player, could improvise well and had a great sense of melody."

At age ten Greg moved with his family to Shilo where his musical training continued. Completing high school he made the move to Winnipeg where his rock 'n' roll career began with the Shags.

"I had already gotten into the Beatles back in Shilo with the Howie brothers, local guitar players in Shilo." Other bands followed such as the Jamieson Roberts Device, Logan Avenue Comfort Station, Gettysbyrg Address, and Wild Rice, before jumping to the big time with the Guess Who in June 1970. He followed that stint up with innovative ensembles Mood Jga Jga, LesQ, Crowcuss and hard rockers Kilowatt, before retiring from live performance to run his home studio Vox Pop, where groups like Crash Test Dummies and New Meanies cut demos. By 1997 he was ready for a change. "I had nothing to lose and nothing going on. I always loved the old hot club swing so I thought, 'I've got to do that!'"

Previously, Greg had played a handful of gigs with well-respected studio and theatrical production guitarist Greg Lowe who, besides composing for radio, television and the stage, had recorded three jazz albums.

"I heard him playing some Djangoesque stuff. He called me and we got together and just started playing all my tunes like 'Queen Jealousy'. We did a few dates together and that was it."

Meantime, Greg began experimenting with the concept that would become Swing Soniq. "My father had taught me the turn-arounds on all those old standards which used diminished chords. I started working on 'After You've Gone', really hitting it hard like Django's band and working out the turn-arounds. But it's hard to play with that kind of power and make it interesting. I wanted a powerful group, an acoustic trio, that was musically interesting and it developed from there." The catalyst was local composer Glenn Buhr. "He knew I was into Django and he wanted to do a Parisian thing over at the St. Norbert Arts Centre. He brought Danny Koulack over and we sized each other up. So Glenn put together a show that was recorded live for CBC. That became our first show and the momentum built from that. Then CBC called us and wanted to record an album, *Moonglow*."

Violin, double bass and banjo player Danny Koulack had worked with Klezmer ensemble Finjan, the Knappen Street All Star Band, as well as recording his own album *Clawhammer Your Way To The Top*.

Released in 1998, *Moonglow* was a breath of musical fresh air, mixing standards like the title song, "After You've Gone" and "I Can't Give You Anything But Love" with songs from Greg's previous musical incarnations including "One Divided", "Gimme My Money", "Ma Cherie" and "Step Aside". The album swings from start to finish with Greg's driving rhythm and vocals and Greg Lowe's Django-inspired soloing, prompting one reviewer to write, "Leskiw's raw vocals bring back the sound and spirit of that jazz great." The band toured extensively over the next two years, performing in concerts and on the jazz festival circuit.

By the new millennium, the group was beginning to suffer personnel problems. Greg Lowe was unable to make all the gigs so viola player extraordinaire Richard Moody of Acoustically Inclined filled in. Danny, too, found himself in demand and several bass players subbed including Gilles Fournier, Bernie Addington

from Vancouver, and more recently Nenad Zdjelar, originally from Yugoslavia. In the end, Lowe and Koulack parted with Greg. "It was a very difficult and painful breakup but I carried on with the name with Richard who has been with me almost five years now." Nenad remains on bass. The addition of Richard Moody, a gifted and intuitive musician, adds a further dimension to Swing Soniq. "He was always into swing. Stephane Grappelli [Django's extraordinary violinist] was always one of his heroes."

Greg still sees a bright future for Swing Soniq. The trio recently won the Cool Jazz FM competition in Winnipeg, with a prize of $15,000 to go toward sessions for a long-overdue second album. The new album will feature more of Greg's extensive back catalogue as well as some new directions. "I feel totally comfortable with this whole concept. It can cover everything I do. I have plans to branch out the Swing Soniq style from where it came from to bring in the country influence and the blues. There isn't much I can't do with this band."

Would Greg go so far as to regard Swing Soniq as his most satisfying musical endeavour? "Mood Jga Jga is a tough one to beat, but Swing Soniq is a close second. Acoustic guitar is my first instrument and I'm back on it. I mean, what's a guy who idolized Django Reinhardt doing in a band like Kilowatt anyway?" ∎

Formed in Winnipeg in 1997 by Greg Leskiw

Members of Swing Soniq were in the Guess Who, Mood Jga Jga, Finjan, Knappen Street All Star Band, and Acoustically Inclined

ALBUM: Moonglow (1998)

COOL FM Jazz Contest winners in 2004

Initially formed to play the St. Norbert Arts Centre

Original member Greg Lowe composed music for the staging of Carol Shield's play *Thirteen Hands*

Performed at every major Canadian jazz festival including the Montreal International Jazz Festival in 2000

Currently recording long-awaited second album

# JANE VASEY

THE BLUES IS LARGELY a male-dominated musical genre. Few women players have ever earned the approving nod of blues aficionados. Winnipegger Jane Vasey changed all that. Both female and classically-trained, she was the antithesis of the typical blues artist. In her seven years at the piano with Toronto's formidable Downchild Blues Band, Jane set the blues world on its ear and carved out a role for a young woman in a man's world.

**SHE HELD HER HEAD AT AN ANGLE WHILE SHE PLAYED, UPRIGHT AND SPARROW-LIKE, AS IF SHE WANTED TO SEE AND HEAR EVERYTHING ONSTAGE WITH A MIXTURE OF CURIOSITY AND ANTICIPATION. HER SKIN WAS PALE, HER EYES GREEN, AND HER HANDS TINY. HOW DID SHE MANAGE TO PLAY SO HARD AND TOUGH WHEN SHE LOOKED SO SMALL AND GENTLE?"**

Born in the south Winnipeg neighbourhood of Crescentwood in 1949, Jane began piano lessons at age six, and quickly discovered a love for music. The family moved to Neepawa in 1955 and Jane continued her music studies. "I remember when my brother-in-law died," says Jane's mother Dorothy Vasey. "Jane went over to the piano and played a whole piece she'd composed." Returning to Winnipeg in 1957, Jane went on to graduate from Kelvin High, going on to earn a BA from the University of Manitoba in 1970. Her music career had already begun after she'd won the Earl Ferguson Award at the Manitoba Music Festival and appeared on CBC TV's *Calling All Children*. Jane played piano for the Royal Winnipeg Ballet School before moving to Toronto, where she furthered her classical studies at the Royal Conservatory of Music, as well as teaching piano lessons and performing with the Global Village Theatre, Toronto Workshop Theatre, and Young Peoples' Theatre.

Jane once told a reporter how she discovered Chicago blues piano master Otis Spann. "A girlfriend of mine, Diane Roblin, brought me over one of his records, and it was like a revelation. It seemed to involve a lot of things I liked about classical music — great runs and phrases that I could really relate to. I turned right on to it." Smitten with the blues, Jane happened to be in Grossman's Tavern in Toronto where she saw the

Downchild Blues Band performing and approached the band members, who were dubious about a female piano player. "She started going out with our sax player and he said, 'Why don't we get Jane in the band?'" remembers Donnie 'Mr. Downchild' Walsh.

Jane proved to be a quick study. "She started listening to blues records and because of her classical training she really picked it up," says Donnie. "She had the feel. Not many people can play the blues. She learned to play like Otis Spann in about an hour and a half. Jane could play like Otis Spann, she could play like Pete Johnson. Then she started to develop her own style after listening to all these other pianists." Jane joined the band in 1973, making her debut on the group's hit single "Flip, Flop, Fly".

For her parents back in Winnipeg the news that Jane had joined a band was a surprise. "Well, it wasn't exactly what we thought she would do," concedes Dorothy.

Jane would go on to wow audiences across North America with her fluid blues style and intuitive feel. "She had a killer left hand for the walking-octave style," says Prairie Oyster piano player Joan Besen, "smooth, fast, and solid." Jane even impressed many of the blues masters including the legendary Roosevelt Sykes. As Donnie Walsh relates, "she sat down and started playing and he went nuts and the crowd went nuts for her. She knocked out Roosevelt Sykes because he appreciated that she could *really* play."

Publicist Richard Flohil once described Jane in performance. "She held her head at an angle while she played, upright and sparrow-like, as if she wanted to see and hear everything onstage with a mixture of curiosity and anticipation. Her skin was pale, her eyes green, and her hands tiny. How did she manage to play so hard and tough when she looked so small and gentle?"

Jane appeared on six Downchild albums: *Dancin', Ready To Go, So Far, We Deliver, Road Fever,* and *Blood Run Hot* and several singles including "I've Got Everything I Need (Almost)," "Tell Your Mother", and her own composition "Trying to Keep Her 88s Straight". She toured North America playing clubs, concerts and festivals and often returned to play in Winnipeg. Being the lone female in an all-male band and in a predominantly male industry never fazed her as Jane earned acceptance once they heard her play. But she always kept her big heart. "One Christmas out on tour she went out and bought every-

one in the band Christmas presents," smiles Donnie.

In 1975 Jane was diagnosed with leukemia. Doctors gave her five years to live; Jane defied them by living six and a half years. Throughout that time only a handful of insiders knew of her affliction, including band mate and boyfriend Donnie Walsh. "We kept it pretty quiet," he remembers. "She knew she was dying so we kind of lived for the moment. We had a great time together and played a lot of great music. You kind of put it out of your mind, but you know it's coming. And then it comes." On tour out west in 1980, Jane had to return to Toronto for treatment. Recalls Donnie, "We were in Nelson, BC when suddenly she got this big pain in her leg and the next day she had to go back. That was the beginning of the end. She came out and toured with us some more but then she got sick in New Brunswick and had to come home. That was probably the last time she went on tour with us." Stoically, Jane continued to perform with the band around Toronto.

"I don't know how she did it, how she managed to get up her strength for that," notes Dorothy. "She never let on that she was sick."

Jane's last public performance was backing up blues great Eddie 'Cleanhead' Vinson at Toronto's Brunswick Hotel in January 1982. Frail and exhausted from her treatment Jane nonetheless amazed everyone in the audience, including Vinson, with her virtuosity and strength. Jane died at home in Toronto on July 6, 1982. The music world mourned her loss. Tributes were given in every newspaper and news program across Canada. Brandon University established a scholarship for piano performance in Jane's name initiated by her parents and endowed from an all-star benefit by the Toronto blues community that had embraced Jane.

"Jane was an inspiration to a lot of people," muses Donnie. "She made it look easy."

"I still have all her records and tapes and I still listen to them," says a proud Dorothy Vasey. ■

Born in Winnipeg

Won the Earl Ferguson Award at the Manitoba Music Festival as a child

ALBUMS: Dancin' (1974); Ready To Go (1975); So Far (1977); We Deliver (1980); Road Fever (1980); Blood Run Hot (1981)

HIT SINGLES: "I've Got Everything I Need (Almost)", "Tell Your Mother", "Trying to Keep Her 88s Straight"

Jane appeared on CBWT's *Calling All Children* television show

Was an accompanist for the Royal Winnipeg Ballet school

Classically trained, Jane learned the blues by studying Otis Spann recordings

Joined Toronto's Downchild Blues Band in 1973

Died of leukemia in Toronto, 1982

# THE WAILIN' JENNYS

THE WAILIN' JENNYS

**O**FTEN THE MOST SATISFYING musical mergers occur without any master plan. Winnipeg-based folk trio The Wailin' Jennys — originally Cara Luft, Ruth Moody and Nicky Mehta — are proof that spellbinding music can result when you simply let it happen.

*"...IT WASN'T UNTIL WE DID THAT FIRST SHOW AND SAW THE AUDIENCE RESPONSE THAT WE KNEW IT WAS SOMETHING SPECIAL. WHEN YOU HAVE VOICES THAT BLEND SO WELL AND WE ALL WRITE SONGS, THAT WAS A BIT OF AN ANOMALY TOO."*

"Nicky and I often played on the same bill," recalls Cara, "but I never met Ruth until the summer of 2001 when she approached Nicky and me at the Winnipeg Folk Festival and said, 'Do you want to sing together?' We just thought it would be one time but people really loved it."

Born in Calgary of folksinger parents, Cara grew up around traditional music. "We didn't have a TV in the house so it was always records, instruments and music. I played autoharp and dulcimer and when everybody turned eleven they got a guitar. I *loved* traditional folk music." Working as a folksinger in Alberta and British Columbia, she moved to Winnipeg in the 1990s on the urging of friends who touted the city's art, culture, and left-wing politics. Performing in coffeehouses while supporting herself with day jobs like selling candies for The Nut Man, Cara established a solid reputation as a guitar player and songwriter, releasing three acclaimed albums including *Tempting the Storm*, and appearing at Lilith Fair and England's prestigious International Guitar Festival.

Winnipegger Nicky Mehta graduated from St. John's-Ravenscourt School and began pursuing a solo career in music following university in Ontario. Nicky plied the folk circuit either solo, with the ensemble Good Blind Soul, or in folk duo Wellspring, releasing *Weather Vane*, an album nominated for a 2002 Western Canada Music Award for Outstanding Roots Recording.

Ruth Moody hails from an artistic family. Born in Australia but raised in Winnipeg, her mother is a music teacher, while her brother Richard is a virtuoso violin player. Ruth studied classical piano and voice until her mid teens, when she became enamored with traditional Irish and Scottish folk music, joining up with Leonard Podolak — son of Winnipeg Folk Festival founder Mitch Podolak — in the Celtic-flavoured group Scruj MacDuhk. Their albums earned the group two Prairie Music Awards and a Juno nomination. Ruth left the group in 2001 to record a solo album, *Blue Muse*.

When Ruth suggested the collaboration, the three all assumed it was a one-off. "I came back from a four-month solo tour and Nicky called and said, 'John Sharples at Sled Dog [a music store] booked us a show in January. We've got to practise.'" Cara observes that "we started singing together and realized that our vocal ranges slotted well together. I'm a natural alto, Nicky's a mezzo, and Ruth's a soprano. But it wasn't until we did that first show and saw the audience response that we knew it was something special. When you have voices that blend so well *and* we all write songs, that was a bit of an anomaly too."

What emerged was a melting pot of influences that shaped the distinctive sound of the group. Cara brought her traditional British folk music sensibilities along with an interest in '70s British folk rock. "I liked Steeleye Span, Pentangle, Martin Carthy. I was a huge Led Zeppelin fan, the folkie side of their sound. Ruth listened a lot to the Beatles. She has all that theoretical background and can explain what it is we're doing. Nicky started singing harmony very young. She listened to a lot of British New Wave in the '80s. So we all have a foot in folk but also other influences. Nicky always claims

Formed in Winnipeg in 2001

Members of the band were in Scruj MacDuhk, and have solo careers

ALBUMS: The Wailin' Jennys (2002); 40 Days (2004)

HIT SINGLE: "Old Man"

Western Canadian Music Award - Best Folk Album (2004)

40 Days recently released in the US, UK and Australia on US roots label Red House Records

Ruth Moody, Nicky Mehta, and Cara Luft all maintain successful solo folk careers

Ruth Moody's brother Richard is a member of Swing Soniq

Cara Luft left the group in November 2004 and was replaced by Montreal-based singer/songwriter Annabelle Chvostek

40 Days nominated for 2005 Juno for best roots/traditional album

she's the least folk of the three of us but that's just because she had less exposure to the traditional stuff than Ruth and me, but her songwriting is very folkie. Between us it's pretty diverse."

The decision to pursue the partnership fulltime came in Florida at the annual Folk Alliance showcase. "The room just went up," laughs Cara. "I had plastered the hotel with these ridiculous posters of us looking like idiots and I guess it piqued people's curiosity. The name kind of caught people's interest, too, and we got a whole summer's worth of bookings as the Wailin' Jennys for 2002.

"We never thought we would be taking the folk world by storm," says Cara. "It was like this train steaming full speed ahead, and suddenly I'm thrown on board without having time to think about it."

They owe their quirky name to John Sharples, owner of Sled Dog Music in Winnipeg. "John initially wanted to call us the Folk Vixens and we said, 'What kind of show do you want this to be, John?!' So then he came up with The Wailin' Jennys and we thought that was brilliant. Two weeks later Waylon Jennings died. I had

already e-mailed all these people going to the Folk Alliance about this new trio, The Wailin' Jennys, and I got notes back saying 'I hope you're going to honour the memory of Waylon Jennings.'" To date the country music legend's estate has expressed no concern over the name. "We've actually had people come to our shows expecting us to play country music," chuckles Cara.

The Jennys' debut recording was a self-titled six-song EP with local producer Lloyd Peterson, owner of Private Ear Studio, featuring original songs and covers. This led to a recording contract with Jericho Beach Records. *40 Days*, recorded at Private Ear with producer David Travers-Smith, was released to glowing reviews in the spring of 2004, earning the trio a Western Canada Music Award. "We wanted a producer who was really good with female harmony vocals and acoustic instruments," says Cara. "We didn't want an over-produced folk-pop album. David knew how to do all those things. He expanded our musical horizons as well and encouraged me to play my electric guitar on one track." The trio recorded

Neil Young's classic "Old Man" for the album and the track drew attention from country music radio, to the surprise of the three. "It's not how we perceive ourselves, but we're open to that," says Cara. "We're discovering we can fit into folk, country, pop, or the Americana thing." The group recently filmed their first video for "Beautiful Dawn," to be aired on Country Music Television.

*40 Days* has been released in the US by Red House Records and in the UK and Australia. The Jennys toured the US in the fall of 2004, with jaunts to the UK and Australia slated for 2005.

In November, Cara Luft announced her departure from the trio to resume her solo career. Ruth and Nicky, however, are determined to carry on, and in early December announced the addition of Montreal singer/songwriter Annabelle Chvostek. She will join the group for its European tour in early 2005. "We expect that our sound is likely to change in some way," says Nicky, "but we are feeling really positive and energized. We're going to be back." ∎

IN THE LATE 1990s, the Watchmen were the band most likely to carry the Winnipeg rock torch into the next millennium from the Guess Who, BTO and Harlequin. Their solid rock sound was born from years of touring and their albums enjoyed gold and platinum status in Canada. "There was a buzz around us," recalls singer Danny Greaves. "It was kind of us and the Crash Test Dummies at the time who were making waves outside Winnipeg."

**"WE KIND OF MISSED A LOT BECAUSE WE WERE OUT ON THE ROAD ALL THE TIME, BUT LOOKING BACK ON IT THERE WAS A RICH HISTORY THERE WE WERE VERY AWARE OF. SOMETHING ABOUT THE COLD WEATHER AND THE ISOLATION."**

Between 1993 and 2003 the Watchmen released five critically acclaimed albums, toured Canada relentlessly, and achieved star status in Australia. "The road really helped us because nobody gave us our career, and so nobody could take it away from us," boasts Danny. "We won our fans over one at a time. If we put out an album that didn't enjoy the same radio or video play as the previous record, the fact that we had toured so steadily enabled us to continue having an audience, even if they weren't playing our songs on the radio."

Emerging from the south Winnipeg neighbourhoods of Tuxedo, River Heights, and Charleswood, the original lineup consisted of Danny Greaves, guitarist Joey Serlin (who named the group from a comic book series), bass player Peter Loewen, and drummer Grant Page, who was replaced soon after by Sammy Kohn. From the outset the group decided to focus almost exclusively on original material. "Songs would start with an initial idea from me or Joey then it would sort of jam out and become what it was after that," says Danny. Rehearsing in the basement of Main Street's funky McLaren Hotel, the Watchmen evolved their sound before taking to the road. "Our agent was Ralph James, the former bass player in Harlequin, who single-handedly was the reason we kept going. We were just kids and he put us on the road, and that was the best thing he could have done. It showed us what was out there and what we could do with our music.

Following a triumphant gig at Toronto's Horseshoe Tavern in 1991, the group picked up management with Tragically Hip's Jake Gold, a record contract with MCA, and a producer in Chris Wardman. Their 1993 debut album, *McLarenFurnaceRoom*, named for their rehearsal space, was the product of four years on the road. "We didn't know what we do now, which was the charm of that record. But Chris really took the bull by the balls and shaped the sound. A lot of people still think it's our best record." Peter Loewen left prior to the second album, *In The Trees*, replaced by Toronto bass player Ken Tizzard. "After that the

four of us never lived in the same city until near the end. By the time we were all here in Toronto it was too late." *In The Trees* became the group's best selling release, with the perennial crowd favourite "Boneyard Tree".

For *Brand New Day* the band wanted to shake things up. "We got cocky after *In The Trees* because it sold a lot. We started bringing keyboards into the sound and taking chances. It was a big eye-opener for us when it didn't do as well. But I definitely don't regret it."

The tour regimen continued as the group went out, playing arenas and theatres in the company of Big Wreck. "That's the way they do it nowadays, groups partnering up and going out in larger venues. But we never really got to the theatre level consistently." On a return to Winnipeg, the Watchmen headlined the 1997 Red River Relief Concert organized by Tom Jackson. "That was kind of cool closing the show in front of 40 or 50,000 people. I threw in Jimmy Cliff's "Many Rivers To Cross" as I recall. It seemed appropriate."

For their next album, *Silent Radar*, the group, now signed with Capitol Records, travelled to grunge rock capital Seattle to work with noted Soundgarden producer Adam Kasper. "That was probably the most fun we had recording. We had so much time and had road tested those songs. And we knew we had a big song in 'Stereo'. It was going over really well live. We spent a lot of money on that album." "Stereo" became an unexpected hit single in Australia, and the group made five forays down under, supporting the likes of Pearl Jam, Green Day and the Foo Fighters. "We were selling 10,000 singles in Australia and we were considered international recording artists. It was

the first time we were getting recognized on the street outside our home town."

Weary of the touring, Sammy Kohn bowed out prior to sessions for their fifth album and rather than replace him in the studio, the three opted to use a drum machine. The move informed the music on *Slo-motion*, with the band moving in a more electronic direction. "Ken had a lot to do with that. He was the first to show us what you could do with a Macintosh computer. It was definitely a huge transition for us. It was about doing something different. Some of those songs, for me, were really beautiful. People were shaken up but we had to do that." The double album divided critics and longtime fans of the group's edgier sound. As Joey admitted, "It was probably the wrong time to put out an electronic record because that sound was on the way out, but we've always been a band who did what they

wanted." The group toured in support of the album before calling it a day in 2003. Ken Tizzard compared the final months to a marriage gone stale.

Danny is currently working with sometime Watchmen bass player Rob Higgins in Doctor, who recently released *High As High Gets*, Ken has a new group, Shadrak, while Joey has been working in film scoring and playing in Redline. Sammy works behind the scenes in the record business. Although the former members of the Watchmen currently live in Toronto, they retain their affection for their hometown.

"Definitely there was a Winnipeg thing happening," confirms Danny. "We kind of missed a lot because we were out on the road all the time, but looking back on it there was a rich history there we were very aware of. Something about the cold weather and the isolation." ∎

Formed in Winnipeg in 1990

Came together in the basement of Main Street's seedy McLaren Hotel,

ALBUMS: McLarenFurnaceRoom (1993); In The Trees (1994); Brand New Day (1996); Silent Radar (1998); Slo-motion (2001)

HIT SINGLES: "Run and Hide", "Incarnate", "Boneyard Tree", "Stereo"

Headlined the Red River Flood Relief Concert in 1997

"Stereo" became a hit single in Australia where the group toured five times

Silent Radar recorded in Seattle with Soundgarden producer Adam Kasper

Managed by Jake Gold of Canadian Idol fame

Broke up in 2003 — members all launched individual careers

# THE WEAKERTHANS

THE WEAKERTHANS

**W**ITH A CHORUS OF "I HATE WINNIPEG" and lyrics like "the Guess Who suck, the Jets were lousy anyway" it's easy to assume that the Weakerthans don't think much of their hometown. Nothing, however, could be further from the truth.

"A couple of people have come up to me in bars slightly drunk and complained about that song," notes leader, guitarist and principal songwriter John K. Samson, "and I always have to bring them back to their junior high school English class to realize that there are characters an author creates. I've never once in my life said I hate Winnipeg. In that song a store clerk, a frustrated driver, and the Golden Boy say it, but I never do." The song was conceived as homage to the city that continues to inspire and inform John's songwriting. "I'm one of the bigger Guess Who fans around and I loved the Jets, too. I certainly meant it as a tribute."

Formed in 1997 by John, the Weakerthans emerged from the underground punk music scene that thrived in Winnipeg in the '80s. "A lot of that scene was centred around the Royal

Albert [Hotel] and Wellington's downtown. The goal was just to play, get your free case of beer, and have fun."

John answered an ad for a bass player for Propagandhi, one of the leading punk outfits, landed the gig and found himself on the road with the trio. He remained with Propagandhi for two albums, contributing three songs to their recordings. "I never really got the hang of the bass. I only played it because everyone I knew was a better guitar player than I was." But the goal was not to be a virtuoso, simply to be involved. "That was the real democratic impulse behind the whole punk scene, that anyone could do it and should if they want to. I think that ethic pervaded the actual politics of the bands that came from that scene as well. We were all politicized." Certainly Propagandhi have maintained a strong socio-political agenda

while selling hundreds of thousands of albums, but John was looking for something else.

"I decided I didn't want to be in a band anymore, but three or four months later I realized I had about ten songs I wanted to record with someone." Veterans of punk band The Red Fisher Show, Jason Tait and bass player John Sutton began working with John on what would become the Weakerthan's debut album, *Fallow*, released in 1997 on Propagandhi's G-7 label.

The album was recorded at Private Ear studios in Winnipeg in the midst of 1997's flood of the century and, according to John, the calamity informed some of the album. "It felt kind of strange seeing the army walking around the streets. When I listened to it I could feel that influence. It's very much a record about Winnipeg with a lot of name checks on it." The title reflects John's mood at that point. "I was trying to get rid of a whole bunch of things I had to deal with before I could move on as a writer."

Following the release of *Fallow* guitarist Stephen Carroll, a friend of John's from Kelvin High School joined the group. A trip to Germany solidified their reputation before touring Canada, and they have continued to tour in Europe twice a year. Their follow-up album, *Left And Leaving*, nominated for a Juno Award for Best Independent Recording, once again mined the local milieu. "The title track was inspired by a heritage building on the Old Market Square, near where I lived on Albert Street. It was burning to the ground. Everyone was standing around

watching. It made me realize I hadn't noticed the building before, but now that it was burning I was devastated by it. So it started me thinking about all the lost stories that this place contained, and the impact of geography and architecture on who we are and what both those things do to community."

The album reflected the maturity of his songwriting and the cohesion within the new four-piece lineup. "It was an important record for us, one we're most affectionate about still because it was the one where we really came together as a band. We toured that album endlessly for about three years. Our current life is still built on that record."

After signing with US-based Epitaph Records, the group recorded *Reconstruction Site* in Toronto at Chemical Sound with producer, Ian Blurton. Again nominated for a Juno, it was the group's most ambitious effort yet. Recorded over a month at a budget twice

that of previous albums and mixed in Seattle by Adam Kasper, whose previous credits include Winnipeg's Watchmen, the Foo Fighters, Pearl Jam and Nirvana, it represents the fulfillment of John's song-writing vision for the group. "In a lot of ways it was the hardest album to make," he points out, "but the one I'm most proud of." The label change offered far wider distribution, with the album getting rave reviews in Britain's leading weekly music journal, *The New Musical Express*, as well as in *Playboy*.

The track that generated the most attention was "One Great City." "It's been an interesting sociological experiment for me to play that song around the world. It's a fairly surreal moment to see a German singing along with it. But I think of Winnipeg as every city, a perfect distillation of anything great and bad about cities. That's important to me that the specific can be universal, and that's the kind of writing I love, writing that can move

people who haven't seen those specifics."

Recently, bass player John Sutton left the group to pursue other interests. In the last few years Tait and Sutton have lived in Toronto. Samson and Carroll remain in Winnipeg. Samson also operates Arbeiter Ring Publishing. The distance has not affected the future of the Weakerthans as they continue to tour worldwide and plan their next album. "We always said that we'll keep doing it until it isn't fun anymore, but it's hard to stop. It's still important to us so I can't imagine stopping."

He continues to be inspired by Winnipeg. "This place has had a profound impact on how I see the world. It's become a huge part of my identity. I guess I've figured out that it's what I'm trying to write about, so I'll be writing about it the rest of my life and I'm kind of content with that knowledge. I think it's important that people try to explain who they are and where they're from." ∎

Formed in Winnipeg in 1997

Members of the band were also in Propagandhi and the Red Fisher Show

ALBUMS: Fallow (1997); Left And Leaving (2000); Reconstruction Site (2003)

Two Prairie Music Awards for Independent Recording and Video

of the Year (2001); Western Canada Music Award (2004)

Leader John K. Samson also operates Arbeiter Ring Publishing in Winnipeg's Exchange district

*Reconstruction Site* was mixed in Seattle by Soundgarden producer Adam Kasper (who also produced the Watchmen)

"One Great City", their paean to Winnipeg, has drawn ire from some fans for its apparent criticism of Winnipeg landmarks

Winnipeg writer Caelum Vatnsdal directed The Weakerthans' two videos

Nominated for 2005 Juno for best video for "Reasons"

# N E I L   Y O U N G

**N**EIL YOUNG IS A ROCK ICONOCLAST never content to rest on his laurels, always searching, stretching, challenging. As a member of two of rock music's most revered outfits — Buffalo Springfield and Crosby, Stills, Nash & Young — his music lit up the Whisky a Go-Go on the Sunset Strip and defined the Woodstock generation in the 1960s. He set the template for the '70s singer-songwriter, recording in a dizzying array of genres from punk, rockabilly, techno-pop, country-rock, to R & B, before a new generation of Nirvana-weaned rockers anointed him the 'Godfather of Grunge'. He has released close to fifty albums in a career that continues to career across a wide musical landscape. Young has done it all, from surfing instrumentals to concept albums and movies. Close friends refer to him as 'Shakey'; his mother called him Neiler. To the rest of the world he is simply one of the most influential and respected artists in rock music history.

**WHAT SET THE SQUIRES APART FROM THE REST WAS THE INCLUSION OF AN EVER-GROWING CATALOGUE OF ORIGINAL SONGS PENNED BY NEIL.**

• The Squires

Charting the mercurial ex-Winnipegger's myriad twists and turns is enough to make anyone dizzy. "I'd rather keep changing and lose a lot of people along the way," he once remarked. "If that's the price, I'll pay it." Neil remains the quintessential enigma and one of rock music's most fascinating mavericks.

Born in Toronto on November 12, 1945, Neil moved to Winnipeg with his mother Rassy in the summer of 1960, following the dissolution of her marriage to noted sports writer Scott Young. For the teenaged Neil, the move was devastating. Quiet and introverted, he found solace in music. Having progressed from ukulele to acoustic guitar in Toronto, Neil acquired his first electric guitar in Winnipeg and wasted little time forming a band: the Jades. The quartet made their debut in January 1961 at an Earl Grey Community Club canteen dance. It would be their one and only performance. For the other three it was hockey; for Neil, it was always about the music. "I knew when I was thirteen or fourteen that that's what I wanted to do," he says. "There was nothing more important in my life than playing music. It took me a long time to grow up because

all my growing-up time was spent on music. All the other things suffered for it."

By 1963, Neil had formed the Squires, a popular south Winnipeg quartet that plied the community club circuit for the next two years. "There was nothing like the community clubs anywhere," says Neil. "It wasn't too long before we had our own little following." What set the Squires apart from the rest was the inclusion of an ever-growing catalogue of original songs penned by Neil. "It's almost like the song feels the need for me to write it and I'm just there," he says. "Songwriting, for me, is like a release." Beginning with Shadows-inspired instrumentals, he soon progressed to lyrics, becoming the Squires' lead vocalist, to the dismay of some early audience members. Following one of his vocal performances, a cover of the Beatles' "She Loves You" complete with a Beatle wig, an audience member hollered out, "Stick to instrumentals!" As Neil recalls, "People told me I couldn't sing, but I just kept at it." CKRC recording engineer Harry Taylor once uttered the now famous pronouncement: "You're a good guitar player kid, but you'll never make it as a singer."

Unfazed, Neil continued with a revolving door of Squires members. Singularly focused, stubborn and uncompromising, his determination drove him onward. "The hardest thing I learned to do was to fire someone," he later said. "If I hadn't been so serious about music I probably wouldn't have had to do that. But knowing where I wanted to go, there was no way I could put up with things that were going to stand in my way. Music had to come first. I had to leave a lot of friends behind, especially in the begin-

ning. I had almost no conscience for what I had to do. I was so driven to make it." Despite several recording dates both in Winnipeg and Thunder Bay, the Squires released only one single on the tiny V Records label, two instrumentals from Neil. "The Sultan", backed by "Aurora", was cut in 1963 at radio station CKRC's two-track studio in downtown Winnipeg and received considerable airplay, allowing the group to venture further afield. In

the fall of 1964 the band played the Flamingo club in Thunder Bay (then Fort William) where, alone on his nineteenth birthday, Neil penned one of his most endearing songs, "Sugar Mountain." It was on another trip to Thunder Bay in April 1965 to play the 4-D coffeehouse that Neil met American folk-rocker Stephen Stills, and an instant bond was formed.

A fan of both rock 'n' roll and acoustic folk music, Neil was already

Born in Toronto; moved to Winnipeg in 1960

BANDS: The Squires, Buffalo Springfield, Crosby, Stills, Nash & Young, Crazy Horse, solo artist

ALBUMS: Buffalo Springfield Again (1967); Everybody Knows This Is Nowhere (1969); After The Gold Rush (1970); Harvest (1972); On The Beach (1974); Tonight's The Night (1975); Decade (1977); Comes A Time (1978); Rust Never Sleeps (1979); This Note's For You (1988); Freedom (1989);

Ragged Glory (1990); Harvest Moon (1992); Sleeps With Angels (1994); Greendale (2003)

HIT SINGLES: "Mr. Soul", "Cinnamon Girl", "Heart of Gold", "Old Man", "Helpless", "Long May You Run", "Comes A Time", "This Note's For You", "Keep On Rockin' In The Free World", "Harvest Moon", "Philadelphia"

Inducted into the Canadian Music Hall of Fame, 1982; Juno Album of the Year (1994); Male Vocalist of the Year

(1995); inducted into the Rock 'n' Roll Hall of Fame (1996)

Has spent 12 years compiling a multi-CD retrospective box set (rumoured to be over ten disks) entitled *Selections From The Neil Young Archives* that includes tracks recorded in Winnipeg in the early 1960s

Dabbles in movies with *Journey Through The Past, Human Highway, Rust Never Sleeps,* and *Greendale*

Prolific beyond belief, Neil is always recording new material experimenting with his own unique blend of folk-rock. "We did classic folk songs with a rock 'n' roll beat and changed the melody," he described. "We changed them totally with rock 'n' roll arrangements. It was a minor key folk, punk, rock kind of thing." Imagine "She'll Be Comin' Round The Mountain" to a Bo Diddley beat. Impressed with the lanky Winnipegger's originality and determination, Stills pushed Young to start thinking about forming a group of their own.

In his beloved hearse 'Mort', Neil relocated to Toronto in the summer of 1965, but not before breaking down in Blind River, Ontario (inspiring his later song "Long May You Run"). Soon after, he jettisoned the remaining Squires to pursue a doomed career as a solo folksinger. "The Squires was the first band that I ever got anything happening with," Neil notes. "We were pretty young and just learning the business and we were pretty naïve, but we had a lot of fun back then. They could have made it. I just wanted it more than they did." Following a brief stint with Rick James in The Mynah Birds, Neil and bass player Bruce Palmer embarked on an overland odyssey in March 1966 in another hearse, bound for Los Angeles in search of Stills. The two finally found him in a traffic jam on LA's Sunset Strip. That same night the Buffalo Springfield was formed.

The Buffalo Springfield would provide Neil's first taste of success and acclaim. Dressed in fringed buckskin, he became

• Buffalo Springfield

the self-styled Hollywood Indian, an image that found him idolized in the teen magazines. Their first single, "Nowadays Clancy Can't Even Sing", was inspired by a former Kelvin High School classmate but it was Stills' "For What It's Worth" that gave

**"...AS PAINFUL AS IT IS TO CHANGE, AND AS RUTHLESS AS I MAY SEEM TO BE IN WHAT I HAVE TO DO TO KEEP GOING, YOU GOTTA DO WHAT YA GOTTA DO."**

the quintet their biggest hit, an enduring anthem of the '60s. Neil quit the group several times before they finally split up in 1968, allowing him the freedom to pursue his own path as a solo artist and member of several groups, including Crazy Horse and the mega-conglomerate Crosby, Stills, Nash & Young as well as brief forays fronting the Stray Gators, Shocking Pinks,

Lost Dogs and International Harvesters. Neil's free-wheeling career left some wreckage behind. "Neil does what Neil wants to do," states CSN&Y's Graham Nash, "and unfortunately it hurts people." Nonetheless, he has remained true to his own musical vision, earning respect from contemporaries for his singular focus. "I don't think I ever did what anybody told me to do," he says. "That's the way it is."

For Neil, change is the constant. "That's the reason I'm still here," he told biographer Jimmy McDonough. "Because as painful as it is to change, and as ruthless as I may seem to be in what I have to do to keep going, you gotta do what ya gotta do." That credo has allowed Neil to overcome huge odds to succeed on his own terms. Observes McDonough, "He was told he couldn't sing, couldn't play guitar, couldn't write. But he's let nothing stop him. Young has not only succeeded, he's prevailed."

*After The Gold Rush* (1970) and *Harvest* (1972) thrust Neil into the rock

stratosphere, a position he continues to maintain, with a prolific output of albums over three decades that other artists can only marvel at. His early '90s explorations into extended guitar workouts set the template for the Seattle grunge movement and he has guested with premier grunge rockers Pearl Jam several times. *Sleeps With Angels* (1994) was inspired by the death of Nirvana's Kurt Cobain who quoted Neil's lyrics from "Hey Hey My My" in his suicide note.

Neil has played Woodstock, Live-Aid and appeared at every Farm-Aid concert since its inception. He organizes the annual Bridge School Benefit Concert series each year to raise money for the San Francisco school for the disabled (his son Ben has cerebral palsy). His song "Philadelphia" from the movie of the same name was nominated for an Academy Award. For the last twelve years Neil has been compiling an exhaustive career retrospective multi-CD set (tipped to be some twelve–fifteen CDs) and accompanying DVD; ever the perfectionist, he has revised the package more times than his record label can recall. Neil is in no hurry, though. His career has hardly slowed down long enough to pause for reflection.

Neil's music has spanned the generations. It is not uncommon to see parents and children together at one of his concerts. As one youthful fan recently gushed, "He's an unpredictable, iconoclastic old guy who can still rock — the *only* old guy who can still rock."

Despite appearing at virtually every major arena, stadium and concert hall round the world, memories of his years toiling on the community club circuit in Winnipeg remain vivid for Neil. "Oh yeah, that's where it all started for me, there's no doubt about that," he says.

Whether he's pining for a "Heart Of Gold", thrashing out searing white hot guitar licks in "Rockin' In The Free World", or railing against the establishment in *Greendale*, Neil Young infuses his music with the same passion he first discovered on that Earl Grey Community Club stage back in 1961. ◼

• Winnipeg rock royalty: Cummings, Young and Bachman together at the 1987 Shakin' All Over concert.

# THEY ALSO SERVED—
# A MANITOBA HONOUR ROLL

## (AN ALPHABETICAL LISTING OF OTHER SIGNIFICANT RECORDING ARTISTS FROM MANITOBA)

James & the Good Brothers' guitarist **Jim Ackroyd** (Winnipeg)

Juno winning singer **Susan Aglukark** (Churchill)

Singer/songwriter **Sam Baardman** (Winnipeg)

'70s rockers **Barrelhouse / Teddy Boys** (Winnipeg)

Juno-nominated children's singer/songwriter **Aaron Burnett** (Winnipeg)

'80s punk/New Wave band **The Cheer** (Winnipeg)

Children's performer **Jake Chenier** (Winnipeg)

Punk pioneers **Chocolate Bunnies From Hell** (Winnipeg)

Country singer **Cindi 'Cain' Churko** (Winnipeg)

Country singer/yodeler **Stu Clayton** (Manitou)

Bluegrass anarchists **The D-Rangers** (Winnipeg)

Fiddling sensation **Andy Desjarlais** (Winnipeg)

Singer/songwriter/producer **Dan Donahue** (Winnipeg)

'80s country group **The Double Eagle Band** (Winnipeg)

Singer/songwriter **Luke Doucet** (Winnipeg)

'90s Rockers **Duotang** (Winnipeg)

'60s band **The Eternals** (Altona/Winnipeg)

Singer/songwriter **Christine Fellows** (Winnipeg)

'60s rock band **The Fifth** (Winnipeg)

Award-winning Klezmer specialists **Finjan** (Winnipeg)

Folk/bluegrass duo **Cathy Fink and Duck Donald** (Winnipeg)

Folksinger **Dan Frechette** (Pinawa)

Francophone folk duo **Gerry & Ziz** (Winnipeg)

'60s band **Gettysbyrg Address** (Winnipeg)

Award-winning Kenora blues sensation **Billy Joe Green** (Winnipeg-based)

Country singer **Rhonda Hart** (Winnipeg)

Singer/songwriter (The Big Beat) **Jeffery Hatcher** (Winnipeg)

Montreal-based jazz drummer **Jim Hillman** (Winnipeg)

Rockers **Inward Eye** (Winnipeg)

Singer/songwriter **Bill Iveniuk** (Winnipeg)

Pop band **Jet Set Satellite** (Winnipeg)

'60s rockers **The Jury** (Winnipeg)

Big Sugar guitarist/singer **Gordie Johnson** (Winnipeg)

Blues musician **Kristi Johnson** (Winnipeg)

Prairie Music Award winning children's entertainers **Just Kiddin'** (Winnipeg)

Rockabilly pioneer **Buddy Knox** (Dominion City)

Buffalo Springfield and Three's a Crowd bass player **Ken Koblun** (Winnipeg)

Singer **Marc LaBossiere** (Winnipeg)

Blues singer/guitarist **J.P 'Paul' LePage** (Morden)

Indie rock trio **Less Travelled** (Winnipeg)

Mother Tucker's Yellow Duck singer/guitarist **Donnie McDougall** (Winnipeg)

'60s rock band **The Mongrels** (Winnipeg)

Hip-hop group **Mood Ruff** (Winnipeg)

Rockers **The New Meanies** (Winnipeg)

Alt. country band **Nathan** (Winnipeg)

'70s rock band **Next** (Winnipeg)

Indie band **Novillero** (Winnipeg)

Arranger/composer/band leader **Ron Paley** (Winnipeg)

Country singer/songwriter **Byron O'Donnell** (Winnipeg)

Mambo kings **Papa Mambo** (Winnipeg)

Indie rock group **The Paperbacks** (Winnipeg)

Country rocker Junior Brown's bass player **Jon Penner** (Morden)

Rock trio **The Perpetrators** (Winnipeg)

Singer/songwriter **Aaron Peters** (Winnipeg)

Sue Foley's guitarist **Lorne Petkau** (Morden)

Guitarist **Jim Pirie** (Winnipeg)

'80s New Wave rockers **Popular Mechanix** (Winnipeg)

Indie rock group **Projektors** (Winnipeg)

Socially-conscious punk band **Propagandhi** (Winnipeg)

Saxophone player/arranger **Dave Pybus** (Winnipeg — a noted musician in Spain)

'60s rockers **The Quid** (Winnipeg)

Jazz stalwart **George Reznick** (Winnipeg)

Country singer **Ashley Robertson** (Winnipeg)

Loverboy bass player **Scott Smith** (Winnipeg)

Singer/songwriter **Shingoose** (Curtis Jonnie - Winnipeg)

Songwriter/producer **Tim Thorney** (Winnipeg)

Rock band **Tin Foil Phoenix/Sonic Bloom** (Winnipeg)

Performer **Vav Jungle** (Winnipeg)

Rock band **Waking Eyes** (Winnipeg)

Blue Rodeo keyboard player **Bobby Wiseman** (Winnipeg)

Lighthouse cellist **Howard Wiseman** (Winnipeg)

Folk trio **The Wyrd Sisters** (Winnipeg)

Jazz bass player extraordinaire **Dave Young** (Winnipeg)